# SOLARO
## STUDY GUIDE

Mathematics 5

**SOLARO Study Guide** is designed to help students achieve success in school. The content in each study guide is 100% curriculum aligned and serves as an excellent source of material for review and practice. To create this book, teachers, curriculum specialists, and assessment experts have worked closely to develop the instructional pieces that explain each of the key concepts for the course. The practice questions and sample tests have detailed solutions that show problem-solving methods, highlight concepts that are likely to be tested, and point out potential sources of errors. **SOLARO Study Guide** is a complete guide to be used by students throughout the school year for reviewing and understanding course content, and to prepare for assessments.

Copyright © 2013 Castle Rock Research Corporation

Rao, Gautam, 1961 –
**SOLARO STUDY GUIDE** – Mathematics 5 (2013 Edition) Common Core State Standards

1. Mathematics – Juvenile Literature. I. Title

**Publisher**
Gautam Rao

Castle Rock Research Corporation
2410 Manulife Place
10180 – 101 Street
Edmonton, AB T5J 3S4

1 2 3 MP 15 14 13

Printed in Canada

Dedicated to the memory of Dr. V. S. Rao

# THE *SOLARO STUDY GUIDE*

The *SOLARO Study Guide* is designed to help students achieve success in school and to provide teachers with a road map to understanding the concepts of the Common Core State Standards. The content in each study guide is 100% curriculum aligned and serves as an excellent source of material for review and practice. The *SOLARO Study Guide* introduces students to a process that incorporates the building blocks upon which strong academic performance is based. To create this resource, teachers, curriculum specialists, and assessment experts have worked closely to develop instructional pieces that explain key concepts. Every exercise question comes with a detailed solution that offers problem-solving methods, highlights concepts that are likely to be tested, and points out potential sources of errors.

The *SOLARO Study Guide* is intended to be used for reviewing and understanding course content, to prepare for assessments, and to assist each student in achieving their best performance in school.

The *SOLARO Study Guide* consists of the following sections:

## TABLE OF CORRELATIONS

The Table of Correlations is a critical component of the *SOLARO Study Guide*.

Castle Rock Research has designed the *SOLARO Study Guide* by correlating each question and its solution to Common Core State Standards. Each unit begins with a Table of Correlations, which lists the standards and questions that correspond to those standards.

For students, the Table of Correlations provides information about how each question fits into a particular course and the standards to which each question is tied. Students can quickly access all relevant content associated with a particular standard.

For teachers, the Table of Correlations provides a road map for each standard, outlining the most granular and measurable concepts that are included in each standard. It assists teachers in understanding all the components involved in each standard and where students are excelling or require improvement. The Table of Correlations indicates the instructional focus for each content strand, serves as a standards checklist, and focuses on the standards and concepts that are most important in the unit and the particular course of study.

Some concepts may have a complete lesson aligned to them but cannot be assessed using a paper-and-pencil format. These concepts typically require ongoing classroom assessment through various other methods.

## LESSONS

Following the Table of Correlations for each unit are lessons aligned to each concept within a standard. The lessons explain key concepts that students are expected to learn according to Common Core State Standards.

As each lesson is tied to state standards, students and teachers are assured that the information will be relevant to what is being covered in class.

## EXERCISE QUESTIONS

Each set of lessons is followed by two sets of exercise questions that assess students on their understanding of the content. These exercise questions can be used by students to give them an idea of the type of questions they are likely to face in the future in terms of format, difficulty, and content coverage.

## DETAILED SOLUTIONS

Some study guides only provide an answer key, which will identify the correct response but may not be helpful in determining what led to the incorrect answer. Every exercise question in the **SOLARO Study Guide** is accompanied by a detailed solution. Access to complete solutions greatly enhances a student's ability to work independently, and these solutions also serve as useful instructional tools for teachers. The level of information in each detailed solution is intended to help students better prepare for the future by learning from their mistakes and to help teachers discern individual areas of strengths and weaknesses.

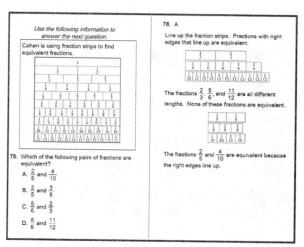

For the complete curriculum document, visit www.corestandards.org/the-standards.

**SOLARO Study Guide**s are available for many courses. Check www.solaro.com/orders for a complete listing of books available for your area.

For more enhanced online resources, please visit www.SOLARO.com.

*Student-Oriented Learning, Assessment, and Reporting Online*

# solaro

SOLARO is an online resource that provides students with regionally and age-appropriate lessons and practice questions. Students can be confident that SOLARO has the right materials to help them when they are having difficulties in class. SOLARO is 100% compliant with each region's core standards. Teachers can use SOLARO in the classroom as a supplemental resource to provide remediation and enrichment. Student performance is reported to the teacher through various reports, which provide insight into strengths and weaknesses.

# TABLE OF CONTENTS

## CREDITS

Every effort has been made to provide proper acknowledgement of the original source and to comply with copyright law. However, some attempts to establish original copyright ownership may have been unsuccessful. If copyright ownership can be identified, please notify Castle Rock Research Corp so that appropriate corrective action can be taken.

Some images in this document may be from www.clipart.com, copyright (c) 2013 Getty images.

.

Some images in this document  may be from www.nasa.com.

Some images may be from National Atmospheric and Oceanic Administration http://www.noaa.gov/.

Some images may be from www.usgs.gov/.

NOTES

Key Tips for Being Successful at School

# KEY TIPS FOR BEING SUCCESSFUL AT SCHOOL

## KEY FACTORS CONTRIBUTING TO SCHOOL SUCCESS

In addition to learning the content of your courses, there are some other things that you can do to help you do your best at school. You can try some of the following strategies:

- **Keep a positive attitude:** Always reflect on what you can already do and what you already know.

- **Be prepared to learn:** Have the necessary pencils, pens, notebooks, and other required materials for participating in class ready.

- **Complete all of your assignments:** Do your best to finish all of your assignments. Even if you know the material well, practice will reinforce your knowledge. If an assignment or question is difficult for you, work through it as far as you can so that your teacher can see exactly where you are having difficulty.

- **Set small goals for yourself when you are learning new material:** For example, when learning the parts of speech, do not try to learn everything in one night. Work on only one part or section each study session. When you have memorized one particular part of speech and understand it, move on to another one. Continue this process until you have memorized and learned all the parts of speech.

- **Review your classroom work regularly at home:** Review to make sure you understand the material you learned in class.

- **Ask your teacher for help:** Your teacher will help you if you do not understand something or if you are having a difficult time completing your assignments.

- **Get plenty of rest and exercise:** Concentrating in class is hard work. It is important to be well-rested and have time to relax and socialize with your friends. This helps you keep a positive attitude about your schoolwork.

- **Eat healthy meals:** A balanced diet keeps you healthy and gives you the energy you need for studying at school and at home.

# HOW TO FIND YOUR LEARNING STYLE

Every student learns differently. The manner in which you learn best is called your learning style. By knowing your learning style, you can increase your success at school. Most students use a combination of learning styles. Do you know what type of learner you are? Read the following descriptions. Which of these common learning styles do you use most often?

- **Linguistic Learner:** You may learn best by saying, hearing, and seeing words. You are probably really good at memorizing things such as dates, places, names, and facts. You may need to write down the steps in a process, a formula, or the actions that lead up to a significant event, and then say them out loud.

- **Spatial Learner:** You may learn best by looking at and working with pictures. You are probably really good at puzzles, imagining things, and reading maps and charts. You may need to use strategies like mind mapping and webbing to organize your information and study notes.

- **Kinesthetic Learner:** You may learn best by touching, moving, and figuring things out using manipulatives. You are probably really good at physical activities and learning through movement. You may need to draw your finger over a diagram to remember it, tap out the steps needed to solve a problem, or feel yourself writing or typing a formula.

# SCHEDULING STUDY TIME

You should review your class notes regularly to ensure that you have a clear understanding of all the new material you learned. Reviewing your lessons on a regular basis helps you to learn and remember ideas and concepts. It also reduces the quantity of material that you need to study prior to a test. Establishing a study schedule will help you to make the best use of your time.

Regardless of the type of study schedule you use, you may want to consider the following suggestions to maximize your study time and effort:

- Organize your work so that you begin with the most challenging material first.

- Divide the subject's content into small, manageable chunks.

- Alternate regularly between your different subjects and types of study activities in order to maintain your interest and motivation.

- Make a daily list with headings like "Must Do," "Should Do," and "Could Do."

- Begin each study session by quickly reviewing what you studied the day before.

- Maintain your usual routine of eating, sleeping, and exercising to help you concentrate better for extended periods of time.

# CREATING STUDY NOTES

## MIND-MAPPING OR WEBBING

Use the key words, ideas, or concepts from your reading or class notes to create a mind map or web (a diagram or visual representation of the given information). A mind map or web is sometimes referred to as a knowledge map. Use the following steps to create a mind map or web:

1. Write the key word, concept, theory, or formula in the centre of your page.

2. Write down related facts, ideas, events, and information, and link them to the central concept with lines.

3. Use coloured markers, underlining, or symbols to emphasize things such as relationships, timelines, and important information.

The following examples of a Frayer Model illustrate how this technique can be used to study vocabulary.

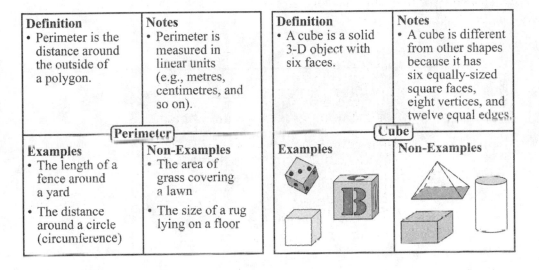

## INDEX CARDS

To use index cards while studying, follow these steps:

1. Write a key word or question on one side of an index card.

2. On the reverse side, write the definition of the word, answer to the question, or any other important information that you want to remember.

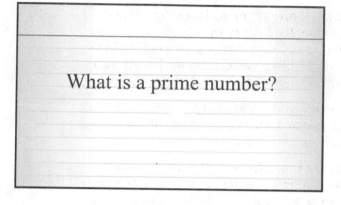

## SYMBOLS AND STICKY NOTES—IDENTIFYING IMPORTANT INFORMATION

Use symbols to mark your class notes. The following are some examples:

- An exclamation mark (!) might be used to point out something that must be learned well because it is a very important idea.

- A question mark (?) may highlight something you are not certain about

- A diamond (◊) or asterisk (*) could highlight interesting information that you want to remember.

Sticky notes are useful in the following situations:

- Use sticky notes when you are not allowed to put marks in books.

- Use sticky notes to mark a page in a book that contains an important diagram, formula, explanation, or other information.

- Use sticky notes to mark important facts in research books.

## MEMORIZATION TECHNIQUES

- **Association** relates new learning to something you already know. For example, to remember the spelling difference between dessert and desert, recall that the word *sand* has only one *s*. So, because there is sand in a desert, the word *desert* has only one *s*.

- **Mnemonic** devices are sentences that you create to remember a list or group of items. For example, the first letter of each word in the phrase "Every Good Boy Deserves Fudge" helps you to remember the names of the lines on the treble-clef staff (E, G, B, D, and F) in music.

- **Acronyms** are words that are formed from the first letters or parts of the words in a group. For example, RADAR is actually an acronym for Radio Detecting and Ranging, and MASH is an acronym for Mobile Army Surgical Hospital. HOMES helps you to remember the names of the five Great Lakes (Huron, Ontario, Michigan, Erie, and Superior).

- **Visualizing** requires you to use your mind's eye to "see" a chart, list, map, diagram, or sentence as it is in your textbook or notes, on the chalkboard or computer screen, or in a display.

- **Initialisms** are abbreviations that are formed from the first letters or parts of the words in a group. Unlike acronyms, an initialism cannot be pronounced as a word itself. For example, GCF is an initialism for **G**reatest **C**ommon **F**actor.

## KEY STRATEGIES FOR REVIEWING

Reviewing textbook material, class notes, and handouts should be an ongoing activity. Spending time reviewing becomes more critical when you are preparing for a test. You may find some of the following review strategies useful when studying during your scheduled study time:

- Before reading a selection, preview it by noting the headings, charts, graphs, and chapter questions.

- Before reviewing a unit, note the headings, charts, graphs, and chapter questions.

- Highlight key concepts, vocabulary, definitions, and formulas.

- Skim the paragraph, and note the key words, phrases, and information.

- Carefully read over each step in a procedure.

- Draw a picture or diagram to help make the concept clearer.

## KEY STRATEGIES FOR SUCCESS: A CHECKLIST

Reviewing is a huge part of doing well at school and preparing for tests. Here is a checklist for you to keep track of how many suggested strategies for success you are using. Read each question, and put a check mark (✓) in the correct column. Look at the questions where you have checked the "No" column. Think about how you might try using some of these strategies to help you do your best at school.

| Key Strategies for Success | Yes | No |
| --- | --- | --- |
| Do you attend school regularly? | | |
| Do you know your personal learning style—how you learn best? | | |
| Do you spend 15 to 30 minutes a day reviewing your notes? | | |
| Do you study in a quiet place at home? | | |
| Do you clearly mark the most important ideas in your study notes? | | |
| Do you use sticky notes to mark texts and research books? | | |
| Do you practise answering multiple-choice and written-response questions? | | |
| Do you ask your teacher for help when you need it? | | |
| Are you maintaining a healthy diet and sleep routine? | | |
| Are you participating in regular physical activity? | | |

Castle Rock Research

$$c^2 - a^2 = b$$

$$5^2 - 3^2 = b$$

$$25 - 9 = b$$

$$16 = b$$

$$\sqrt{16} = b$$

# OPERATIONS AND ALGEBRAIC THINKING

## Table of Correlations

| Standard | | Concepts | Exercise #1 | Exercise #2 |
|---|---|---|---|---|
| **5.OA** | Operations and Algebraic Thinking | | | |
| 5.OA.1 | Use parentheses, brackets, or braces in numerical expressions, and evaluate expressions with these symbols. | Order of Operations | 1, 2 | 21 |
| | | Multiplying with Easy Multiplication Facts | 3, 4 | 22 |
| 5.OA.2 | Write simple expressions that record calculations with numbers, and interpret numerical expressions without evaluating them. | Writing Expressions with Variables | 5 | 24 |
| | | Describing Expressions in Words | 6, 7, 8 | 23 |
| 5.OA.3 | Generate two numerical patterns using two given rules. Identify apparent relationships between corresponding terms. Form ordered pairs consisting of corresponding terms from the two patterns, and graph the ordered pairs on a coordinate plane. | Extend a Decreasing Pattern | 9, 10, 11 | 25 |
| | | Extend a Growing Pattern | 12, 13 | 26 |
| | | Connecting Terms with a Term Number | 14, 15 | 27 |
| | | Creating Number and Geometric Patterns | 16, 17 | 28 |
| | | Compare Increasing Patterns | 18 | 29 |
| | | Making a Line Graph from a Table of Values | 19, 20 | 30 |

5.OA.1    *Use parentheses, brackets, or braces in numerical expressions, and evaluate expressions with these symbols.*

## ORDER OF OPERATIONS

The standard order of operations is as follows:

1. Perform any calculations inside brackets (parentheses).
2. Perform any calculations involving multiplication and division, working from left to right.
3. Perform any calculations involving addition and subtraction, working from left to right.

*Example*

Using the rules for order of operations, determine the value of the expression $4 \times 3 + 15 \div 5$.

*Solution*

**Step 1**

Complete the multiplication and division first, in the order they appear, from left to right.

It may be helpful to put brackets around the multiplication and division operations.

$(4 \times 3) + (15 \div 5)$

Perform the operations inside the two sets of brackets.

$(4 \times 3) + (15 \div 5)$
$= 12 + 3$

**Step 2**

Complete the addition and subtraction next, in the order they appear, from left to right.

$12 + 3$
$= 15$

## MULTIPLYING WITH EASY MULTIPLICATION FACTS

Sometimes, when you are multiplying, if you do not know the answer you can use easier multiplication facts to help you.

*Example*

If you need to solve $8 \times 6$, you can use the easier facts $8 \times 5$ and $8 \times 1$.

You know that $6 = 5 + 1$. This means that instead of multiplying $8 \times 6$, you multiply $8 \times 5$ and $8 \times 1$ and then add the answers together.

$8 \times 5 = 40$
$8 \times 1 = 8$
$40 + 8 = 48$

You can use an area model to show that this is true. Start by drawing a grid that is 6 squares long and 8 squares high.

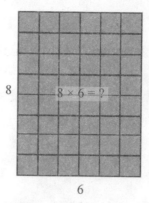

You can divide this square into two parts. One part shows 8 × 5 and the other part shows 8 × 1. When you add them together you can see that the total area is 48.

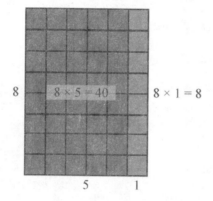

This means that 8 × 6 = 48.

You can use any multiplication facts that you know to help you find the answer to a harder question. There may be many different easy multiplication facts you can use to solve one problem.

*Example*

The given table shows that there is more than one way to solve 8 × 6 using easier facts. Find all the different numbers that make 6, then choose the ones that are easiest for you.

| 6 = 1 + 5 | Multiply 8 × 1 and 8 × 5 and add the answers together. | 8 × 1 = 8<br>8 × 5 = 40<br>8 + 40 = 48 |
|---|---|---|
| 6 = 3 + 3 | Multiply 8 × 3 and 8 × 3 and add the answers together. | 8 × 3 = 24<br>8 × 3 = 24<br>24 + 24 = 48 |
| 6 = 7 − 1 | Multiply 8 × 7 and 8 × 1 and subtract the answers. | 8 × 7 = 56<br>8 × 1 = 8<br>56 − 8 = 48 |

*Example*

Use easier facts to solve 7 × 9.

*Solution*

Think of different numbers that make 9 and choose the ones that are easiest for you. In this case, use 10 – 1 = 9.

To solve 7 × 9, first multiply 7 × 10 and 7 × 1. Then, subtract the two numbers to find the answer.
7 × 10 = 70
7 × 1 = 7
70 – 7 = 63

This means that 7 × 9 = 63.

---

*5.OA.2*   *Write simple expressions that record calculations with numbers, and interpret numerical expressions without evaluating them.*

## WRITING EXPRESSIONS WITH VARIABLES

An expression is a number sentence that has numbers and operations (such as + , – , × , and ÷ ) but no equal sign. Examples of expressions are 2 + 7 and (3 × 4) – 8. Sometimes, expressions have variables. For example, in the expression 16 – 2$a$, the letter $a$ is a variable because it can represent any number.

When you multiply or divide by a variable in an expression, you do not need to use the symbols × and ÷ . For example, the expression 2 × $a$ can be written as 2$a$, and the expression 2 ÷ $a$ can be written as $\frac{2}{a}$.

If you have a description of an expression, you can write it using numbers and variables. For example, the phrase "a number plus one" is the same as the expression $x + 1$ because the variable $x$ can represent any number. When writing an expression with numbers and variables, follow these steps:

1. Read the sentence carefully, and decide which operations to use.
2. Choose a variable, and write the expression.

*Example*

Write an expression that matches the phrase "7 less than a number."

*Solution*

**Step 1**
Decide which operation to use.
The words "less than" mean that you will use subtraction. You will subtract 7 from the variable.

**Step 2**
Choose a variable, and write the expression.
You can use $b$ as the variable.
The expression is $b – 7$.

---

*Example*

Write an expression that matches the phrase "9 added to 4 times a number."

*Solution*

**Step 1**

Decide which operations to use.

This expression will have two operations:

- The word "times" means that you will use multiplication.
- The word "added" means that you will use addition.

You will multiply the variable by 4. Then, you will add 9.

**Step 2**

Choose a variable, and write the expression.

You can use $m$ as the variable. When you multiply 4 by $m$, you do not need to use the multiplication symbol. You can write it as $4m$. Then, add 9.

The expression is $4m + 9$.

## DESCRIBING EXPRESSIONS IN WORDS

An expression is a way to show a mathematical relationship using numbers and variables. A variable is a letter that stands in place of an unknown number. For example, the expression $7 + m$ represents a number that is an unknown amount more than 7.

To describe an expression in words, you need to know the different ways to describe each operation.

## ADDITION

Some of the words that are used to describe addition are *sum*, *added to*, *plus*, and *more than*.

*Example*

The expression $a + 9$ can be described in several different ways:

- The sum of 9 and a number
- 9 added to a number
- A number plus 9
- 9 more than a number

## SUBTRACTION

Some of the words that are used to describe subtraction are *difference*, *subtracted from*, *minus*, and *less than*.

*Example*

The expression $x - 12$ can be described in several different ways:

- The difference of a number and 12
- 12 subtracted from a number
- A number minus 12
- 12 less than a number

When describing subtraction expressions, the order of the numbers is important. The phrase "12 subtracted from a number" means $x - 12$, but "a number subtracted from 12" means $12 - x$.

## MULTIPLICATION

Some of the words that are used to describe multiplication are *product*, *times*, and *multiplied by*. If a number is being multiplied by 2, you can use the word *double*, and if a number is being multiplied by 3, you can use the word *triple*.

*Example*

The expression $3r$ can be described in several different ways:

- The product of 3 and a number
- 3 times a number
- 3 multiplied by a number
- Triple a number

## DIVISION

Some of the words that are used to describe division are *quotient*, *divided by*, and *split*. If a number is being divided by 2, you can use the words *half of*. A number divided by 3 is a *third of*, and a number divided by 4 is a *quarter of*.

*Example*

The expression $\frac{s}{2}$ can be described in several different ways:

- The quotient of a number and 2
- A number divided by 2
- A number split 2 ways
- A number split into 2 groups
- Half of a number

In division expressions, the order is important. The phrase "a number divided by 2" means $s \div 2$ or $\frac{s}{2}$,

but "2 divided by a number" means $2 \div s$ or $\frac{2}{s}$.

# EXPRESSIONS WITH TWO OPERATIONS

Expressions can show more than one operation. When you describe expressions with two operations, your description needs to make it clear which operation is happening first. The easiest way to do this is to use the terms *sum* and *difference* to describe the addition and subtraction.

*Example*

The expression $\frac{6}{p} + 1$ shows that you need to divide $6 \div p$ and then add 1 to the total. If you say "6 divided by a number plus 1," it is impossible to tell if you are describing $(6 \div p) + 1$ or $6 \div (p + 1)$.

The phrase "the sum of 6 divided by a number and 1" makes it clear that the division comes first and then the addition.

---

*5.OA.3*   *Generate two numerical patterns using two given rules. Identify apparent relationships between corresponding terms. Form ordered pairs consisting of corresponding terms from the two patterns, and graph the ordered pairs on a coordinate plane.*

# EXTEND A DECREASING PATTERN

A **shrinking pattern** decreases in value or size with each term. For example, 17, 15, 13, 11 is a shrinking pattern that decreases by 2 each time.

A pattern can shrink by using subtraction or division.

If you want to extend the pattern 54, 51, 48, 45, 42, you first need to determine how the numbers change from term to term. For this pattern of numbers, you can subtract one number from the number before it in the pattern.
54 – 51 = 3
51 – 48 = 3
48 – 45 = 3
45 – 42 = 3

Once you have determined how the numbers change, you can continue subtracting 3 from each term to get the next term.

A table of values can help you organize your results.

| Term Number | Term |
|:---:|:---:|
| 6 | 39(42 – 3) |
| 7 | 36(39 – 3) |
| 8 | 33(36 – 3) |
| 9 | 30(33 – 3) |
| 10 | 27(30 – 3) |

*Example*

Anna counts these numbers aloud.

65, 55, 45, 35, _____, _____

What are the next two numbers that Anna should say?

*Solution*

### Step 1
Determine how the terms are changing.

65 – 55 = 10
55 – 45 = 10
45 – 35 = 10

Anna's pattern is decreasing by 10.

### Step 2
Continue the pattern.

Continue to subtract 10 from the last number to determine the missing numbers.

35 – 10 = 25
25 – 10 = 15

The next two numbers, in order, that Anna should say are 25 and 15.

## EXTEND A GROWING PATTERN

A growing pattern increases in value or size with each term. For example, 5, 10, 15, 20 is a growing pattern that increases by 5 with each new term. A pattern can grow by using addition or multiplication.

To extend a pattern use the following steps:

1. Determine how each number is changing. This can be done by subtracting two numbers that are side by side.
2. Once you know how each term changes continue the pattern from the last given digit.

*Example*

Peter built these shapes with colored links.

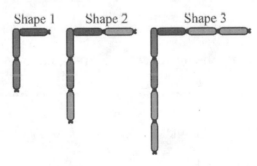

Shape 1     Shape 2     Shape 3

How many links will be in shape 4?

*Solution*

**Step 1**

Count the number of links in each shape.

- In shape 1, there are three links.
- In shape 2, there are five links.
- In shape 3, there are seven links.

The pattern grows by adding two links to each shape to make the next shape.

**Step 2**

Continue the pattern.

Shape four: 7 + 2 = 9

There will be nine links in shape 4.

---

*Example*

A pattern of numbers:  4, 8, 12, 16

When the given pattern is extended, what will the next two numbers be?  Explain your work.

*Solution*

**Step 1**

Determine how the numbers change from term to term.

One way to do this is to subtract each two numbers that are side by side.

8 – 4 = 4

12 – 8 = 4

16 – 12 = 4

Since this is a growing pattern, each number is four more than the previous number.

**Step 2**

Continue to add 4.

16 + 4 = 20

20 + 4 = 24

When the pattern is extended, the next two terms will be 20 and 24.

---

## CONNECTING TERMS WITH A TERM NUMBER

A pattern is made up of terms and term numbers.  **Terms** are the numbers in a pattern, and the **term number** tells the number's position in a pattern.

The term number of 3 is 1.

3, 6, 9, 12 …

The term number of 12 is 4.

## USING TABLES

**Tables** can be used to record the term numbers and their terms. It is sometimes easier to see the relationships between the **term numbers** and the **terms** in a table.

*Example*

    12, 10, 8, 6

    Record the given set of numbers in a table of values.

*Solution*

### Step 1

Count the number of terms to create a table outline.

There are 4 terms in the number pattern.

| Term Number | Term |
|:-----------:|:----:|
| 1 | |
| 2 | |
| 3 | |
| 4 | |

### Step 2

Match each term with its term number and fill in the table.

| Term Number | Term |
|:-----------:|:----:|
| 1 | 12 |
| 2 | 10 |
| 3 | 8 |
| 4 | 6 |

## CREATING NUMBER AND GEOMETRIC PATTERNS

To create a pattern, start with a pattern rule and then follow that rule. A pattern rule explains how the pattern is made.

*Example*

Create a geometric pattern that uses big squares and little squares.

The pattern rule could be 2 big squares, 3 little squares, repeat.

This is what the pattern will look like:

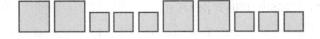

*Example*

Start at 45 and make a pattern of numbers for five counts. Show your pattern of numbers in the chart below. Explain the pattern rule you used.

| 1st | 2nd | 3rd | 4th | 5th | 6th |
|-----|-----|-----|-----|-----|-----|
| 45 |  |  |  |  |  |

*Solution*

Example pattern

| 1st | 2nd | 3rd | 4th | 5th | 6th |
|-----|-----|-----|-----|-----|-----|
| 45 | 38 | 31 | 24 | 17 | 10 |

Example explanation

The pattern rule I used to make this pattern of numbers is subtract 7 from each number to get the next number.

## COMPARE INCREASING PATTERNS

**Increasing patterns** have numbers that increase in value with each term of the pattern. It is sometimes called a **growing pattern**.

Depending on the number used to increase the patterns they will look different. You can compare different increasing patterns to see how they are growing.

*Example*

Compare the following skip counting patterns.
100, 110, 120, 130, 140
100, 105, 110, 115, 120

*Solution*

To compare the number patterns, look to see what number the pattern is increasing by.

In the first pattern, each number is increasing by 10.

In the second pattern, each number is increasing by 5.

The first pattern is increasing by double the amount of the second pattern.

## MAKING A LINE GRAPH FROM A TABLE OF VALUES

Patterns can be recorded in a table of values. They can also be made into line graphs.

To draw a graph from a table of values, follow these steps:

1. Make ordered pairs from the numbers in the table of values. The first number will come from the left column, and the second number will come from the right column.
2. Plot the points on your graph, and connect them with a line.

Make sure to give the graph a title, and label the *x*- and *y*-axes.

*Example*

Every week, Samantha puts $5.00 into her piggy bank. The amount of money in her piggy bank each week makes a pattern.

5, 10, 15, 20, 25

A table of values with this information is given.

| Week | Amount of Money ($) |
|------|---------------------|
| 1 | 5.00 |
| 2 | 10.00 |
| 3 | 15.00 |
| 4 | 20.00 |
| 5 | 25.00 |

To make a graph, put the number of weeks along the bottom (*x*-axis) and the amount of money in the piggy bank on the left side (*y*-axis).

Draw a point to show that Samantha had $5.00 in the first week. You can do this by plotting the point (1, 5) on the graph. In the second week, she had $10.00. Draw a point at (2, 10).

Each point will be an ordered pair with a number from the left column and a number from the right column. You need to make an ordered pair from each row of the table. The last three ordered pairs from this table are (3, 15), (4, 20), and (5, 25).

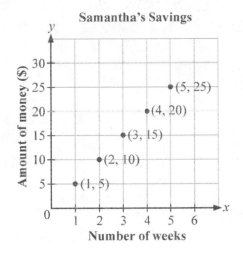

After all the points are plotted, draw a line to connect them.

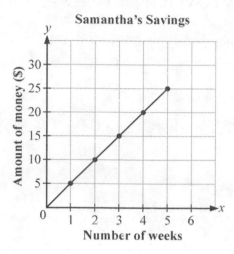

Samantha's Savings

# EXERCISE #1—OPERATIONS AND ALGEBRAIC THINKING

1. If 5 × 7 + 18 = 53, then what is the value of 5 + 7 × 18?
   A. 26
   B. 53
   C. 131
   D. 216

2. What is the value of the expression 8 × 2 + 23 − 56 ÷ 7?
   A. 27
   B. 29
   C. 31
   D. 33

*Use the following information to answer the next question.*

Mario is doing his math homework, and he cannot think of the answer to one of the multiplication questions. He decides to use easier multiplication facts to help him. He uses the facts 3 × 5 and 3 × 3.

3. Mario could use these multiplication facts to find the answer to
   A. 3 × 8
   B. 5 × 3
   C. 6 × 8
   D. 8 × 9

*Use the following information to answer the next question.*

Mila is trying to find the answer to the expression 6 × 9. She wants to use two easier facts to help her. She decides to use 6 × 10 = 60 as one fact.

4. Which other multiplication fact should Mila use to help her answer 6 × 9?
   A. 6 × 1
   B. 6 × 5
   C. 9 × 1
   D. 9 × 10

5. Which of the following expressions matches the phrase "a number multiplied by 6"?
   A. $\dfrac{6}{b}$
   B. $\dfrac{b}{6}$
   C. $6b$
   D. $6 + b$

6. Which of the following phrases describes the expression $\dfrac{4}{n}$?
   A. A number divided by 4
   B. A number split 4 ways
   C. One quarter of a number
   D. The quotient of 4 and a number

7. Which of the following phrases describes the expression $9 + y$?
   A. The sum of a number and $y$
   B. The product of a number and $y$
   C. The quotient of a number and $y$
   D. The difference of a number and $y$

8. Which of the following phrases matches the expression $3w - 5$?

   A. The difference between three times a number and 5

   B. The difference between five times a number and 3

   C. Three times a number subtracted from 5

   D. Five times a number subtracted from 3

*Use the following information to answer the next question.*

Rachel created this pattern:  29, 22, 15, 8…

9. What will the next number in this shrinking pattern be?

   A. 1                                             B. 3

   C. 5                                             D. 7

10. The next number in the shrinking pattern 75, 70, 65, 60, 55, 50 is _____.

*Use the following information to answer the next question.*

Yuki made a pattern out of strawberry stickers.

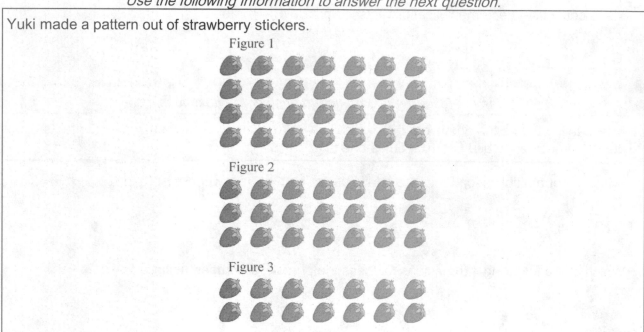

Figure 1

Figure 2

Figure 3

11. If Yuki continues the pattern, how many strawberry stickers will she need to make the next figure?

*Use the following information to answer the next question.*

Arthur arranges a group of squares in a pattern.

Figure 1    Figure 2    Figure 3    Figure 4    Figure 5

12. Which of the following sets of squares continues the given pattern?

A.

B. 

C. 

D. 

*Use the following information to answer the next question.*

Mr. Scott writes the following number pattern on the board:

67, 77, 87, 97, _____, _____

13. In order, which two numbers belong in the blanks?

A. 97 and 107

B. 107 and 117

C. 107 and 127

D. 117 and 127

*Use the following information to answer the next question.*

In his math class, Mr. Stevens writes a pattern of numbers on the chalkboard.

100, 150, 200, 250, 300

14. Which of the following tables correctly matches the term values shown with their corresponding term numbers?

A.
| Term number | 1 | 2 | 3 | 4 | 5 |
|---|---|---|---|---|---|
| Term | 100 | 250 | 200 | 150 | 300 |

B.
| Term number | 1 | 2 | 3 | 4 | 5 |
|---|---|---|---|---|---|
| Term | 100 | 150 | 200 | 250 | 300 |

C.
| Term number | 1 | 2 | 3 | 4 | 5 |
|---|---|---|---|---|---|
| Term | 300 | 100 | 250 | 150 | 200 |

D.
| Term number | 1 | 2 | 3 | 4 | 5 |
|---|---|---|---|---|---|
| Term | 300 | 150 | 200 | 250 | 100 |

*Use the following information to answer the next question.*

Mr. Murphy writes a pattern of numbers on the chalkboard of his classroom.

15, 25, 35, 45, 55

15. For the given pattern, which of the following tables correctly matches the term values with their corresponding term numbers?

A.
| Term number | 1 | 2 | 3 | 4 | 5 |
|---|---|---|---|---|---|
| Term | 15 | 25 | 35 | 45 | 55 |

B.
| Term number | 1 | 2 | 3 | 4 | 5 |
|---|---|---|---|---|---|
| Term | 15 | 35 | 55 | 45 | 25 |

C.
| Term number | 1 | 2 | 3 | 4 | 5 |
|---|---|---|---|---|---|
| Term | 25 | 35 | 15 | 55 | 45 |

D.
| Term number | 1 | 2 | 3 | 4 | 5 |
|---|---|---|---|---|---|
| Term | 45 | 15 | 35 | 55 | 45 |

*Use the following information to answer the next question.*

Alexander's teacher asked him to draw a geometric pattern that followed the pattern rule "add two to each figure to get the next figure."

16. Which of the following patterns did Alexander draw?

A.

B.

C.

D.

*Use the following information to answer the next question.*

Leon makes a repeating pattern that starts with the numbers 10, 20, and 30.

17. Which of the following patterns did Leon make?

A. 10, 20, 30, 40, 50, 60, 70, 80, 90

B. 10, 20, 30, 10, 20, 30, 10, 20, 30

C. 10, 20, 30, 20, 30, 40, 30, 40, 50

D. 10, 20, 30, 20, 40, 60, 40, 60, 90

*Use the following information to answer the next question.*

Derritt is comparing two increasing patterns.

18. His first step should be to

A. Extend each pattern

B. Determine how each pattern increases

C. Create a pattern using the same pattern rule

D. Compare the first two numbers of each pattern.

*Use the following information to answer the next question.*

Luis collects the tabs from rootbeer cans to donate to charity. His mother always buys rootbeer in boxes of 6. He makes a table to show the relationship between the number of boxes and the number of tabs.

| Number of Boxes | Number of Tabs |
|:---:|:---:|
| 1 | 6 |
| 2 | 12 |
| 3 | 18 |
| 4 | 24 |

19. Which of the following graphs shows the information in Luis's table?

A.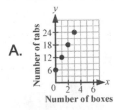

B.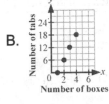

C.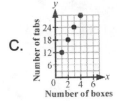

D.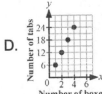

*Use the following information to answer the next question.*

Mr. Louis is planning some drills for basketball practice. The players will be in groups of 3, and each group will have 1 ball. He makes a table to show how many balls he will need.

| Number of Players | Number of Balls |
|:---:|:---:|
| 3 | 1 |
| 6 | 2 |
| 9 | 3 |
| 12 | 4 |
| 15 | 5 |

20. If Mr. Louis makes a graph of this information, which of the following points will be on the graph?

    A. (1, 3)                      B. (3, 1)

    C. (3, 6)                      D. (6, 3)

# EXERCISE #1—OPERATIONS AND ALGEBRAIC THINKING ANSWERS AND SOLUTIONS

| | | | |
|---|---|---|---|
| 1. C | 6. D | 11. 7 | 16. D |
| 2. C | 7. A | 12. B | 17. B |
| 3. A | 8. A | 13. B | 18. B |
| 4. A | 9. A | 14. B | 19. D |
| 5. C | 10. 45 | 15. A | 20. B |

## 1. C

In order to solve the equation, you must follow the rules of order of operations. Multiplication must always be done before addition or subtraction.

$5 + 7 \times 18$

$7 \times 18 = 126$

$5 + 126 = 131$

Therefore, the value of $5 + 7 \times 18$ is 131.

## 2. C

**Step 1**

According to the order of operations, do the multiplications and divisions first, in the order they appear, from left to right.

It may be helpful to put brackets around the multiplication and division parts of the expression.

$(8 \times 2) + 23 - (56 \div 7)$
$= 16 + 23 - 8$

**Step 2**

According to the order of operations, do the additions and subtractions next, in the order they appear, from left to right.

$\underline{16 + 23} - 8$
$= 39 - 8$
$= 31$
$8 \times 2 + 23 - 56 \div 7 = 31$

## 3. A

Mario is using the facts **3 × 5** and **3 × 3**. The number 3 is in both of these facts, so he is multiplying 3 times something. If he multiplies $3 \times \mathbf{5}$ and then $3 \times \mathbf{3}$, he can add the answers together to find $3 \times 8$ because $5 + 3 = 8$.

Mario could use the facts $3 \times 5$ and $3 \times 3$ to find the answer to $3 \times 8$.

## 4. A

Mila is trying to use $6 \times 10 = 60$ to help find the answer to $6 \times 9$.

The number 9 can be broken down as $9 = 10 - 1$. To find the answer to $6 \times 9$, she can multiply $6 \times 10$ and $6 \times 1$ and subtract to find the answer.
$6 \times 10 = 60$
$\phantom{6}6 \times 1 = 6$
$60 - 6 = 54$

This means that $6 \times 9 = 54$. The other multiplication fact that Mila should use is $6 \times 1$.

## 5. C

**Step 1**

Decide which operation to use.

The words "multiplied by" mean that you will use multiplication. You will multiply 6 by the variable.

**Step 2**

Write the expression.

When you multiply by a variable, the number comes first and the variable comes second. You do not need to use the multiplication symbol.

Write $6 \times b$ as $6b$.

## 6. D

The expression $\dfrac{4}{n}$ is the same as $4 \div n$.

The phrases "a number divided by 4," "a number split 4 ways," and "one quarter of a number" all describe the expression $n \div 4$, or $\dfrac{n}{4}$.

Of the given phrases, the only one that describes the expression $\frac{4}{n}$ is "the quotient of 4 and a number."

## 7. A

The operation in the expression is addition.

The word *product* is used for multiplication. The word *quotient* is used for division. The word *difference* is used for subtraction.

Of the given words, only the word *sum* is used for addition. The phrase "the sum of a number and *y*" describes $9 + y$.

## 8. A

In the expression $3w - 5$, 3 is being multiplied by *w*, so the phrase needs to say "three times a number." The number 5 is being subtracted from $3w$. In this case, the order of the words is important. If you said "three times a number subtracted from 5," the expression would be $5 - 3w$.

The only phrase that matches the expression is "The difference between three times a number and 5."

## 9. A

### Step 1
Find the pattern rule.
Determine how the numbers shrink from each number to the next.
$29 - 7 = 22$
$22 - 7 = 15$
$15 - 7 = 8$
The pattern rule is to start at 29 and subtract 7 from the previous number.

### Step 2
Use the pattern rule to find the next number in the sequence.
Subtract 7 from the 8.
$8 - 7 = 1$
The next number in the pattern is 1.

## 10. 45

### Step 1
Find the pattern rule.
Determine how the numbers shrink from one number to the next.
$75 - 5 = 70$
$70 - 5 = 65$
$65 - 5 = 60$
The pattern rule is to start at 75 and subtract 5.

### Step 2
Use the pattern rule to find the next number in the pattern.
Subtract 5 from 50.
$50 - 5 = 45$
The next number in the shrinking pattern is 45.

## 11. 7

### Step 1
Before you can extend the pattern, you need to determine the pattern rule.

One way to do this is to count the number of stickers in each figure and then compare the number of stickers in each figure.

Another way is to count the number of stickers in each row (7) and then to compare the number of rows in each of the different figures.

- Figure 1 has 28 stickers (4 rows).
- Figure 2 has 21 stickers (3 rows).
  $28 - 7 = 21$
- Figure 3 has 14 stickers (2 rows).
  $21 - 7 = 14$

The pattern rule is to subtract 7 (one row) from each figure to make the next figure.

### Step 2
Continue the pattern by subtracting 7 (1 row) from figure 3 to get the number of stickers needed for figure 4.
Figure 4 will have 7 stickers (1 row).
$14 - 7 = 7$

## 12. B

Each set in the pattern increases by 2 squares.

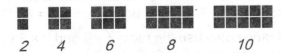

2    4    6    8    10

The next set of squares will have 12 squares.

### 13. B

In order, the next two numbers in the number pattern are 107 and 117.

This number pattern counts forward by 10s. The digits in the tens place go up by 1, and the digits in the ones place stay the same (always end in 7).

The first blank in the number pattern will be 10 greater than 97.
97 + 10 = 107

The second blank in the number pattern will be 10 greater than 107.
107 + 10 = 117

### 14. B

The given pattern is 100, 150, 200, 250, 300.

In the pattern, the first term is 100, the second term is 150, the third term is 200, the fourth term is 250, and the fifth term is 300.

The following table is the only table that displays this information correctly:

| Term number | 1 | 2 | 3 | 4 | 5 |
|---|---|---|---|---|---|
| Term | 100 | 150 | 200 | 250 | 300 |

### 15. A

In the given pattern, the first term is 15, the second term is 25, the third term is 35, the fourth term is 45, and the fifth term is 55.

The following table is the only table that correctly displays this information:

| Term number | 1 | 2 | 3 | 4 | 5 |
|---|---|---|---|---|---|
| Term | 15 | 25 | 35 | 45 | 55 |

### 16. D

The pattern rule Alexander was given was "add two to each figure to get the next figure." The following pattern follows this pattern rule. There are three squares in the first figure, five squares in the next figure, and seven squares in the last figure.

### 17. B

In a repeating pattern, the numbers continue to repeat over and over.

The number pattern 10, 20, 30, 10, 20, 3010, 20, 30 is the only pattern that repeats the numbers 10, 20, and 30 over and over.

### 18. B

The first step of comparing two increasing patterns is to determine how each pattern increases.

After Derritt determines how the patterns increase, he can compare them to one another and make conclusions.

### 19. D

**Step 1**

Make ordered pairs from the numbers in the table of values.

The first number will come from the left column, and the second number will come from the right column.

The four points in Luis's table are (1, 6), (2, 12), (3, 18), and (4, 24).

**Step 2**

Draw the graph.

Give the graph a title, and label the x- and y-axes.

Draw a point for each of the ordered pairs in the table of values.

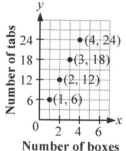

Rootbeer Tabs for Charity

## 20. B

### Step 1

Make ordered pairs from the numbers in the table of values.

When Mr. Louis makes the graph, he will have one ordered pair for each row in his table.

The first number of the pair will come from the left column, and the second number will come from the right column. The pairs will be (3, 1), (6, 2), (9, 3), (12, 4), and (15, 5).

### Step 2

Plot the points on your graph, and connect them with a line.

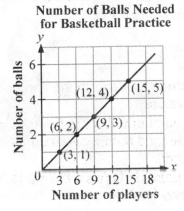

The point (3, 1) is the only option given that will be on the graph.

# EXERCISE #2—OPERATIONS AND ALGEBRAIC THINKING

21. The value of the expression 20 – 9 + 2 × 3 is
    A. 5
    B. 7
    C. 17
    D. 39

*Use the following information to answer the next question.*

Leah cannot remember the answer to 6 × 4, so she wants to use easier facts. To do this, she needs to find other numbers that make 4. Then, she can multiply 6 by those other numbers.

22. Which of the following pairs of facts **cannot** help Leah find the answer?
    A. 6 × 1, 6 × 2
    B. 6 × 1, 6 × 3
    C. 6 × 2, 6 × 2
    D. 6 × 5, 6 × 1

23. The expression $\frac{a}{8}$ matches the phrase
    A. eight times a number
    B. a number divided by 8
    C. eight added by a number
    D. the difference of 8 and a number

24. Which of the following expressions matches the phrase "2 more than a number"?
    A. $z + 2$
    B. $z - 2$
    C. $2 - z$
    D. $2 \times z$

*Use the following information to answer the next question.*

Here is a pattern of stars.

Row 1 ☆☆☆☆☆☆☆☆☆☆☆☆☆☆☆☆

Row 2 ☆☆☆☆☆☆☆☆☆☆☆☆☆☆

Row 3 ☆☆☆☆☆☆☆☆☆☆☆☆

Row 4 ☆☆☆☆☆☆☆☆☆☆

Row 5 ☆☆☆☆☆☆☆☆

25. If the pattern continues, how many stars will be in Row 7 and Row 8?
    A. 6 and 4
    B. 4 and 2
    C. 4 and 0
    D. 2 and 0

James is writing a pattern. He writes the first three numbers of the pattern in this table.

| Term | Term Number |
|------|-------------|
| 1 | 8 |
| 2 | 11 |
| 3 | 14 |
| 4 | |
| 5 | |
| 6 | |

**26.** Determine the pattern, and find the next three term numbers.

*Use the following information to answer the next question.*

John is given a sequence of numbers: 2, 4, 6, 8, 10

**27.** For the given sequence, which of the following tables correctly matches the term values with their corresponding term numbers?

**A.**

| Term number | 1 | 2 | 3 | 4 | 5 |
|-------------|----|----|----|----|----|
| Term | 10 | 6 | 8 | 2 | 4 |

**B.**

| Term number | 1 | 2 | 3 | 4 | 5 |
|-------------|----|----|----|----|----|
| Term | 4 | 8 | 6 | 2 | 10 |

**C.**

| Term number | 1 | 2 | 3 | 4 | 5 |
|-------------|----|----|----|----|----|
| Term | 2 | 4 | 6 | 8 | 10 |

**D.**

| Term number | 1 | 2 | 3 | 4 | 5 |
|-------------|----|----|----|----|----|
| Term | 10 | 8 | 6 | 4 | 2 |

*Use the following information to answer the next question.*

Mr. Ren asked his students to create a decreasing pattern that started at 105 and decreased by 10 for 4 counts.

Sam handed in this pattern: 105, 100, 95, 90

Clara handed in this pattern: 105, 104, 103, 102

Kelsey handed in this pattern: 105, 95, 85, 75

Anthony handed in this pattern: 105, 90, 75, 60

28. Which student handed in the correct pattern?
   A. Sam
   C. Kelsey
   B. Clara
   D. Anthony

*Use the following information to answer the next question.*

Both of the given patterns are skip counting forward.

A.  15, 20, 25, 30
B.  7, 14, 21, 28

29. Which of the following statements about the given patterns is **true**?
   A. Both patterns are increasing by the same amount.
   B. Pattern B is increasing more than pattern A.
   C. Pattern A is increasing more than pattern B.
   D. Neither pattern is an increasing pattern.

*Use the following information to answer the next question.*

Sophia is trying to grow her hair. She reads that human hair grows an average of 0.5 in per month. She makes a table of values to show how long it will take her hair to grow 2 in.

| Number of Months | Hair Growth (in) |
|:---:|:---:|
| 1 | 0.5 |
| 2 | 1.0 |
| 3 | 1.5 |
| 4 | 2.0 |

30. Which of the following graphs shows the information in Sophia's table?

A.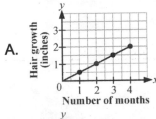

B.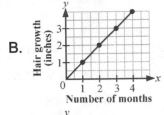

C.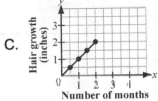

D.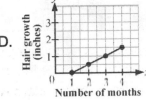

# EXERCISE #2—OPERATIONS AND ALGEBRAIC THINKING
## ANSWERS AND SOLUTIONS

| | | | |
|---|---|---|---|
| 21. C | 24. A | 27. C | 30. A |
| 22. A | 25. B | 28. C | |
| 23. B | 26. See solution | 29. B | |

## 21. C

Follow the order of operations.

**Step 1**

Working from left to right, first multiply or divide. It may be helpful to put brackets around the multiplication part of the expression.

$20 - 9 + (2 \times 3)$
$20 - 9 + (2 \times 3 = 6)$
$20 - 9 + 6$

**Step 2**

Working from left to right, add or subtract.

$20 - 9 = 11$
$11 + 6 = 17$

The value of the expression $20 - 9 + 2 \times 3$ is 17.

## 22. A

Since $4 = 1 + 3$, she can multiply $6 \times 1$ and $6 \times 3$ and then add the answers together.

Since $4 = 2 + 2$, she can multiply $6 \times 2$ and $6 \times 2$ and then add the answers together.

Since $4 = 5 - 1$, she can multiply $6 \times 5$ and $6 \times 1$ and then subtract the answers.

There is no way to make 4 by using the numbers 1 and 2, so Leah cannot use the facts $6 \times 1$ and $6 \times 2$ to find $6 \times 4$.

## 23. B

When an expression is written as a fraction, it shows division. The number you are dividing is on top, and the number you are dividing by is on the bottom.

In the expression $\frac{a}{8}$, the variable $a$ represents a number. A number is being divided by 8.

## 24. A

**Step 1**

Decide which operation to use.

The words "more than" mean that you will use addition.

You will add 2 to the variable.

**Step 2**

Write the expression.

$z + 2$

## 25. B

**Step 1**

Count the number of stars in each row to determine the pattern rule.

- In Row 1, there are 16 stars.
- In Row 2, there are 14 stars.
- In Row 3, there are 12 stars.
- In Row 4, there are 10 stars.
- In Row 5, there are 8 stars.

The pattern rule is subtract 2 from each term to get the next term.

**Step 2**

Apply the pattern rule for three more terms (rows 6, 7, and 8).

$8 - 2 = 6$
$6 - 2 = 4$
$4 - 2 = 2$

There will be 4 stars in Row 7 and 2 stars in Row 8.

## 26.

**Step 1**

Determine what the question is asking.

There is a pattern of how the numbers are changing. Determine the pattern, and apply it to the next two numbers in the table.

### Step 2

Plan your strategy.

Determine how much the numbers are increasing by.

8 + 3 = 11
11 + 3 = 14

The numbers are increasing by 3.

### Step 3

Solve.

Find more terms by following the pattern. Add 3 to each term number.

14 + 3 = 17
17 + 3 = 21
21 + 3 = 24

| Term | Term Number |
|------|-------------|
| 1 | 8 |
| 2 | 11 |
| 3 | 14 |
| 4 | 17 |
| 5 | 20 |
| 6 | 23 |

### Step 4

Check your answer.

Redo the addition to make sure that it is correct.

### 27. C

In the given sequence, the first term is 2, the second term is 4, the third term is 6, the fourth term is 8, and the fifth term is 10. Therefore, the table that correctly displays this information is shown in C.

### 28. C

Compare the patterns to determine which student handed in the correct pattern.

Sam's pattern decreased by 5 for 4 counts.

Clara's pattern decreased by 1 for 4 counts.

Kelsey's pattern decreased by 10 for 4 counts.

Anthony's pattern decreased by 15 for 4 counts.

Kelsey handed in the correct pattern.

### 29. B

Pattern A is increasing by 5, and pattern B is increasing by 7. This means that pattern B is increasing more than pattern A.

### 30. A

### Step 1

Make ordered pairs from the numbers in the table of values.

The first number will come from the left column, and the second number will come from the right column.

The four points Sophia will plot on her graph are (1, 0.5), (2, 1), (3, 1.5), and (4, 2).

### Step 2

Draw the graph.

Give the graph a title, and label the x- and y-axes.

Draw a point for each of the ordered pairs.

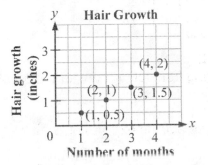

Since hair grows continuously, join the points with a line.

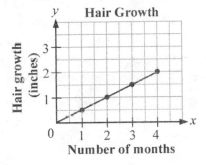

# NOTES

Number and Operations in Base Ten

# NUMBER AND OPERATIONS IN BASE TEN

## Table of Correlations

| Standard | | Concepts | Exercise #1 | Exercise #2 |
|---|---|---|---|---|
| **5.NBT** | Number and Operations in Base Ten | | | |
| 5.NBT.1 | Recognize that in a multi–digit number, a digit in one place represents 10 times as much as it represents in the place to its right and 1/10 of what it represents in the place to its left. | Understanding Place Value to a Million | 31, 32 | 89 |
| 5.NBT.2 | Explain patterns in the number of zeros of the product when multiplying a number by powers of 10, and explain patterns in the placement of the decimal point when a decimal is multiplied or divided by a power of 10. Use whole–number... | Dividing Numbers by Various Powers of Ten | 33, 34 | 90 |
| | | Using Mental Strategies to Multiply Whole Numbers by 0.1, 0.01, and 0.001 | 35, 36 | 91 |
| | | Using Mental Math Strategies to Multiply Whole Numbers by 10, 100, and 1,000 | 37, 38 | 92 |
| | | Multiplying Decimals by 10, 100, 1,000, and 10,000 | 39, 40 | 93 |
| | | Writing Positive Powers of 10 | 41, 42 | 94 |
| 5.NBT.3A | Read, write, and compare decimals to thousandths. Read and write decimals to thousandths using base-ten numerals, number names, and expanded form. | Place Value in Decimal Numbers | 43, 44 | 95 |
| | | Reading and Writing Decimal Numbers | 45, 46 | 96 |
| | | Representing Decimal Numbers to the Thousandths | 47, 48 | 97 |
| 5.NBT.3B | Read, write, and compare decimals to thousandths. Compare two decimals to thousandths based on meanings of the digits in each place, using >, =, and < symbols to record the results of comparisons. | Compare Decimals using Place Value | 49, 50 | 98 |
| | | Ordering Decimal Numbers to the Thousandths | 51, 52 | 99 |
| 5.NBT.4 | Use place value understanding to round decimals to any place. | Rounding Decimals to the Nearest Tenth | 53, 54 | 100 |
| | | Rounding Decimals to the Nearest Hundredth | 55, 56 | 101 |
| | | Round Two Place Decimals to Nearest Whole Number | 57, 58 | 102 |
| 5.NBT.5 | Fluently multiply multi–digit whole numbers using the standard algorithm. | Multiplying a Two-Digit Number by Another Two-Digit Number | 59, 63 | 103 |
| | | Multiplying Two-Digit Numbers by Two-Digit Numbers without Regrouping | 60, 61 | 104 |
| | | Solving Problems Involving Multiplication | 62, 63 | 105 |
| | | Multiplying a Four-Digit Number by a One-Digit Number | 64, 65 | 106 |
| | | Multiplying Three-Digit Whole Numbers by Two-Digit Whole Numbers | 66, 67 | 107 |
| 5.NBT.6 | Find whole–number quotients of whole numbers with up to four–digit dividends and two–digit divisors, using strategies based on place value, the properties of operations, and/or the relationship between multiplication and... | Division Of Whole Numbers | 68 | 112 |
| | | Representing Division Using an Area Model | 69, 70 | 108 |
| | | Dividing Three-Digits by Two-Digits | 71, 72 | 109 |
| | | Dividing Multi-Digit Numbers by One-Digit Numbers | 73, 74 | 110 |

| | | Dividing Four-Digit Numbers by Two-Digit Numbers | 75, 76 | 111, 112 |
|---|---|---|---|---|
| 5.NBT.7 | Add, subtract, multiply, and divide decimals to hundredths, using concrete models or drawings and strategies based on place value, properties of operations, and/or the relationship between addition and subtraction; relate the strategy to a... | Multiplying Decimals by One-Digit Whole Numbers | 77, 78, 88 | 113 |
| | | Adding Decimals to 100ths | 86, 87 | 116 |
| | | Subtracting Decimals to 100ths | 84, 85 | 117 |
| | | Multiplying Decimals by Decimals | 83 | 118 |
| | | Dividing Decimals by Decimals | 79, 80 | 114 |
| | | Dividing Decimals by Whole Numbers | 81, 82 | 115 |

**5.NBT.1** *Recognize that in a multi-digit number, a digit in one place represents 10 times as much as it represents in the place to its right and 1/10 of what it represents in the place to its left.*

## UNDERSTANDING PLACE VALUE TO A MILLION

Understanding place values and period names will help you find the value of a large whole number.

Large numbers are broken up into groups with three digits each. Each group is called a **period**. From right to left, the first period is the ones period, followed by the thousands period. Each period is then broken down into three place values: ones, tens, and hundreds.

To determine the value of a digit in a given place value, use the following steps:

1. Place the number into a place value chart.
2. Identify the value of the digit.

*Example*

Determine the value of the digit 8 in the number 678234.

*Solution*

Place the number in a place value chart.

| Thousands | | | Ones | | |
|---|---|---|---|---|---|
| H | T | O | H | T | O |
| 6 | 7 | 8 | 2 | 3 | 4 |

The digit 8 is in the ones position of the thousands period.

Therefore, the digit 8 has a value of 8,000.

---

**5.NBT.2** *Explain patterns in the number of zeros of the product when multiplying a number by powers of 10, and explain patterns in the placement of the decimal point when a decimal is multiplied or divided by a power of 10. Use whole–number...*

## DIVIDING NUMBERS BY VARIOUS POWERS OF TEN

When dividing a number by a multiple of 10, the decimal point moves as many places to the left as there are zeros. The new number (quotient) is smaller in value.

The following examples demonstrate the rule for dividing numbers by a multiple of 10.

$$123 \div 100 = 1.23$$
$$123{,}000 \div 1{,}000 = 123$$
$$12.3 \div 100 = 0.123$$
$$0.123 \div 1{,}000 = 0.000123$$

$123 \div 100 = 1.23$
    1 2

$123\ 000 \div 1\ 000 = 123.000$
    1 2 3

$12.3 \div 100 = 0.123$
    1 2

$0.123 \div 1\ 000 = 0.000123$
    1 2 3

A power of ten is repeated multiplication of the number 10. For example, $10^3$ is a power of ten. It is the same as $10 \times 10 \times 10 = 1{,}000$. The number 1,000 is a multiple of 10.

Dividing decimals by powers of ten is no different than dividing decimals by multiples of 10. Instead of counting the zeros to determine how many places the decimal moves to the left, look at the exponent on the base 10. The exponent indicates how many places the decimal moves to the left.

The numbers in the previous examples can be written with powers of 10.

$123 \div 10^2 = 1.23$

$123\,000 \div 10^3 = 123.000$

$12.3 \div 10^2 = 0.123$

$0.123 \div 10^3 = 0.000123$

The answers are exactly the same as the answers in the first example.

To divide a number by a power of 10, follow these steps:

1. Identify the exponent on the base 10.
2. Move the decimal.

*Example*

What is the result when 192.37 is divided by $10^3$?

*Solution*

**Step 1**

Identify the exponent of the base 10.

The exponent is 3. This indicates that the decimal moves 3 places to the left.

**Step 2**

Move the decimal.

.192.37

$192.37 \div 10^3 = 0.19237$

Since $10^1 = 10$, the exponent 1 is usually not written. The movement of the decimal still follows the rule, so the decimal moves one place to the left.

*Example*

What is the result when 392.83 is divided by 10?

*Solution*

**Step 1**

Identify the exponent of the base 10.

When there is no exponent on the base, the exponent is assumed to be 1. This indicates that the decimal moves one place to the left.

**Step 2**

Move the decimal.

The equation $392.83 \div 10 = 39.283$ is the same as $392.83 \div 10^1 = 39.283$.

---

Any base with an exponent of 0 is equal to 1 (e.g., $2^0 = 1$, $5^0 = 1$, $10^0 = 1$). The movement of the decimal still follows the rule, so the decimal does not move.

*Example*

What is the result when 69.37 is divided by $10^0$?

*Solution*

**Step 1**

Identify the exponent of the base 10.

Since the exponent is 0, the value of $10^0$ is 1.

**Step 2**

Move the decimal.

Because $10^0$ has a value of 1, the decimal does not move.

$69.37 \div 10^0 = 69.37 \div 1 = 69.37$

---

## USING MENTAL STRATEGIES TO MULTIPLY WHOLE NUMBERS BY 0.1, 0.01, AND 0.001

To make problem solving easier, it is helpful to use a general rule or mental strategy instead of always having to rely on a calculator. There is a general rule to use when you are multiplying any whole number by 0.1, 0.01, or 0.001.

The rule states that you first count the number of decimal places that the decimal number has. Then, you move the decimal point of the whole number that number of places to the left.

- The decimal number 0.1 has one decimal place after the decimal. Move the decimal in the whole number one place to the left.

  51 × 0.1 becomes 5.1

- The decimal number 0.01 has two decimal places after the decimal. Move the decimal in the whole number two places to the left.

  51 × 0.01 becomes 0.51

- The decimal number 0.001 has three decimal places after the decimal. Move the decimal in the whole number three places to the left. You need to add a zero to hold the place when you move three places.

  51 × 0.001 becomes 0.051

*Example*

Explain the mental strategy that can be used to quickly determine the product of the expression 3,526 × 0.001.

*Solution*

The mental strategy you can use is the rule for multiplying any whole number by 0.1, 0.01, or 0.001; count the number of decimal places in the decimal number, and move the decimal point in the whole number that number of places to the left.

**Step 1**

Count the number of decimal places in the decimal number.

There are 3 decimal places (0 tenths, 0 hundredths, and 1 thousandths).

**Step 2**

Move the decimal in the whole number three places to the left. 3526

3,526 × 0.001 = 3.526

---

## Using Mental Math Strategies to Multiply Whole Numbers by 10, 100, and 1,000

One mental math strategy you can use is to look for patterns when multiplying whole numbers by multiples of 10. Look at the pattern that forms when you multiply the same number by 1, 10, 100, and 1,000.

4 × 1 = 4
4 × 10 = 40
4 × 100 = 400
4 × 1 0 = 4 0

| Multiplier | Explanation | Example |
|---|---|---|
| × 10 | There is one zero in 10. Add one zero to the end of the other number. | 36 × 10 = 360 |
| × 100 | There are two zeros in 100. Add two zeros to the end of the other number. | 93 × 10 = 9 30 |
| × 1 0 | There are three zeros in 1000. Add three zeros to the end of the other number. | 7 × 10 = 70 |

One mental strategy for quickly and easily multiplying numbers by 10, 100, or 1,000 is to count the number of zeros. Then, add the same number of zeros to the end of the other number.

*Example*

In a concert hall there are 73 rows with 100 seats.

In total, how many seats are there in the concert hall?

*Solution*

73 × 100 = □

**Step 1**
Count the number of zeros in 100.
There are 2 zeros.

**Step 2**
Add 2 zeros to 73.
73 × 100 = 7,300.
There are 7,300 seats in total.

## MULTIPLYING DECIMALS BY 10, 100, 1,000, AND 10,000

When you multiply decimal numbers by the whole numbers 10, 100, 1,000, or 10,000, you will always move the decimal point to the right.

A mental math strategy you can use to multiply decimals is to count the number of zeros, then move the decimal point that many places to the right. Sometimes you may have to add zeros to the given decimal number to hold the place value.

*Example*

The following examples show these mental multiplication strategies for the decimal number 1.42. The arrows show how the decimal point moves. Remember that you do not need to put a decimal point after a whole number.

- 1.42 × 10 becomes 14.2

  Move the decimal point 1 digit to the right because there is 1 zero in the whole number 10.

- 1.42 × 100 becomes 142.

  Move the decimal point 2 digits to the right because there is 2 zeros in the whole number 100.

- 1.42 × 1 000 becomes 1.420

  Move the decimal point 3 digits to the right because there is 3 zeros in the whole number 1,000. You will have to add a 0 to the right of the digit 2 so that you are able to move the decimal point 3 digits to the right.

- 1.42 × 10 000 becomes 14200.

  Move the decimal point 4 digits to the right because there are 4 zeros in the number 10,000. You will have to add 2 zeros to the right of the digit 2 so that you are able to move the decimal point 4 digits to the right.

### Example

Mr. Barker writes a problem on the board every morning for the class to solve. Today's problem says to multiply 0.75 by 1,000.

Use a mental strategy to find the answer to the expression 0.75 × 1,000.

### Solution

**Step 1**
Count the number of zeros in 1,000.
There are three zeros.

**Step 2**
Move the decimal point.
Since there are three zeros, move the decimal point 3 digits to the right.
Since there are only 2 digits after the decimal point in the given number (0.75), you need to add a zero to the end of the number to show that there are no ones in the new number. Do not put a decimal point after a whole number.
0.75 × 1,000 = 750

---

## WRITING POSITIVE POWERS OF 10

A power has a base and an exponent. To write a number as a power, you need to write it using exponents.

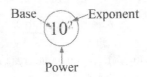

Powers are used to shorten large numbers. They allow you to represent a number such as 1,000,000 without having to write out each zero. Powers do this by multiplying a number by itself. For example, $10^2$ means 10 multiplied by itself 2 times. The power $10^5$ means 10 multiplied by itself 5 times. The following table shows five powers of 10:

| Power | Multiplication | Number |
|-------|----------------|--------|
| $10^1$ | 10 | 10 |
| $10^2$ | 10 × 10 | 100 |
| $10^3$ | 10 × 10 × 10 | 1,000 |
| $10^4$ | 10 × 10 × 10 × 10 | 10,000 |
| $10^5$ | 10 × 10 × 10 × 10 × 10 | 100,000 |

For each power, the exponent is equal to the number of zeros in the number. For example, $10^7$ will have 7 zeros after the 1, and $10^{23}$ will have 23 zeros after the 1.

When writing a positive power of 10, first determine the exponent. To do this, count the number of zeros in the given number. Once you have determined the exponent, write it above the base of 10.

*Example*

Write 10,000 by using exponents.

*Solution*

**Step 1**

Determine the base.

The base of the power is always 10.

**Step 2**

Determine the exponent.

Count the number of zeros.

There are 4 zeros in 10,000, so 4 is the exponent.

**Step 3**

Write the power.

Written with an exponent, the number 10,000 is $10^4$.

---

*5.NBT.3A  Read, write, and compare decimals to thousandths.  Read and write decimals to thousandths using base-ten numerals, number names, and expanded form.*

# Place Value in Decimal Numbers

The pattern showing the relationship among place values is the same in decimal numbers as it is in whole numbers.  As you move from right to left in the place value chart, multiply the place value on the right by 10 to get the place value immediately to the left.  For example, 10 thousandths make 1 hundredth, 10 hundredths make 1 tenth, and 10 tenths make 1 whole.

| Place value position | Ones | . | Tenths | Hundredths | Thousandths |
|---|---|---|---|---|---|
| Base ten block | | . | | | |
| Value | 1 | . | 0.1 | 0.01 | 0.001 |
| Shape | Large cube | . | Flat | Rod | Small cube |

×10    ×10    ×10

*Example*

Describe the place value of each digit in the number 1.438 using base ten materials.

*Solution*

| Ones | • | Tenths | Hundredths | Thousandths |
|------|---|--------|------------|-------------|
|      | • |        |            |             |
| 1    | • | 0.1    | 0.01       | 0.001       |
| 1 one | • | 4 tenths | 3 hundredths | 8 thousandths |

First, remember that the decimal place is in between the ones and the tenths place.

The digit 1 is in the ones place. The value is 1 × 1, or 1.

The digit 4 is in the tenths place. The value is 4 × 0.1, or 0.4.

The digit 3 is in the hundredths place. The value is 3 × 0.01, or 0.03.

The digit 8 is in the thousandths place. The value is 8 × 0.001, or 0.008.

Therefore, 1 + 0.4 + 0.03 + 0.008 = 1.438

## READING AND WRITING DECIMAL NUMBERS

In order to read and write decimal numbers, you must have an understanding of place value to the right of the decimal. The decimal point separates whole numbers from numbers that are less than one. The numbers to the right of the decimal show parts of a whole and are read according to their place value locations.

- The first number to the right of the decimal point is the tenths place value.
- The second number to the right of the decimal point is the hundredths place value.
- The third number to the right of the decimal point is the thousandths place value.

You can use a place value chart to help you place the numbers correctly.

*Example*

To write the number 2.345 in a place value chart, keep the place values in mind. The digit 3 represents three tenths, the digit 4 represents four hundredths, and the digit 5 represents five thousandths.

| Ones | Decimal | Tenths | Hundredths | Thousandths |
|------|---------|--------|------------|-------------|
| 2    | .       | 3      | 4          | 5           |

When reading decimal numbers to the thousandths, you read from the left to the right and say "and" when you read the decimal. To read the number 2.345, you say "two and three hundred forty-five thousandths." To read the number 2.334, you say "two and three hundred thirty-four thousandths."

*Example*

Write the number five and one hundred five thousandths as a numeral.

*Solution*

The number before the word "and" is a whole number. It is written to the left of the decimal point: 5.

"One hundred five thousandths" will be written to the right of the decimal point. Since there are thousandths in the number, there must be 3 digits to the right of the decimal point. One hundred five thousandths is written as .105.

Putting the whole number and decimal together, five and one hundred five thousandths is written as a numeral as 5.105.

---

# REPRESENTING DECIMAL NUMBERS TO THE THOUSANDTHS

Decimal numbers are used to represent parts of a whole. Two ways to represent decimal numbers are with place value charts and in expanded form.

## PLACE VALUE CHARTS

You can represent a decimal number by writing the digits in their correct positions in a place value chart.

*Example*

The decimal number 3.645 can be represented in a place value chart by the following placement of the digits:

- The 3 represents 3 wholes. The digit 3 is written in the ones position.
- The 6 represents 6 tenths. The digit 6 is written in the tenths position.
- The 4 represents 4 hundredths. The digit 4 is written in the hundredths position.
- The 5 represents 5 thousandths. The digit 5 is written in the thousandths position.

| Ones | . | Tenths (Tths) | Hundredths (Hths) | Thousandths (Thths) |
|------|---|---------------|-------------------|---------------------|
| 3 | . | 6 | 4 | 5 |

---

# EXPANDED FORM

Decimal numbers can also be represented using expanded form. Expanded form takes a decimal number and shows it expanded (or stretched out) into an expression based on the place value of each digit. The values of all the digits are then added.

*Example*

To write out the decimal number 4.563 using expanded form, start with the largest place value, which is the ones. Replace all of the other digits in the decimal with zeros. Remember that having zeros after the decimal point does not change the value of the number, so they can be left out. Continue to write the values of the other digits in the given decimal number.

- The largest place value is the ones. The digit 4 is written as 4.000 or 4.
- The next largest place value is the tenths. The digit 5 is written as 0.500 or 0.5.
- The next largest place value is the hundredths. The digit 6 is written as 0.060 or 0.06.
- The last place value is the thousandths. The digit 3 is written as 0.003.

Write all of the place values in a number sentence to represent the decimal number.
4.563 = 4 + 0.5 + 0.06 + 0.003

---

*5.NBT.3B Read, write, and compare decimals to thousandths. Compare two decimals to thousandths based on meanings of the digits in each place, using >, =, and < symbols to record the results of comparisons.*

# COMPARE DECIMALS USING PLACE VALUE

Decimal numbers are compared based on their place values. When comparing decimal numbers, you need to compare each individual **place value**, beginning with the tenths.

It is important to align the decimal points before comparing. You can write the numbers below each other, and then use a **place value chart** to help organize your numbers.

When comparing decimal numbers, the following symbols can be used:

> **Greater than**

< **Less than**

= **Equal to**

- Start at the beginning of the whole number (the highest place value). If one number has a **greater** whole number than another, then that number is the **larger** number.
- If the whole number is the same, move onto the next place value: the **tenths**. The decimal that has the **greatest** number in the tenths place is the **largest**.
- If the numbers in the tenths place are equal, then compare the **hundredths** until one decimal is larger or there are no more place values left to compare.

*Example*

Compare the decimals 0.410, 0.415, 0.414 using a **place value chart**.

*Solution*

### Step 1

Place the numbers in the place value chart.

| O | . | Tths | Hths | Thths |
|---|---|------|------|-------|
| 0 | . | 4 | 1 | 0 |
| 0 | . | 4 | 1 | 5 |
| 0 | . | 4 | 1 | 4 |

### Step 2

Compare the decimals.

Begin with the highest place value. From the place value chart, you can see that the numbers are the same in the ones, the tenths, and the hundredths place value positions.

When comparing the digits in the thousandths (Thths) place, 5 > 4 > 0.

This means that the number with a 5 in the thousandths place is the largest number, the number with a 4 in the thousandths place is the second largest number, and the number with a 0 in the thousandths place is the smallest number.
0.415 > 0.414 > 0.410

## ORDERING DECIMAL NUMBERS TO THE THOUSANDTHS

There are two different ways to order decimal numbers. Decimal numbers can be placed in descending order or in ascending order:

- Descending order is from greatest value to least value.
- Ascending order is from least value to greatest value.

To order decimal numbers to the thousandths, use the following steps:

1. Place the decimal numbers into a place value chart.
2. Compare the digits in the decimal numbers from left to right.
3. Order the decimal numbers.

*Example*

Place the decimal numbers 0.405, 0.45, and 0.445 in ascending order.

*Solution*

### Step 1

Place the decimal numbers into a place value chart.

| O | . | Tth | Hth | Thth |
|---|---|-----|-----|------|
| 0 | . | 4 | 0 | 5 |
| 0 | | 4 | 5 | |
| 0 | | 4 | 4 | 5 |

**Step 2**

Compare the digits in the decimal numbers from left to right.

Compare the ones. All of the decimals have a 0 in the ones place value position.

Compare the tenths. All of the decimals have a 4 in the tenths place value position.

Compare the hundredths.

5 > 4 > 0

Therefore, 0.45 has the greatest value and 0.405 has the least value.

**Step 3**

Order the decimal numbers in ascending order. Ascending order is from least to greatest.

In ascending order, the decimal numbers are 0.405, 0.445, and 0.45.

---

*5.NBT.4    Use place value understanding to round decimals to any place.*

## ROUNDING DECIMALS TO THE NEAREST TENTH

When rounding decimal numbers to the nearest tenth, you need to look at the digit in the hundredths place.

If the digit in the hundredths place is 5 or greater than 5, round the tenths digit up to the next number and drop the number that is in the hundredths place.

*Example*

| Ones | . | Tenths | Hundredths |
|------|---|--------|------------|
| 1 | . | 2 | 6 |

In the number 1.26, the digit 6 > 5, so the 2 in the tenths place rounds up to a 3 and the 6 is dropped.

Rounded to the nearest tenth, 1.26 → 1.3.

---

If the digit in the hundredths place is less than 5, leave the tenths digits as it is and drop the number that is in the hundredths place.

*Example*

| Ones | . | Tenths | Hundredths |
|------|---|--------|------------|
| 3 | . | 8 | 4 |

In the number 3.84, the digit 4 < 5, so the 8 stays as it is and the 4 is dropped.

Rounded to the nearest tenth, 3.84 → 3.8.

*Example*

Mrs. Wilson bought a basket of peaches that had a mass of 5.73 kg.

Rounded to the nearest tenth of a kilogram, what is the mass of the peaches?

*Solution*

To solve this problem, you need to know the place value positions of tenths and hundredths.

The 3 in 5.73 is in the hundredths position.

Since it is less than 5, the 7 in the tenths position stays as it is and the 3 is dropped.

Rounded to the nearest tenth, the mass of the peaches is 5.7 kg.

## ROUNDING DECIMALS TO THE NEAREST HUNDREDTH

To round decimals to the nearest hundredth, you must have an understanding of place value to the right of the decimal point. Keep in mind that the first number to the right of the decimal point is the tenths place value, the second number is the hundredths place value, and the third number is the thousandths place value.

| O | . | Tths | Hths | THths |
|---|---|------|------|-------|
|   | . |      |      |       |

When rounding decimal numbers to the nearest hundredth, you need to look at the digit in the thousandths place.

If the digit in the thousandths place is 5 or greater than 5, round the hundredths digit up to the next number, and drop the number that is in the thousandths place.

*Example*

In the decimal number 1.268, the digit 8 is greater than 5 (8 > 5), so the 6 in the hundredths place rounds up to 7, and the 8 is dropped.

Rounded to the nearest hundredth, 1.268 → 1.27.

If the digit in the thousandths place is less than 5, leave the hundredths digit as it is, and drop the number that is in the thousandths place.

*Example*

In the decimal number 3.842, the digit 2 is less than 5 (2 < 5), so the digit 4 in the hundredths place stays the same, and the 2 is dropped.

Rounded to the nearest hundredth, 3.482 → 3.48.

*Example*

Rounded to the nearest hundredth, what does the decimal number 42.476 become?

*Solution*

When you are rounding a number to the nearest hundredth, look at the digit in the thousandths place.

| T | O | . | Tths | Hths | THths |
|---|---|---|------|------|-------|
| 4 | 2 | . | 4    | 7    | 6     |

Since 6 > 5, 7 hundredths round up to 8 hundredths, and the 6 thousandths are dropped.

42.476 → 42.48

When rounded to the nearest hundredth, the decimal number 42.476 becomes 42.48.

---

## Round Two Place Decimals to Nearest Whole Number

When rounding decimal numbers to the nearest whole number, focus on the first digit to the right of the decimal point in the tenths place. If the digit in the tenths place is between 5 and 9, round the whole number to the next whole number and drop the decimal point and any numbers to the right of the decimal point.

*Example*
Round 34.82 to the nearest whole number.

*Solution*

To round to the nearest whole number means to determine whether the number is closer to 34 or to 35.

Since 8 > 5, round the 4 of 34 up to 5, and drop the .82.
34.82 → 35

---

If the digit in the tenths place is 0-5, leave the whole number as it is, and drop the decimal point and any numbers to the right of the decimal point.

*Example*
Round 15.48 to the nearest whole number.

*Solution*

To round to the nearest whole number, determine whether the number is closer to 15 or to 16.

Since 4 < 5, the 5 of 15 stays the same and the .48 is dropped.

15.48 → 15

---

*5.NBT.5    Fluently multiply multi–digit whole numbers using the standard algorithm.*

## Multiplying a Two-Digit Number by Another Two-Digit Number

To multiply a two digit whole number by a two-digit number, follow these steps:

1. Multiply the first number by the ones of the second number.
2. Multiply the first number by the tens of the second number.
3. Add the two products.

*Example*
What is the product of 67 × 48?

*Solution*

Think of the multiplier 48 as 4 tens (40) and 8 ones.

**Step 1**
Multiply 67 by the ones of 48.

  67
× 8

Multiply the 8 by the digit in the ones place.
8 × 7 = 56

Regroup the answer as 5 tens and 6 ones. Write the 6 in the ones place. Carry the 5 tens over to the tens place.

  5
  67
× 8
   6

Multiply 8 by the digit in the tens place.
8 × 6 = 48

Add this to the 5 tens that you carried over.
48 + 5 = 53

  5
  67
× 8
536

**Step 2**
Multiply 67 by the tens of 48.

  67
× 40

If you multiply 67 × 4 and add a zero on the end, that is the same as multiplying 67 × 40. Put a 0 in the ones place, then multiply 67 × 4.

  67
× 40
   0

Multiply 4 by the digit in the ones place.
4 × 7 = 28

Regroup the answer as 2 tens and 8 ones. Write the 8 in the tens place. Carry the 2.

  2
  67
× 40
  80

Multiply 4 by the digit in the tens place.
4 × 6 = 24

Add this to the 2 tens that you carried over.
24 + 2 = 26

  2
  67
× 40
2,680

**Step 3**
Add the products.
536 + 2,680 = 3,216

```
    67
  × 48
  3,216
```

---

## MULTIPLYING TWO-DIGIT NUMBERS BY TWO-DIGIT NUMBERS WITHOUT REGROUPING

To multiply a two-digit whole number by a two-digit number, follow these steps:

1. **Multiply** the multi-digit number by the ones.
2. **Multiply** the multi-digit number by the tens.
3. **Add** the two products.

*Example*
Solve 34 × 21 = □

*Solution*
Think of the multiplier 21 as 2 tens and 1 one.

**Step 1**
Multiply the multi-digit number by the ones.

```
  34
 × 1
```

You know that any number times 1 is always equal to itself.

```
  34
 × 1
  34
```

**Step 2**
Multiply the multi-digit number by the tens.

```
   34
 × 20
```

Start multiplying from the right; you know that any number multiplied by 0 is always equal to 0. Without doing any calculations, you can write a 0 in the ones position.

```
   34
 × 20
    0
```

Start multiplying the tens.
4 × 2 = 8. 4 ones (4) multiplied by 2 tens (20) equals 8 tens (80). The 8 can be written directly below the tens place value.

```
   34
 × 20
   80
```

2 × 3 = 6. 2 tens (20) multiplied by 3 tens (30) equals 6 hundreds (600). The 6 can be written directly below the hundreds place value.

```
    34
  × 20
    80
 +600
   680
```

**Step 3**
Add the products.

680 + 34 = 714
34 × 21 = 714

---

## SOLVING PROBLEMS INVOLVING MULTIPLICATION

To solve problems that involve multiplication, follow these steps:

1. Identify the important information.
2. Line up the numbers based on their place value.
3. Multiply the digit in the ones place by all the digits in the multi-digit number. Regroup where necessary.
4. Multiply the digit in the tens place by all the digits in the multi-digit number. Regroup where necessary.
5. Add the products.

*Example*

Corey has a box that contains 294 marbles. He wants to know the weight of the box, but his scale cannot weigh objects that heavy. He puts one marble on the scale and finds that it weighs 19 g.

If all the marbles are the same size, what is the total weight of all the marbles in the box?

*Solution*

**Step 1**
Identify the given information, and determine what the problem is asking.
Each marble weighs 19 g, and there are 294 marbles. You need to find the weight of all the marbles.

**Step 2**
Line up the two numbers using place value.

294
× 19

**Step 3**
Multiply the ones. Regroup where necessary.

$$\begin{array}{r} {}^{8\,3} \\ 294 \\ \times\ \ \ \ 9 \\ \hline 2{,}646 \end{array}$$

**Step 4**
Multiply the tens. Regroup where necessary.

$$\begin{array}{r} 294 \\ \times\ 10 \\ \hline 2{,}940 \end{array}$$

**Step 5**
Add the two products together.

$$\begin{array}{r} {}^{1} \\ 2646 \\ +2{,}940 \\ \hline 5{,}586 \end{array}$$

The total weight of the marbles is 5,586 g.

---

# MULTIPLYING A FOUR-DIGIT NUMBER BY A ONE-DIGIT NUMBER

Use the following steps to multiply a four-digit number by a one-digit number:

1.  Line up the numbers according to place value.
2.  Multiply the one-digit number by the ones place value.  Regroup if necessary.
3.  Multiply the one-digit number by the tens place value.  Regroup if necessary.
4.  Multiply the one-digit number by the hundreds place value.  Regroup if necessary.
5.  Multiply the one-digit number by the thousands place value.  Regroup if necessary.

*Example*
Multiply 3 × 1,223.

*Solution*

### Step 1
Multiply the one-digit number by the ones.

$3 \times 3 = 9$

Place the product under the ones place value.

```
  1,223
×     3
      9
```

### Step 2
Multiply the one-digit number by the tens.

$3 \times 2 = 6$

Place the product under the tens place value.

```
  1,223
×     3
     69
```

### Step 3
Multiply the one-digit number by the hundreds.

$3 \times 2 = 6$

Place the product under the hundreds place value.

```
  1,223
×     3
    669
```

### Step 4
Multiply the one-digit number by the thousands.

$3 \times 1 = 3$

Place the product under the thousands place value.

```
  1,223
×     3
  3,669
```

---

# MULTIPLYING THREE-DIGIT WHOLE NUMBERS BY TWO-DIGIT WHOLE NUMBERS

To multiply a three-digit whole number by a two-digit number, follow these steps:

1.  Line up the numbers based on their place value.
2.  Multiply the three-digit number by the digit in the ones place.
3.  Multiply the three-digit number by the digit in the tens place.
4.  Add the two products.

*Example*

Calculate the product of 145 × 22.

*Solution*

**Step 1**

Line up the numbers based on their place value.

```
  145
× 22
```

Think of the multiplier 22 as 2 tens (20) and 2 ones.

**Step 2**

Multiply the three-digit number by the digit in the ones place.
Multiply 145 by the 2 ones.

```
  1
145
× 2
───
290
```

**Step 3**

Multiply the three-digit number by the digit in the tens place.
Multiply 145 by the 2 tens.

```
   1
 145
× 20
─────
2,900
```

**Step 4**

Add the two products.
290 + 2,900 = 3,190

```
   145
 × 22
 ─────
   290
+2,900
 ─────
 3,190
```

*5.NBT.6*  *Find whole–number quotients of whole numbers with up to four–digit dividends and two–digit divisors, using strategies based on place value, the properties of operations, and/or the relationship between multiplication and...*

# DIVISION OF WHOLE NUMBERS

As in multiplication, the best step to begin with when dividing large whole numbers is estimation.

*Example*
Calculate the quotient to 6 337 ÷ 30.

*Solution*
Begin by estimating the solution.  Round each number to the highest place value.  To estimate 6 337 ÷ 30, round 6,337 down to 6 0.
6 0 ÷ 30 = 200

To calculate the quotient of 6 337 ÷ 30, round 6 337 down to 6 0.

| | |
|---|---|
| $$\begin{array}{r} 30\,)\overline{6\,337} \\ -6\,000 \mid 200 \\ \hline 337 \end{array}$$ | There are about 200 groups of 30 in 6 0, so multiply 200 by 30 and subtract this product from 6 337 as shown.  The **remainder** from this step is 337. |
| $$\begin{array}{r} 30\,)\overline{6\,337} \\ -6\,000 \mid 200 \\ \hline 337 \\ -300 \mid 10 \\ \hline 37 \end{array}$$ | There are about 10 groups of 30 in 337, so multiply 10 × 30 and subtract this product from 337 as shown.  The remainder from this step is 37. |
| $$\begin{array}{r} 30\,)\overline{6\,337} \\ -6\,000 \mid 200 \\ \hline 337 \\ -300 \mid 10 \\ \hline 37 \\ -30 \mid 1 \\ \hline 7 \end{array}$$ | There is 1 group of 30 in 37, so multiply 1 × 30 and subtract this product from 37.  There is still 7 remaining, but since 7 is less than 30, 7 is the remainder. Add the numbers down the side of your calculation.  The calculated quotient is 211 with a remainder of 7. |

*Alternate Solution:*

| | |
|---|---|
| $$\begin{array}{r} 211 \\ 30\,)\overline{6\,337} \\ -6\,0 \\ \hline 33 \\ -30 \\ \hline 37 \\ -30 \\ \hline 7 \end{array}$$ | 63 ÷ 30 = 2 with a remainder of 3<br>33 ÷ 30 = 1 with a remainder of 3<br>37 ÷ 30 = 1 with a remainder of 7<br><br>Therefore, the calculated quotient is 211 with a remainder of 7. |

This calculation of 211 is reasonable because it is very close to your estimate of 200.

# REPRESENTING DIVISION USING AN AREA MODEL

Division equations can be represented by an area model. An area model follows the same idea as the area formula, which is $A$ = length × width.

When using an area model to represent division, the dividend is used to represent the area (the total), and the divisor represents the width. Divide the area of the rectangle by the width to find the length.

$\frac{area}{width}$ = length

*Example*

To represent the equation 255 ÷ 5 using an area model, draw a rectangle with a width of 5 and an area of 255.

| 5 | 255 |
|---|---|

It is difficult to divide a large number like 255 by 5. To make it easier, you can split 255 into smaller parts that are easier to divide. The easiest way is to split it up into hundreds, tens, and ones.
255 = 200 + 50 + 5

Now, you can split your rectangle into smaller parts that are easier to divide.

| 5 | 200 | 50 | 5 |
|---|---|---|---|

To find the length of the whole rectangle, you can find the length of each smaller part and then add them together. That means that 255 ÷ 5 is the same as 200 ÷ 5 plus 50 ÷ 5 plus 5 ÷ 5.

| | 40 | | 10 | | 1 |
|---|---|---|---|---|---|
| 5 | 200 | 5 | 50 | 5 | 5 |
| | 200 ÷ 5 = 40 | | 50 ÷ 5 = 10 | | 5 ÷ 5 = 1 |

You can write the quotients above the rectangles to show the length of each part.

| | 40 | 10 | 1 |
|---|---|---|---|
| 5 | 200 | 50 | 5 |

Add these all together to find the total length.
$l$ = 40 + 10 + 1
$l$ = 51

The answer was found using the area model to represent the equation 255 ÷ 5 = 51.

# DIVIDING THREE-DIGITS BY TWO-DIGITS

Dividing a three-digit dividend by a two-digit divisor is similar to dividing a three-digit dividend by a one-digit divisor. The difference is that, instead of finding the number of times the one-digit divisor can go into each individual number, you need to find the number of times the two-digit divisor can go into the first two digits of the dividend.

*Example*

To solve a three-digit by one-digit division problem like $484 \div 4$, you need to change it into a long division equation and see how many times 4 can go into each digit.

$$\begin{array}{r} 1\phantom{00} \\ 4\overline{)484} \\ \underline{-4}\phantom{00} \\ 0\phantom{00} \end{array}$$

Drop down the 8, and see how many times 4 will go into 8.

$$\begin{array}{r} 12\phantom{0} \\ 4\overline{)484} \\ \underline{-4}\downarrow\phantom{0} \\ 08\phantom{0} \\ \underline{-8}\phantom{0} \\ 0\phantom{0} \end{array}$$

Drop down the 4, and see how many times 4 will go into 4.

$$\begin{array}{r} 121 \\ 4\overline{)484} \\ \underline{-4}\downarrow\phantom{0} \\ 08\phantom{0} \\ \underline{-8}\downarrow \\ 04 \\ \underline{-4} \\ 0 \end{array}$$

The solution to the division problem is $484 \div 4 = 121$.

---

*Example*

Division with a two-digit divisor uses a similar process. To divide $484 \div 42$, start by putting it into a long division equation. This time, you need to see how many times 42 can go into 48.

$$\begin{array}{r} 1\phantom{00} \\ 42\overline{)484} \\ \underline{-42}\phantom{0} \\ 6\phantom{0} \end{array}$$

Drop down the 4, and calculate the number of times 42 will go into 64.

$$\begin{array}{r} 11 \\ 42\overline{)484} \\ \underline{-42}\downarrow \\ 64 \\ \underline{-42} \\ 22 \end{array}$$

Since you cannot make another group of 42, there is a remainder of 22.

Therefore, 484 ÷ 42 = 11 R22.

---

Estimation, trial and error, and multiplication facts can be used when you are unsure of how many times the divisor will go into the dividend.

*Example*

Find the quotient of 851 ÷ 17.

*Solution*

**Step 1**

Rewrite the problem as a long division equation.

$17\overline{)851}$

**Step 2**

Determine the number of times 17 will go into 851.

It is not easy to see the number of times 17 will go into 85. Rounding the two numbers will make it easier to solve. Round 17 to 20 and 85 to 90. Then, it is easier to see that 20 goes into 90 four times. Check using multiplication to see if 17 will go into 85 four times.

$$\begin{array}{r} \overset{2}{17} \\ \times\ 4 \\ \hline 68 \end{array}$$

Subtract 68 from 85 to see if you can make one more group of 17.

$$\begin{array}{r} \overset{7}{85} \\ -\ 68 \\ \hline 17 \end{array}$$

Because the difference is 17, you know that 17 can go into 85 one more time. The divisor 17 will go into 85 five times.

$$\begin{array}{r} 5\phantom{00} \\ 17\overline{)851} \\ \underline{85\phantom{0}} \\ 0 \end{array}$$

Drop down the 1.

$$\begin{array}{r} 5\phantom{00} \\ 17\overline{)851} \\ \underline{85\ \downarrow} \\ 1 \end{array}$$

Since the divisor 17 cannot go into 1, there is a remainder of 1.

851 ÷ 17 = 5 R1

---

# DIVIDING MULTI-DIGIT NUMBERS BY ONE-DIGIT NUMBERS

When you divide a whole number, you are breaking the whole number into smaller parts. The starting group is called the **dividend**. The number of small parts the dividend is being broken into is called the **divisor**. The number of objects in each smaller group is called the **quotient**.

$$\text{Divisor} - 4\overset{\overset{\textstyle 2 \;\text{Quotient}}{}}{\smash{)}\,8} - \text{Dividend}$$
$$\frac{8}{0}$$

$$\text{Dividend} \quad \text{Quotient}$$
$$8 \div 4 = 2$$
$$\text{Divisor}$$

To divide a multi-digit number by a one-digit number, follow these steps:

1. Write the division sentence as long division.
2. Find out how many times the divisor goes into the first digit of the dividend. Write the answer on top. (Sometimes, the divisor will be too large to fit into the first digit. If this is the case, find out how many times the divisor goes into the first two digits of the dividend).
3. Multiply the number on top by the divisor. Write the answer below. Subtract.
4. Bring down the next number from the dividend. Write it next to the answer from step 4. This is the new dividend.
5. Repeat steps 2, 3, and 4 until the new dividend is 0. The final answer will be left on top.

*Example*
Divide 8,274 by 3.

*Solution*
### Step 1
Write the division sentence as long division.

$$3\overline{\smash{)}8\,274}$$

### Step 2
Find out how many times the divisor goes into the first digit of the dividend. Write the answer on top.

$$\overset{\textstyle 2}{3\overline{\smash{)}8\,274}}$$

The number 3 goes into 8 two times. Write the number 2 above the 8.

### Step 3
Multiply the number on top by the divisor. Write your answer below. Subtract.

$$\overset{\textstyle 2}{3\overline{\smash{)}8\,274}}$$
$$\underline{-6}$$
$$2$$

Since 3 × 2 = 6, write 6 below the 8. Subtract to find a difference of 2.

**Step 4**

Bring down the next number from the dividend. Write it next to the answer from step 3. This is the new dividend.

```
    2
3)8 274
 −6↓
   2 2
```

Bring down the 2.

**Step 5**

Repeat steps 2, 3, and 4 until the new dividend is 0. The final answer will be left on top.

The number 3 goes into 22 seven times. $3 \times 7 = 21$

Write the 7 on top, and subtract 21 from 22. Bring down the next digit from the dividend.

```
    2 7
3)8 274
 −6↓
   2 2
  −2 1↓
     17
```

The number 3 goes into 17 five times. $3 \times 5 = 15$

Write the 5 on top, and subtract 15 from 17. Bring down the next digit from the dividend.

```
    2 75
3)8 274
 −6↓
   2 2
  −2 1↓
     17
    −15↓
      24
```

The number 3 goes into 24 eight times. $3 \times 8 = 24$

Write the 8 on top, and subtract 24 from 24. Since the new dividend is 0, and there are no more digits to bring down from the dividend, the final answer is the number left on top.

```
    2 758
3)8 274
 −6↓
   2 2
  −2 1↓
     17
    −15↓
      24
     −24
       0
```

The number 8,274 divided by 3 is 2,758.

---

## DIVIDING FOUR-DIGIT NUMBERS BY TWO-DIGIT NUMBERS

Dividing a four-digit number by a two-digit number is very similar to dividing a four-digit number by a one-digit number. The difference is that instead of finding the number of times the one-digit divisor can go into each individual number, you need to find the number of times the two-digit divisor can go into the first two digits of the dividend. Because you are working with larger numbers, you may need to use trial and error or estimation to find out how many times a divisor fits into the dividend.

To divide a four-digit number by a two-digit number, follow these steps:

1. Write the division sentence as long division.
2. Find out how many times the divisor goes into the first two digits of the dividend. Write your answer on top. (Sometimes the divisor will be too large to fit into the first two digits. If this is the case, find out how many times the divisor goes into the first three digits of the dividend).
3. Multiply the number on top by the divisor. Write your answer below and subtract.
4. Bring down the next number from the dividend. Write it next to your answer from step 4. This is your new dividend.
5. Repeat steps 2, 3, and 4 until you reach 0. The final answer will be left on top.

*Example*

Divide 6,358 by 22.

*Solution*

### Step 1

Write the division sentence as long division.

$$22\overline{)6,358}$$

### Step 2

Find out how many times the divisor goes into the first two digits of the dividend. Write your answer on top.

The divisor, 22, goes into 63 two times.

$$\begin{array}{r} 2\phantom{,358} \\ 22\overline{)6,358} \end{array}$$

### Step 3

Multiply the number on top, 2, by the divisor. Write your answer below. Subtract.

Since 22 × 2 = 44, write 44 below the 63. Subtract to find a difference of 19.

$$\begin{array}{r} 2\phantom{,358} \\ 22\overline{)6,358} \\ -44\phantom{58} \\ \hline 19\phantom{58} \end{array}$$

### Step 4

Bring down the next number from the dividend. Write it next to your answer from step 4. This is your new dividend.

Bring down the 5.

$$\begin{array}{r} 2\phantom{,358} \\ 22\overline{)6,358} \\ -44\phantom{58} \\ \hline 195\phantom{8} \end{array}$$

**Step 5**
Repeat steps 2, 3, and 4 until you reach 0. The final answer will be left on top.

```
       289
22)6,358
  - 44
    195
  - 176
    198
  - 198
      0
```

The number 6,358 divided by 22 is 289.

---

*5.NBT.7* *Add, subtract, multiply, and divide decimals to hundredths, using concrete models or drawings and strategies based on place value, properties of operations, and/or the relationship between addition and subtraction; relate the strategy to a...*

## MULTIPLYING DECIMALS BY ONE-DIGIT WHOLE NUMBERS

Multiplying decimal numbers by natural numbers is similar to multiplying whole numbers by whole numbers. When you are multiplying decimal numbers, follow the same procedure you would when multiplying whole numbers. However, when multiplying decimals, you need to put the decimal point in its correct place after you have completed the multiplication steps for the problem.

To determine where the decimal point belongs, count the number of digits to the right of the decimal in the number you are multiplying. Your solution should have the same number of digits to the right of the decimal point as there are in your decimal number.

*Example*

Emma has 8 straws. Each straw is 15.5 cm long. She decides to place the straws in a line on the table.

How long will the line of straws be if the straws are placed end to end?

*Solution*

**Step 1**
Multiply the length of one straw (15.5 cm) by the number of straws (8).
Write the numbers vertically.
Place the 8 below the 5 that is in the tenths place.

```
15.5
×  8
```

**Step 2**
Multiply 15.5 by 8, regrouping where necessary.

```
 44
15.5
×  8
─────
1,240
```

## Step 3

Place the decimal point in the solution.

Since there is one digit to the right of the decimal point in 15.5, you need to have one digit to the right of the decimal point in your answer.

$$1,240 \rightarrow 124.0$$
$$15.5 \times 8 = 124.0$$

When the straws are placed end to end, the combined length of the 8 straws will be 124 cm.

---

## ADDING DECIMALS TO 100THS

When adding decimal numbers using place value follow the following steps:

- First, estimate the answer. Round each decimal number to the nearest whole number.
- Second, add the two rounded numbers to get an estimate of the sum.
- Third, do the actual calculation from right to left, don't forget to regroup where necessary. Line up the two decimals at the decimal point.

*Example*

Ally solved the addition equation $1.15 + 1.75 = \square$ using the following steps:

She rounded each decimal to the nearest whole number. $1.15 \rightarrow 1, 1.75 \rightarrow 2$.

She then added the two estimated numbers. $1 + 2 = 3$.

To determine the actual answer she first lined up the decimals based on their place value.

$$
\begin{array}{r}
1.15 \\
+1.75 \\
\end{array}
$$

She added from right to left.

Hundredths: $5 + 5 = 10$ the 10 hundredths need to be grouped as 1 tenth and 0 hundredths. The 0 is written in the hundredths place value.

Tenths: $1 + 1 + 7 = 9$ the 9 tenths is written directly below the tenths place value.

Ones: $1 + 1 = 2$ the 2 is written in the ones place value. Remember to keep the decimal in the same place as the decimals being added.

$$
\begin{array}{r}
1.15 \\
+1.75 \\
\hline
2.90 \\
\end{array}
$$

---

## SUBTRACTING DECIMALS TO 100THS

Subtracting decimal numbers is the same as subtracting whole numbers. The steps for subtracting decimal numbers are:

- Align decimal numbers in a vertical column. All the digits of the same place value and decimal points form a straight line.
- Fill in any missing spaces to the right of the decimal with zeros.
- Subtract the same as for whole numbers.
- Carry the decimal down, such that it is aligned with the decimals above.

## Example

Kenton had $3.29 in his pocket. He gave $1.07 to his little brother.

How much money does Kenton have left?

## Solution

To solve this problem you need to subtract the two money amounts.

**Step 1**

Line up the decimals based on their place value.

```
  3.29
- 1.07
```

**Step 2**

Subtract the decimal numbers from right to left.

Subtract the hundredths: 9 – 7 = 2. The 2 is written directly below the hundredth place value.

Subtract the tenths: 2 – 0 = 2. The 2 is written directly below the tenths place value.

Subtract the ones: 3 – 1 = 2. The 2 is written directly below the ones place value. Remember to keep the decimal in the same position as the decimals being subtracted.

```
  $3.29
- $1.07
  $2.22
```

Kenton had $2.22 left.

---

## MULTIPLYING DECIMALS BY DECIMALS

To multiply decimal numbers by thousandths, follow these steps:

1. Remove the decimal points.
2. Line up the numbers based on place value.
3. Multiply the two whole numbers together.
4. Add the products together. (Only if you are multiplying by a hundred or thousandth).
5. Place the decimal back into the product.

To replace the decimal in the product, count the number of digits to the right of each of the original decimals. Add the totals together. This will tell you how many digits should be after the decimal point. If there are not enough digits in the product, add zeros right after the decimal point.

## Example

What is the product of 0.134 × 0.2?

## Solution

**Step 1**

Remove the decimal point.

The zeros before the decimal point can be removed as well because having a zero in front does not change the value of the number.

134 × 2 =

**Step 2**

Line up the numbers based on place value.

```
  134
×   2
```

## Step 3
Multiply the two whole numbers together.

$$\begin{array}{r} 134 \\ \times\ 2 \\ \hline 268 \end{array}$$

## Step 4
Replace the decimal into the product.

Count the number of digits to the right of each of the original decimals. The first decimal number has 3 digits to the right of the decimal point. The second decimal has 1 digit to the right of the decimal point. Added together, the new decimal should have 4 digits after the decimal point.

Because there are only 3 digits in the product, place a 0 in front of the 2 so that there will be 4 digits.
$0.134 \times 0.2 = 0.0268$

---

*Example*

What is the product of $0.123 \times 0.311 = \square$?

*Solution*

### Step 1
Remove the decimal point.

The zeros before the decimal point can be removed as well because having a zero in front does not change the value of the number.
$123 \times 311 =$

### Step 2
Line up the numbers based on place value.

$$\begin{array}{r} 123 \\ \times\ 311 \end{array}$$

### Step 3
Multiply the two whole numbers together.

Start by multiplying 1 by the top number.

$$\begin{array}{r} 123 \\ \times\ 1 \\ \hline 123 \end{array}$$

Multiply 10 by the top number. Remember to add a zero on the right side before multiplying to hold the place value of the tens. Continue multiplying the top number by 1.

$$\begin{array}{r} 123 \\ \times\ 10 \\ \hline 1,230 \end{array}$$

Multiply 300 by the top number. Remember to add two zeros on the right side before multiplying to hold the place value of the hundreds. Continue multiplying the top number by 3.

$$\begin{array}{r} 123 \\ \times\ 300 \\ \hline 36,900 \end{array}$$

### Step 4
Add the products together.

$$\begin{array}{r} 123 \\ {}^{1}1,230 \\ +\ 36,900 \\ \hline 38,253 \end{array}$$

**Step 5**

Replace the decimal into the product.

Count the number of digits to the right of each of the original decimals. Both decimal numbers have 3 digits to the right of the decimal point. Added together, the new decimal should have 6 digits after the decimal point.

Because there are only 5 digits in the product, you need to place a 0 in front of the 3 so that there will be 6 digits.
$0.123 \times 0.311 = 0.038253$

## DIVIDING DECIMALS BY DECIMALS

Dividing decimals by decimals is similar to dividing whole numbers. Follow these steps to divide decimals by decimals:

1. Convert the divisor to a whole number by moving the decimal point. What is done to the divisor must also be done to the dividend. For example, if you move the decimal point two places to the right in the divisor, you must also move the decimal point two places to the right in the dividend.
2. Set up the division equation. Remember to place the decimal point into the quotient by lining up the decimal points above and below the division sign.
3. Perform the division.

*Example*

Solve the expression $14.64 \div 2.4$.

*Solution*

**Step 1**

Since the diviser is not a whole number, make it a whole number by moving the decimal point one place to the right.

The divisor is 2.4. Move the decimal point one place to the right, and it becomes 24. Because you moved the decimal point one place to the right in the divisor, you must do the same thing to the dividend. The dividend is 14.64. After you move the decimal point one place to the right, the dividend becomes 146.4.

**Step 2**

Set up the division equation, and line up the decimal points above and below the division sign.

$$24\overline{)146.4}$$

**Step 3**

Divide the two decimals normally, as if they were two whole numbers.

$$
\begin{array}{r}
6.1 \\
24\overline{)146.4} \\
-144\phantom{.0} \\
\hline
2\,4 \\
-2\,4 \\
\hline
0
\end{array}
$$

$14.64 \div 2.4 = 6.1$

*Example*

What is the quotient of 2.592 ÷ 0.54?

*Solution*

**Step 1**

Rewrite the divisor as a whole number.

The divisor is 0.54. Move the decimal point two places to the right.

$0.54 \rightarrow 54$

Move the decimal point two places to the right in the dividend as well.

$2.592 \rightarrow 259.2$

**Step 2**

Set up the division equation. Line up the decimal points above and below the division sign.

$$54\overline{)259.2}$$

**Step 3**

Perform the division.

```
        4.8
54   )259.2
     -216 ↓
       432
      -432
         0
```

The quotient is 4.8.

---

## DIVIDING DECIMALS BY WHOLE NUMBERS

To divide decimal numbers by whole numbers, use the following steps:

1. Remove the decimal point from the number, and divide as a whole number.
2. Set up the long-division equation.
3. Determine the quotient.
4. Place the decimal point into the quotient in the same place as in the original number.

If the placement of the decimal point is incorrect, the value of the answer will be incorrect.

*Example*

Solve 1.59 ÷ 3.

*Solution*

**Step 1**

Remove the decimal point from the decimal number.

$1.59 \rightarrow 159$

**Step 2**

Set up the long-division equation.

$$3\overline{)159}$$

## Step 3

Determine how many times 3 can go into 15.

The number 3 can go into 15 five times.  Write the 5 above the 5 in the dividend.

Multiply 3 by 5, and subtract the product from 15.

Bring down the 9.

```
    5
3)159
 − 15
     9
```

## Step 4

Determine how many times 3 can go into 9.

The number 3 can go into 9 three times.  Write the 3 beside the 5 in the quotient.

Multiply 3 by 3, and subtract the product from 9.

```
   53
3)159
 − 15
     9
    −9
     0
```

## Step 5

Add the decimal back into the dividend, and add a decimal into the quotient.

The original dividend had two decimal places, so the quotient will also have two decimal places.

Since there must always be a number to the left of a decimal, add a 0 to the left of the decimal in the quotient.

```
  0.53
3)1.59
 − 15
     9
    −9
     0
```

# EXERCISE #1—NUMBER AND OPERATIONS IN BASE TEN

31. What digit is in the tens place value in the number 245,697?
    A. 5
    B. 6
    C. 7
    D. 9

32. In which of the following sets of numbers is the digit 4 in the same place value position for every number in the set?
    A. 96,407, 43,543, 26,421
    B. 86,194, 576,436, 26,421
    C. 23,407, 875,436, 126,421
    D. 572,194, 254,250, 975,436

33. What is the value of the expression $31.09 \div 10^2$?
    A. 0.03109
    B. 0.3109
    C. 3.109
    D. 31.09

34. What is the value of the expression $1.97 \div 10$?
    A. 0.0197
    B. 0.197
    C. 1.97
    D. 19.7

35. What is the value of the expression $63 \times 0.1$?
    A. 0.063
    B. 0.63
    C. 6.3
    D. 63

36. The value of the expression $56 \times 0.1$ is
    A. 0.056
    B. 0.56
    C. 5.6
    D. 56

37. What is $18 \times 100$?
    A. 80
    B. 180
    C. 1,800
    D. 180,000

38. What is the product of $100 \times 5$? _____

39. What is the value of the expression $5,129.73 \times 10$?
    A. 5.12973
    B. 51.2973
    C. 512.973
    D. 51,297.3

40. What is the product of $0.25 \times 100$?
    A. 250
    B. 2,500
    C. 25,000
    D. 250,000

41. Which number is equal to the power $10^4$?
    A. 4,000
    B. 10,000
    C. 40,000
    D. 100,000

42. Which power represents 100,000?
    A. $6^{10}$
    B. $5^{10}$
    C. $10^5$
    D. $10^6$

43. In the number 854.902, the value of the digit 2 is
    A. $\dfrac{2}{100}$
    B. $\dfrac{20}{100}$
    C. $\dfrac{2}{1,000}$
    D. $\dfrac{200}{1,000}$

44. Express the value of 2 in the number 1.324 in words.

45. What is fourteen and ninety-seven thousandths written as a decimal number?

**46.** Express the number 0.101 in words.

**47.** Write the decimal number that is represented by the expanded notation $1 + \dfrac{8}{100} + \dfrac{5}{1,000}$.

**48.** What decimal number represents the expanded notation $50 + 6 + \dfrac{8}{10} + \dfrac{9}{1,000}$?

*Use the following information to answer the next question.*

Mr. James gave his students the following list of decimals: 3.221, 4.859, 4.872, 3.564.
He asked his students to identify the decimal with the least value. The answers of four students are shown here.

- Alison: The decimal with the least value is 4.872.
- Hannah: The decimal with the least value is 3.221.
- Martin: The decimal with the least value is 3.564.
- Jason: The decimal with the least value is 4.859.

**49.** Which student identified the decimal with the **least** value?
   **A.** Hannah                 **B.** Alison
   **C.** Martin                  **D.** Jason

*Use the following information to answer the next question.*

During a lesson on decimals, some Grade 5 students said the following statements:

- Alan said that 0.234 is greater than 0.412.
- Peter said that 0.999 is less than 0.128.
- Brittany said that 0.558 is greater than 0.047.
- Madison said that 0.065 is less than 0.031.

**50.** Which of the students' statements is **true**?
   **A.** Madison             **B.** Brittany
   **C.** Peter                 **D.** Alan

51. Ordered from **least** to **greatest**, the decimals 4.531, 4.211, 4.307, and 4.444 are

    A. 4.211, 4.307, 4.444, and 4.531

    B. 4.307, 4.444, 4.531, and 4.211

    C. 4.211, 4.444, 4.531, and 4.307

    D. 4.531, 4.444, 4.307, and 4.211

*Use the following information to answer the next question.*

James was given the decimals 2.333, 2.338, 2.331, 2.334.  He orders them from **least** to **greatest**.

52. What should James's list of decimals look like?

    A. 2.333, 2.331, 2.334, 2.338

    B. 2.331, 2.333, 2.334, 2.338

    C. 2.338, 2.334, 2.331, 2.333

    D. 2.334, 2.331, 2.338, 2.333

*Use the following information to answer the next question.*

A set of numbers is given.

103.980, 103.099, 103.482, 103.917

53. Round the numbers to the nearest tenth, and write them in ascending order.

Elisa is practicing for the long jump for the track and field day at her school. At practice, her first jump was 2.86 m, and her second jump was 3.24 m.

54. Rounded to the nearest tenth, what is the difference between Elisa's two jumps?

55. Rounded to the nearest hundredth, what is the sum of 10.958 and 13.998?

Four boys ran as a team in a 4 × 100 m relay race.  The time, in seconds, each boy took to run his 100 m is given.

- Chung:  13.298
- Ryan:  13.909
- David:  13.004
- Greg:  12.921

56. Rounding each time to the nearest hundredth of a second, how long did it take the boys' team to run the relay race?

57. Akeela's school is 18.45 km from her house.  Rounded to the nearest kilometer, how far is Akeela's house from her school?

*Use the following information to answer the next question.*

Stuart works at a pet store.  He unloads a total of 614.995 kg of dog food from the delivery truck in one day.

58. Rounded to the nearest whole number, what is the total weight of dog food that Stuart unloaded?

59. The product of 39 × 52 is
    A. 273                         B. 793
    C. 1,418                       D. 2,028

60. What is the product of 12 × 34?
    A. 408                         B. 400
    C. 108                         D. 84

61. The product of 31 × 14 is
    A. 438
    B. 434
    C. 155
    D. 138

*Use the following information to answer the next question.*

> A school was making a photo collage of its student population. One hundred twenty-five students each brought three pictures to add to the collage.

62. How many pictures were there in total?
    A. 375
    B. 395
    C. 455
    D. 615

63. What is the product of 76 × 84?
    A. 6,384
    B. 6,080
    C. 984
    D. 912

64. What is 6 × 1,243?
    A. 7,458
    B. 7,218
    C. 6,248
    D. 6,218

65. What is 2 multiplied by 2,863? _____

66. What is the product of 591 × 43?
    A. 24,000
    B. 24,413
    C. 24,445
    D. 25,413

67. The product of 176 × 11 is
    A. 1,936
    B. 1,836
    C. 352
    D. 242

*Use the following information to answer the next question.*

> At a particular candy store, a machine sorts 10,057 candies and puts them into bags. There are 28 candies in each bag.

68. When the machine is finished sorting, how many candies will be left over?
    A. 0
    B. 2
    C. 5
    D. 8

**69.** Which of the following area models represents 288 ÷ 4 ?

**A.**
| | 5 | 2 | 2 |
|---|---|---|---|
| 4 | 20 | 8 | 8 |

**B.**
| | 50 | 2 | 2 |
|---|---|---|---|
| 4 | 200 | 8 | 8 |

**C.**
| | 5 | 20 | 2 |
|---|---|---|---|
| 4 | 20 | 80 | 8 |

**D.**
| | 50 | 20 | 2 |
|---|---|---|---|
| 4 | 200 | 80 | 8 |

*Use the following information to answer the next question.*

Peggy has 555 bottle caps in her collection. She wants to put them into groups of 5 to sell at the county fair. She writes an equation to help her divide the bottle caps.

**70.** Which of the following area models represents Peggy's equation?

**A.**
| | 100 | 10 | 1 |
|---|---|---|---|
| 5 | 500 | 50 | 5 |

**B.**
| | 10 | 10 | 1 |
|---|---|---|---|
| 5 | 50 | 50 | 5 |

**C.**
| | 1 | 1 | 1 |
|---|---|---|---|
| 5 | 5 | 5 | 5 |

**D.**
| | 10 | 10 | 10 |
|---|---|---|---|
| 5 | 50 | 50 | 50 |

**71.** What is the remainder of the equation 852 ÷ 36? _____

**72.** What is the quotient of the division equation 585 ÷ 13 = □? _____ _____

**73.** When 3,462 is divided by 4, the quotient is

**A.** 265, with a remainder of 4
**B.** 365, with a remainder of 4
**C.** 465, with a remainder of 2
**D.** 865, with a remainder of 2

*Use the following information to answer the next question.*

Candice bought 8 stereos on sale for a total of $2,680. She paid the same price for each stereo.

**74.** How much did each of Candice's stereos cost? $_____

**75.** The quotient of 9,386 ÷ 20 is

**A.** 368, with a remainder of 6
**B.** 400, with a remainder of 6
**C.** 450, with a remainder of 6
**D.** 469, with a remainder of 6

**76.** The quotient of 6,417 ÷ 31 is _____.

**77.** What is the product of 9.9 × 8? _____

78. What is $3.27 multiplied by 3?
    A. $9.81                              B. $9.60
    C. $6.81                              D. $6.60

79. The solution to the expression 22.223 ÷ 3.13 is
    A. 7.0                                B. 7.1
    C. 7.4                                D. 7.7

80. When the number 578.042 is divided by 0.01, the decimal moves
    A. two places to the left             B. five places to the left
    C. two places to the right            D. five places to the right

*Use the following information to answer the next question.*

Candice bought 3 backpacks on sale for a total of $27.33.  She paid the same price for each backpack.

81. How much did each backpack cost?
    A. $9.11                              B. $9.00
    C. $8.11                              D. $8.00

82. To the nearest hundredth, the solution to the expression 1.05 ÷ 5 is _____.

83. What is the product of the equation $0.341 \times 0.637 = \square$? _____

84. What is the difference between the decimals 4.61 and 1.50? _____

85. Expressed to the nearest hundredth, the difference between 6.34 and 2.10 is _____.

86. The sum of the decimals 2.41 and 1.58 is _____.

87. What is the sum of the decimals 3.01 and 5.86? _____

88. Valerie has 7 HDTV sets in her electronics store.  If each television costs $3,149.98, the total cost of all 7 television sets is
    A. $220,498.60                        B. $22,050.00
    C. $22,049.86                         D. $2,204.99

# EXERCISE #1—NUMBER AND OPERATIONS IN BASE TEN
## ANSWERS AND SOLUTIONS

| | | | |
|---|---|---|---|
| 31. D | 46. See solution | 61. B | 76. 207 |
| 32. C | 47. See solution | 62. A | 77. 79.2 |
| 33. B | 48. See solution | 63. A | 78. A |
| 34. B | 49. A | 64. A | 79. B |
| 35. C | 50. B | 65. 5726 | 80. C |
| 36. C | 51. A | 66. D | 81. A |
| 37. C | 52. B | 67. A | 82. 0.21 |
| 38. 500 | 53. See solution | 68. C | 83. 0.217217 |
| 39. D | 54. See solution | 69. D | 84. 3.11 |
| 40. B | 55. See solution | 70. A | 85. 4.24 |
| 41. B | 56. See solution | 71. 24 | 86. 3.99 |
| 42. C | 57. See solution | 72. 45 | 87. 8.87 |
| 43. C | 58. See solution | 73. D | 88. C |
| 44. See solution | 59. D | 74. 335 | |
| 45. See solution | 60. A | 75. D | |

## 31. D

**Step 1**

Place the number into a place value chart.

| Thousands | | | Ones | | |
|---|---|---|---|---|---|
| H | T | O | H | T | O |
| 2 | 4 | 5 | 6 | 9 | 7 |

**Step 2**

Identify the place value of each digit in the number 245,697.

- The digit 7 is in the ones position.
- The digit 9 is in the tens position.
- The digit 6 is in the hundreds position.
- The digit 5 is in the thousands position.
- The digit 4 is in the ten thousands position.
- The digit 2 is in the hundred thousands position.

The digit 9 is in the tens position in the number 245,697.

## 32. C

**Step 1**

Make a place value chart to compare the digits in each number.

| | Thousands | | | Ones | |
|---|---|---|---|---|---|
| H | T | O | H | T | O |
| | 9 | 6 | 4 | 0 | 7 |
| | 4 | 3 | 5 | 4 | 3 |
| | 2 | 6 | 4 | 2 | 1 |

The digit 4 is not in the same place value position in the numbers 96,407, 43,543, and 26,421.

| | Thousands | | | Ones | |
|---|---|---|---|---|---|
| H | T | O | H | T | O |
| | 8 | 6 | 1 | 9 | 4 |
| 5 | 7 | 6 | 4 | 3 | 6 |
| | 2 | 6 | 4 | 2 | 1 |

The digit 4 is not in the same place value position in the numbers 86,194, 576,436, and 26,421.

| | Thousands | | | Ones | |
|---|---|---|---|---|---|
| H | T | O | H | T | O |
| | 2 | 3 | 4 | 0 | 7 |
| 8 | 7 | 5 | 4 | 3 | 6 |
| 1 | 2 | 6 | 4 | 2 | 1 |

The digit 4 is in the same place value position in the numbers 23,407, 875,436, and 126,421.

| Thousands | | | Ones | | |
|---|---|---|---|---|---|
| H | T | O | H | T | O |
| 5 | 7 | 2 | 1 | 9 | 4 |
| 2 | 5 | 4 | 2 | 5 | 0 |
| 9 | 7 | 5 | 4 | 3 | 6 |

The digit 4 is not in the same place value position in the numbers 572,194, 254,250, and 975,436.

**Step 2**
Identify the value of the digit 4.
In the numbers 23,407, 875,436, and 126,421, the digit 4 is in the hundreds place and has a value of 400 in each number.

**33. B**

To divide a number by 10, move the decimal 1 place to the left.

To divide by $10^2$, move the decimal 2 places to the left.
$31.09 \div 10^2 = 0.3109$

**34. B**

To divide a number by 10, move the decimal 1 place to the left.
$1.97 \div 10 = 0.197$

**35. C**

When a number is multiplied by 0.1, the decimal point in the number is moved one place to the left.
$63 \times 0.1 = 6.3$

**36. C**

When a number is multiplied by 0.1, the decimal point in the number moves one place to the left.
$56 \times 0.1 = 5.6$

**37. C**

When you are multiplying by multiples of 10, the multiple and the answer always contain the same number of zeros.

Determine how many zeros are in the multiple. Add this amount of zeros to the product.

Since there are two zeros in 100, add two zeros to 18.
$18 \times 100 = 1,800$

**38. 500**

There are two zeros after the 1. To find the product, simply place two zeros after the 5.
$100 \times 5 = 500$

**39. D**

When a number is multiplied by 10, the decimal moves 1 place to the right.
$5,129.73 \times 10 = 51,297.3$

**40. B**

$0.25 \times 100 = 2500$
Since you are multiplying, the decimal point will move to the right.

Since there are four zeros in 10,000, the decimal point will move four places to the right.

**41. B**

When writing a positive power of 10, the base is always 10. The exponent on a positive power of 10 indicates how many zeros are in the number. The exponent has a 4, which means the number will have four zeros in it.

The power $10^4$ is written as the number 10,000.

**42. C**

To write 100,000 using exponents, count the number of zeros. There are 5 zeros in 100,000, so the exponent will be 5.

When writing a positive power of 10, the base is always 10.

Therefore, 100,000 can be written as $10^5$.

**43. C**
**Step 1**
Place the number 854.902 in a place value chart.

| H | T | O | . | Tth | Hth | Thth |
|---|---|---|---|---|---|---|
| 8 | 5 | 4 | . | 9 | 0 | 2 |

**Step 2**
Since the digit 2 is in the thousandths position, the value of the 2 is two thousandths or $\dfrac{2}{1,000}$.

**44.**

**Step 1**
Make a place value chart to determine the values of the digits.

| O | . | Tth | Hth | Thth |
|---|---|-----|-----|------|
| 1 | . | 3 | 2 | 4 |

**Step 2**
Write in words.
In the place value chart, the 2 is in the hundredths place.
The value of 2 in the number 1.324 is two hundredths.

**45.**

**Step 1**
Since the word *fourteen* comes before the word *and*, fourteen is a whole number. It is written as 14, with the decimal point located immediately to the right.

**Step 2**
Since the words *ninety-seven thousandths* end with the word *thousandths*, there must be three digits to the right of the decimal.

- The 7 of $\dfrac{97}{1,000}$ is in the thousandths place.

- The 9 is in the hundredths place.

- There are no tenths in $\dfrac{97}{1,000}$, so put a zero in the tenths place as a placeholder.

**Step 3**
The given chart shows the placement of the digits representing the number fourteen and ninety-seven thousandths.

| T | O | . | Tths | Hths | Thths |
|---|---|---|------|------|-------|
| 1 | 4 | . | 0 | 9 | 7 |

Fourteen and ninety-seven thousandths is written as the decimal number 14.097.

**46.**

**Step 1**
Determine the whole number.
Since there is no whole number, start with the fractional amount.

**Step 2**
Determine the fractional amount.
The numerator of the fractional amount, 101, is expressed in words as one hundred one.
Since there are three digits to the right of the decimal, the denominator of the fractional amount is expressed in words as thousandths.
Expressed in words, the decimal number 0.101 is one hundred one thousandths.

**47.**

**Step 1**
Use a place value chart to help you see the different place values represented in the expanded notation.
Since there are no tenths represented in the expanded notation, you need to place a zero (place holder) in the tenths position.

| O | . | Tth | Hth | Thth |
|---|---|-----|-----|------|
| 1 | . | 0 | .8 | 5 |

**Step 2**
Write the number as a decimal.
The decimal number represented by the expanded notation $1 + \dfrac{8}{100} + \dfrac{5}{1,000}$ is 1.085.

**48.**

**Step 1**
Place each digit into a place value chart.
The given chart shows the position and value of the digits in the expanded notation.
Since there are no hundredths in the expanded notation, place a zero in the hundredths place as a place holder.

| T | O | . | Tth | Hth | Thth |
|---|---|---|-----|-----|------|
| 5 | 6 | . | 8 | 0 | 9 |

**Step 2**
Determine the decimal number.
The decimal number that represents the expanded notation $50 + 6 + \dfrac{8}{10} + \dfrac{9}{1,000}$ is 56.809.

## 49. A

### Step 1
Place each decimal in a place value chart.

| Ones | | | . | Parts of a Whole | | |
|---|---|---|---|---|---|---|
| H | T | O | . | Tth | Hth | Thth |
| | | 3 | . | 2 | 2 | 1 |
| | | 4 | . | 8 | 5 | 9 |
| | | 4 | . | 8 | 7 | 2 |
| | | 3 | . | 5 | 6 | 4 |

### Step 2
Compare the decimals from left to right. Compare the digits in the ones place. Since 3 < 4, neither 4.859 nor 4.872 has the least value.

Compare the digit in the tenths place of 3.221 and 3.564. Since 2 < 5, then 3.221 < 3.564. The decimal with the least value is 3.221. Therefore, Hannah's answer is correct.

## 50. B

### Step 1
Compare the decimals in Alan's statement. Since there is a 0 in the ones place of each decimal, compare the digits in the tenths places.

| Ones | | | . | Parts of a Whole | | |
|---|---|---|---|---|---|---|
| H | T | O | . | Tth | Hth | Thth |
| | | 0 | . | 2 | 3 | 4 |
| | | 0 | . | 4 | 1 | 2 |

Since 4 > 2, 0.412 is greater than 0.234. Alan's statement is incorrect.

### Step 2
Compare the decimals in Peter's statement. Since there is a 0 in the ones place of each decimal, compare the digits in the tenths places.

| Ones | | | . | Parts of a Whole | | |
|---|---|---|---|---|---|---|
| H | T | O | . | Tth | Hth | Thth |
| | | 0 | . | 9 | 9 | 9 |
| | | 0 | . | 1 | 2 | 8 |

Since 9 > 1, 0.999 is greater than 0.128. Peter's statement is incorrect.

### Step 3
Compare the decimals in Brittany's statement. Since there is a 0 in the ones place of each decimal, compare the digits in the tenths places.

| Ones | | | . | Parts of a Whole | | |
|---|---|---|---|---|---|---|
| H | T | O | . | Tth | Hth | Thth |
| | | 0 | . | 5 | 5 | 8 |
| | | 0 | . | 0 | 4 | 7 |

Since 5 > 0, 0.558 is greater than 0.047. Brittany's statement is correct.

### Step 4
Compare the decimals in Madison's statement. Since there is a 0 in the tenths place of each decimal, compare the digits in the hundredths places.

| Ones | | | . | Parts of a Whole | | |
|---|---|---|---|---|---|---|
| H | T | O | . | Tth | Hth | Thth |
| | | 0 | . | 0 | 6 | 5 |
| | | 0 | . | 0 | 3 | 1 |

Since 6 > 3, 0.065 is greater than 0.031. Madison's statement is incorrect.

## 51. A

### Step 1
Place each decimal into a place value chart.

| O | . | Tth | Hth | Thth |
|---|---|---|---|---|
| 4 | . | 5 | 3 | 1 |
| 4 | . | 2 | 1 | 1 |
| 4 | . | 3 | 0 | 7 |
| 4 | . | 4 | 4 | 4 |

### Step 2
Compare the decimals.

Start at the greatest place value, and compare the single digits. All the decimal numbers have the same number in the ones place (4), so compare the digits in the tenths place.
2 < 3 < 4 < 5

### Step 3
Order the decimals.

Ordered from least to greatest, the given decimals are 4.211, 4.307, 4.444, and 4.531.

## 52. B

### Step 1

Place the decimals in a place value chart.

| O | . | Tth | Hth | Thth |
|---|---|-----|-----|------|
| 2 | . | 3 | 3 | 3 |
| 2 | . | 3 | 3 | 8 |
| 2 | . | 3 | 3 | 1 |
| 2 | . | 3 | 3 | 4 |

### Step 2

Compare the digits in the decimal numbers from left to right.

Start on the left with the greatest place value. The greatest place value is the ones position. Each of the numbers has a 2 in the ones position. Because these numbers are all the same, move to the next greatest place value position.

The next greatest place value is the tenths. All the decimals have a 3 in the tenths place value. Because these numbers are all the same, move to the next greatest place value position.

The next greatest place value is the hundredths. All the decimals have a 3 in the hundredths place. Because these numbers are all the same, move to the next greatest place value position.

The next greatest place value is the thousandths. Compare the digits in the thousandths place.
$8 > 4 > 3 > 1$
The decimal 2.338 has the greatest value, and the decimal 2.331 has the least value.

### Step 3

Order the decimals from least to greatest

To order the decimals, you have to compare the value of each decimal. Start with the highest place value. In this case, the decimals all have the same decimals except for in the thousandths place. Use the single digits in the thousandths place to order the decimals.
$1 < 3 < 4 < 8$
From least to greatest, the decimals are 2.331, 2.333, 2.334, and 2.338.

## 53.

### Step 1

Round each number to the nearest tenth. Remember to look only at the digit in the place value to the right of the tenths, which is the hundredths place value.

- Since $8 > 5$, $103.980 \to 104.0$.
- Since $9 > 5$, $103.099 \to 103.1$.
- Since $8 > 5$, $103.482 \to 103.5$.
- Since $1 < 5$, $103.917 \to 103.9$.

### Step 2

Write the numbers in ascending order (from least to greatest value).
103.1, 103.5, 103.9, 104.0

## 54.

### Step 1

Calculate the difference between the two jumps, regrouping where necessary.

```
  3.24
 −2.86
  0.38
```

The difference between Elisa's two jumps is 0.38 m.

### Step 2

Round the difference to the nearest tenth.
Since $8 > 5$, $0.38 \to 0.4$
Rounded to the nearest tenth, the difference between the two jumps is 0.4 m.

## 55.

### Step 1

Calculate the sum of the two numbers, regrouping when necessary.

```
  1 11
 10.958
+13.998
 24.956
```

### Step 2

Round the sum to the nearest hundredth.
The digit 6 is in the thousandths place. Because 6 is greater than 5, the digit in the hundredth place (5) is rounded up.
$24.956 \to 24.96$

**56.**

**Step 1**

Round each time to the nearest hundredth.

- Chung: 13.298 → 13.30 because 8 > 5
- Ryan: 13.909 → 13.91 because 9 > 5
- David: 13.004 → 13.00 because 4 < 5
- Greg: 12.921 → 12.92 because 1 < 5

**Step 2**

Calculate the sum of the four rounded times, regrouping when necessary.

```
 12
 13.30
 13.91
 13.00
+12.92
 53.13
```

It took the boys' team 53.13 seconds to complete the relay race.

**57.**

**Step 1**

Identify the digit in the ones place using a place value chart.

| T | O | . | Tth | Hth |
|---|---|---|-----|-----|
| 1 | 8 | . | 4 | 5 |

The digit in the ones place is 8.

**Step 2**

Round to the nearest whole number.

Since the 4 in the tenths place is less than 5, the 8 ones remain the same. The digits to the right of the decimal are dropped.

18.45 → 18

Rounded to the nearest kilometer, Akeela's house is 18 km from her school.

**58.**

**Step 1**

Identify the digit in the ones place.

| H | T | O | . | Tth | Hth | Thth |
|---|---|---|---|-----|-----|------|
| 6 | 1 | 4 | . | 9 | 9 | 5 |

The digit in the ones place is 4.

**Step 2**

Round the number to the nearest whole number.

Since the 9 in the tenths place is greater than 5, the 4 ones round up to 5 ones. Drop the decimal and all the digits to the right of the decimal. 614.995 → 615 because 9 > 5.

Rounded to the nearest whole number, Stuart unloaded 615 kg of dog food.

**59. D**

**Step 1**

Multiply 39 by 2.

```
  1
  39
× 2
  78
```

**Step 2**

Multiply 39 by 50.

```
   4
   39
× 50
1,950
```

**Step 3**

Add the two products

78 + 1,950 = 2,028

**60. A**

**Step 1**

Multiply the ones.

Multiply 4 by 12.

```
  12
× 4
  48
```

**Step 2**

Multiply the tens.

There is a 3 in the tens place, which equals 30. Multiply 30 by 12.

```
   12
× 30
  360
```

**Step 3**

Add the two products.

360 + 48 = 408

## 61. B

**Step 1**
Multiply the ones.
In this case, multiply 31 by 4.

```
  31
×  4
───
 124
```

**Step 2**
Multiply the tens.
There is a 1 in the tens place value, which equals 10, so multiply 31 by 10.

```
  31
× 10
───
 310
```

**Step 3**
Add the two products.
124 + 310 = 434

## 62. A

**Step 1**
Place the three-digit number above the one-digit number. The digits in the ones place must be lined up. Draw a line under the bottom number.

```
125
× 3
```

**Step 2**
Begin by multiplying the ones digits.
(5 × 3 = 15)
This number (15) is larger than 9, so the 1 needs to be placed above the tens column. Place the 5 below the line in the ones column.

```
  1
125
× 3
───
  5
```

**Step 3**
Multiply the digit in the tens place by the one-digit number.
(2 × 3 = 6)
Add the 1 to the 6.
1 + 6 = 7

```
  1
125
× 3
───
 75
```

**Step 4**
Multiply the digit in the hundreds place by the one-digit number.
(1 × 3 = 3)

```
  1
125
× 3
───
375
```

The correct answer is 375.

## 63. A

**Step 1**
Multiply 4 by 76.

```
 ²76
×   4
────
 304
```

**Step 2**
Multiply 80 by 76.

```
 ⁴76
×  80
─────
6,080
```

**Step 3**
Add the two products.
6,080 + 304 = 6,384

## 64. A

**Step 1**
Multiply the one-digit number by the ones.
6 × 3 = 18
Write the 8 below the line of the ones place, and carry the 1 to the top of the tens place.

```
    1
1243
×   6
────
    8
```

**Step 2**
Multiply the one-digit number by the tens. Remember to add the 1 that was carried over from the ones.
6 × 4 = 24
24 + 1 = 25
Write the 5 below the line of the tens place, and carry the 2 to the top of the hundreds place.

```
   21
1243
×   6
────
   58
```

### Step 3

Multiply the one-digit number by the hundreds. Remember to add the 2 that was carried over from the tens.

$6 \times 2 = 12$
$12 + 2 = 14$

Write the 4 below the line of the hundreds place, and carry the 1 to the top of the thousands place.

```
 121
1243
×   6
 458
```

### Step 4

Multiply the one-digit number by the thousands. Remember to add the 1 that was carried over from the hundreds.

$6 \times 1 = 6$
$6 + 1 = 7$

Write the 7 below the line of the thousands place.

```
 121
1243
×   6
7,458
```

### 65  5726

#### Step 1

Multiply the one-digit number by the ones.

$2 \times 3 = 6$

Place the 6 below the line of the ones place value.

```
2863
×   2
   6
```

#### Step 2

Multiply the one-digit number by the tens.

$2 \times 6 = 12$

Place the 2 below the line of the tens place, and carry the 1 to the top of the hundreds place.

```
  1
2863
×   2
  26
```

### Step 3

Multiply the one-digit number by the hundreds. Do not forget to add the 1 that was carried over from the tens.

$2 \times 8 = 16$
$16 + 1 = 17$

Place the 7 below the line of the hundreds place, and carry the 1 to the top of the thousands place.

```
 11
2863
×   2
 726
```

### Step 4

Multiply the one-digit number by the thousands. Do not forget to add the 1 that was carried over from the hundreds.

$2 \times 2 = 4$
$4 + 1 = 5$

Place the 5 below the line of the thousands place.

```
 11
2863
×   2
5,726
```

### 66.  D

#### Step 1

Estimate the product to predict a reasonable answer.

Round both numbers to the highest place value.

$43 \rightarrow 40$
$591 \rightarrow 600$
$600 \times 40 = 24,000$

#### Step 2

Multiply the ones. Regroup where necessary.

```
 2
591
× 3
1,773
```

## Step 3

Multiply the tens. Regroup where necessary.

$$\begin{array}{r} \overset{3}{591} \\ \times\ 40 \\ \hline 23{,}640 \end{array}$$

When multiplying by the tens position, it is important to remember that even though it may seem that you are only multiplying by a single digit, you are really multiplying by 10. In this case, you are multiplying 4 tens, which is equal to 40. A zero must be added before multiplying to hold the place value of the ones position.

## Step 4

Add the products together.
1,773 + 23,640 = 25,413

## Step 5

Compare the estimated product to the calculated product, and determine the reasonableness of the answer.

The calculated answer of 25,413 is close to the estimated answer of 24,000, so the answer of 25,413 is reasonable.

## 67. A

Think of the multiplier 11 as one 10 and one 1.

Multiply the multi-digit number by the number in the ones place.

176
× 1

- 6 × 1 = 6
  The 6 is written directly below the ones place value.

  $$\begin{array}{r} 176 \\ \times\ 1 \\ \hline 6 \end{array}$$

- 7 × 1 = 7
  The 7 tens is written directly below the tens place value.

  $$\begin{array}{r} 176 \\ \times\ 1 \\ \hline 76 \end{array}$$

- 1 × 1 = 1
  The 1 hundred is written directly below the hundreds place value.

  $$\begin{array}{r} 176 \\ \times\ 1 \\ \hline 176 \end{array}$$

Multiply the multi-digit number by the number in the tens place.

176
× 10

You know that anything multiplied by 0 will always equal 0. Without doing any multiplication, you can automatically write a 0 directly below the ones place value. This will keep the value of the 10 while simply multiplying the multi-digit number by 1.

$$\begin{array}{r} 176 \\ \times\ 10 \\ \hline 0 \end{array}$$

Now, begin multiplying the tens.

- 6 × 1 = 6
  The 6 is written directly below the tens place value.

  $$\begin{array}{r} 176 \\ \times\ 10 \\ \hline 60 \end{array}$$

- 7 × 1 = 7
  The 7 tens is written directly below the hundreds place value.

  $$\begin{array}{r} 176 \\ \times\ 10 \\ \hline 760 \end{array}$$

- 1 × 1 = 1
  The 1 hundred is written directly below the thousands place value.

  $$\begin{array}{r} 176 \\ \times\ 10 \\ \hline 1{,}760 \end{array}$$

Add the products.

$$\begin{array}{r} 1760 \\ +\ 176 \\ \hline 1{,}936 \end{array}$$

$$\begin{array}{r} 176 \\ \times\ 11 \\ \hline 1{,}936 \end{array}$$

The product of 176 × 11 is 1,936.

## 68. C

To determine how many candies will be left over, calculate how many bags will be needed to sort 10,057 candies.

Divide the total number of candies (10,057) by the number of candies that will go into each bag (28). The quotient will show how many bags will be used, and the remainder will show how many candies will be left over.

$$
\begin{array}{r}
359 \\
28\overline{)10057} \\
-84 \phantom{00} \\
\hline
165 \phantom{0} \\
-140 \phantom{0} \\
\hline
257 \\
-252 \\
\hline
5
\end{array}
$$

After all the candies are bagged, there will be 5 candies left over.

### 69. D

**Step 1**
Write the larger number in expanded notation. Split the larger number into hundreds, tens, and ones.
288 = 200 + 80 + 8

**Step 2**
Draw an area model.
Write the smaller number along the width of the rectangle. Write the ones, tens, and hundreds of the larger number inside the rectangle.
This area model represents 288 ÷ 4.

| | 50 | 20 | 2 |
|---|---|---|---|
| 4 | 200 | 80 | 8 |

If you need help, this is how the quotients are found:
200 ÷ 4 = 50
80 ÷ 4 = 20
8 ÷ 4 = 2
All the individual quotients are written on top of the area being divided.

**Step 3**
To find the quotient of 288 ÷ 4, add the individual quotients from the expanded area.
50 + 20 + 2 = 72
288 ÷ 4 = 72

### 70. A

**Step 1**
Write the larger number in expanded notation. Split the larger number into hundreds, tens, and ones.
555 = 500 + 50 + 5

**Step 2**
Draw the area model.
Write the smaller number along the width of the rectangle. Write the hundreds, tens, ones of the larger number inside the rectangle.
This is the area model that represents Peggy's equation.

| | 100 | 10 | 1 |
|---|---|---|---|
| 5 | 500 | 50 | 5 |

If you need help, this is how the quotients are found:
500 ÷ 5 = 100
50 ÷ 5 = 10
5 ÷ 5 = 1

**Step 3**
To find the quotient of 555 ÷ 5, add the individual quotients from the expanded area.
100 + 10 + 1 = 111
555 ÷ 5 = 111

### 71. 24

Write the long division equation.
$36\overline{)852}$

Determine the quotient and remainder.

The number 36 cannot go into 8, but it goes into 85 twice.

Multiply 36 by 2, and write the product directly below 85. Subtract the two numbers, and write the difference below. Bring down the 2.

$$
\begin{array}{r}
2 \phantom{0} \\
36\overline{)852} \\
-72\downarrow \\
\hline
132
\end{array}
$$

Determine how many times 36 can go into 132. It can go into 132 three times. Write the 3 in the quotient. Multiply 36 by 3, and write the product directly below 132. Subtract the two numbers, and write the difference below. Since 36 cannot go into 24, the remainder is 24.

$$\begin{array}{r} 23 \\ 36\overline{)852} \\ 72\downarrow \\ \hline 212 \\ 132 \\ -108 \\ \hline 24 \end{array}$$

$852 \div 36 = 23 \text{ R}24$

The quotient of $852 \div 36$ is 23 with a remainder of 24.

## 72. 45

**Step 1**
Write the division equation.
$13\overline{)585}$

**Step 2**
Determine the quotient.
The number 13 cannot go into 5, but it can go into 58. It goes into 58 four times.

$$\begin{array}{r} 4 \\ 13\overline{)585} \\ -52\downarrow \\ \hline 65 \end{array}$$

Write a 4 in the quotient, and multiply 13 by 4. Write the product directly below 58. Subtract the two numbers, and write the difference below. Bring down the 5.

$$\begin{array}{r} 45 \\ 13\overline{)585} \\ -52\downarrow \\ \hline 65 \\ -65 \\ \hline 0 \end{array}$$

Determine how many times 13 goes into 65. It goes into 65 five times. Write a 5 in the quotient, and write the product directly below. Subtract the two numbers. If the difference is zero, then the division is complete.
$585 \div 13 = 45$

## 73. D

**Step 1**
Set up the division equation.
Write the divisor (4) in front of the division bracket and the dividend (3,462) below the division bracket.
$\text{divisor}\overline{)\text{dividend}}$
$4\overline{)3,462}$

**Step 2**
Determine if the first digit in the dividend can be divided by the divisor. If not, use the first two digits of the dividend.
The first digit in the dividend (3) is smaller than 4 (the divisor).
You will need to use the first two digits of the dividend (34).

**Step 3**
Determine how many times the divisor can go into the first two numbers of the dividend.
The number 4 can go into 34 eight times.
Multiply the 4 by the 8, and write the product (32) below the dividend.

$$\begin{array}{r} 8 \\ 4\overline{)3,462} \\ 32 \end{array}$$

**Step 4**
Subtract the two numbers.
$34 - 32 = 2$
Bring down the number 6. Thus, 26 will be the new dividend.

$$\begin{array}{r} 8 \\ 4\overline{)3,462} \\ -32 \\ \hline 26 \end{array}$$

**Step 5**
Repeat the previous steps until you cannot divide any longer.
The answer will be above the dividend.

```
    865
4)3,462
  -32
   26
  -24
   22
  -20
    2
```

The quotient is 865, with a remainder of 2.

74. **335**

**Step 1**
Write the division sentence as long division.

```
8)2,680
```

**Step 2**
Find out how many times the divisor goes into the dividend. Write your answer on top.
Since 8 does not go into the first digit (2), you must look at the first two digits (26). The number 8 goes into 24 three times, so write the number 3 above the 6.

```
    3
8)2,680
```

**Step 3**
Multiply the number on top by the divisor. Write your answer below, and subtract. Since 8 × 3 = 24, write 24 below 26. Subtract to find a difference of 2.

```
    3
8)2,680
  -24
    2
```

**Step 4**
Bring down the next number from the dividend. Bring down the 8. Write it next to your answer from step 3. This is your new dividend.

```
    3
2)2,680
  -24
   28
```

**Step 5**
Repeat steps 2, 3, and 4 until you reach 0.
The final answer will be left on top.

```
   335
8)2,680
  -24
   28
  -24
   40
  -40
    0
```

Each of the stereos cost Candice $335.

75. **D**

**Step 1**
Start by dividing 20 into the largest place value, the thousands place value position of the four-digit number.
Divide 20 into 9,000.
Since 20 goes into 9,000 450 times, subtract this product from 9,386. The remainder from this step is 386.

```
20)9,386
  -9,000  (450)
```

**Step 2**
Divide 20 into the hundreds place value position.
Divide 20 into 300.
Since 20 goes into 300 15 times, subtract this product from 386. The remainder from this step is 86.

```
20)9,386
  -9,000  (450)
     386
    -300  (15)
```

## Step 3

Divide 20 into the tens place value position.

Divide 20 into 80.

Since 20 goes into 80 four times, subtract this product from 86. There is still 6 remaining. Because 6 is less than 20, there will be a remainder of 6.

```
20)9,386
  -9,000  (450)
     386
    -300  (15)
      86
     -80  (4)
       6
```

## Step 4

Add the numbers down the side of your calculation, and put the sum on top of the long division symbol.

450 + 15 + 4 = 469

```
       469
20)9,386
  -9,000
     386
    -300
      86
     -80
       6
```

The calculated quotient is 469, with a remainder of 6.

## 76.  207

### Step 1

Set up the division equation.

Write the divisor (31) in front of the division bracket and the dividend (6,417) below the division bracket.

divisor)dividend

31)6,417

## Step 2

Divide 31 into 64.

The number 31 can go into 64 twice. Place a 2 on top of the division bracket.

31 × 2 = 62

Place the 62 under the 64, and subtract the two numbers.

64 − 62 = 2

Drop down the 1.

```
      2
31)6417
  -62↓
    21
```

## Step 3

Divide 31 into 21.

The number 31 cannot go into 21. It is important to place a 0 beside the 2 on top of the division bracket.

31 × 0 = 0

Place the 0 under the 21, and subtract the two numbers.

21 − 0 = 21

Drop down the 7.

```
     20
31)6417
  -62↓
    21
    -0↓
    217
```

## Step 4

Divide 31 into 217.

The number 31 goes into 217 seven times. Place a 7 beside the 0 on top of the division bracket.

31 × 7 = 217

Place the 217 under the 217, and subtract the two numbers.

217 − 217 = 0

There is no remainder. The division statement is done.

```
     207
31)6417
  -62↓
    21
    -0↓
    217
   -217
      0
```

6,417 ÷ 31 = 207

## 77. 79.2

Since there is one digit to the right of the decimal in the number 9.9, there must also be one digit to the right of the decimal in the product.

$$\begin{array}{r} 9.9 \\ \underline{\times\ 8} \\ 79.2 \end{array}$$

The product of 9.9 × 8 is 79.2.

## 78. A

**Step 1**
Place the dollar amount ($3.27) above the one-digit number (3) so that the ones line up.

$$\begin{array}{r} 3.27 \\ \underline{\times\ 3} \end{array}$$

**Step 2**
Take the decimal out of the dollar amount.

$$\begin{array}{r} 327 \\ \underline{\times\ 3} \end{array}$$

**Step 3**
Multiply the ones.
$7 \times 3 = 21$
Place the 1 ones (in 21) below the line.
Place the 2 tens (in 21) above the 2 tens.

$$\begin{array}{r} \overset{2}{3}27 \\ \underline{\times\ 3} \\ 1 \end{array}$$

**Step 4**
Multiply the tens.
$2 \times 3 = 6$
Add the 2 tens that were carried to the tens place.
$6 + 2 = 8$
Place the 8 below the line in the tens column.

$$\begin{array}{r} 327 \\ \underline{\times\ 3} \\ 81 \end{array}$$

**Step 5**
Multiply the hundreds.
$3 \times 3 = 9$
Place the 9 below the line in the hundreds column.

$$\begin{array}{r} 327 \\ \underline{\times\ 3} \\ 981 \end{array}$$

**Step 6**
Place the decimal back into the dollar amount. The decimal should be in the same place as the original decimal.

$$\begin{array}{r} 3.27 \\ \underline{\times\ 3} \\ 9.81 \end{array}$$

## 79. B

**Step 1**
Rewrite the divisor as a whole number.
The divisor is 3.13. To rewrite 3.13 as a whole number, move the decimal point two places to the right.
$3.13 \rightarrow 313$
What you do to the divisor, you must also do to the dividend. Move the decimal point two places to the right in the dividend.
$22.223 \rightarrow 2{,}222.3$

**Step 2**
Set up the division equation. Line up the decimal points above and below the division sign.
Divide.

$$\begin{array}{r} 7.1 \\ 313\overline{)2{,}222.3} \\ \underline{2{,}191} \\ 313 \\ \underline{313} \\ 0 \end{array}$$

$2{,}222.3 \div 313 = 7.1$

## 80. C

A decimal number that is used as a divisor needs to be made into a whole number first. This is done by multiplying the decimal divisor by a power of ten for each place value to the right of the decimal point.

To remove the decimal, 0.01 must be multiplied by 100 because the last digit, 1, is in the hundredths place.
$0.01 \times 100 = 1$

This means that the decimal moved two places to the right.

## 81. A

Use long division to divide the total amount Candice spent on the backpacks by 3.

$$
\begin{array}{r}
9.11 \\
3\overline{)27.33} \\
\underline{27} \\
0\ 3 \\
\underline{3} \\
0
\end{array}
$$

Each backpack cost $9.11.

## 82. 0.21

### Step 1
Set up the long division equation.
Take out the decimal while dividing. It will be added in again at the end.

$$5\overline{)105}$$

### Step 2
Determine how many times 5 can go into 10. The number 5 can go into 10 twice. Write a 2 above the 10 in the dividend. Next, multiply 5 by 2, and subtract the product from 10. Finally, bring down the 5.

$$
\begin{array}{r}
21 \\
5\overline{)105} \\
\underline{-10} \\
5
\end{array}
$$

### Step 3
Determine how many times 5 can go into 5. The number 5 can go into 5 once. Write the 1 above the 5 in the dividend. Next, multiply 5 by 1, and subtract the product from 5.

$$
\begin{array}{r}
21 \\
5\overline{)105} \\
\underline{-10} \\
5 \\
\underline{-5} \\
0
\end{array}
$$

### Step 4
Add the decimal back into the dividend, and add a decimal into the quotient.
The dividend had two decimal places, so the quotient will also have two decimal places.

$$
\begin{array}{r}
0.21 \\
5\overline{)1.05} \\
\underline{-10} \\
5 \\
\underline{-5} \\
0
\end{array}
$$

## 83. 0.217217

### Step 1
Remove the decimal points.
The zeros before the decimal point can be removed as well because having a zero in front does not change the value of the number.

$$341 \times 637 =$$

### Step 2
Line up the numbers based on place value.

$$
\begin{array}{r}
341 \\
\times\ 637
\end{array}
$$

### Step 3
Multiply the two whole numbers.
Start by multiplying 7 by the top number.

$$
\begin{array}{r}
\overset{2}{3}41 \\
\times\quad 7 \\
\hline
2,387
\end{array}
$$

Multiply 30 by the top number.
Remember to add a zero on the right side before multiplying to hold the place value of the tens. Continue to multiply the top number by 3.

$$
\begin{array}{r}
\overset{1}{3}41 \\
\times\qquad 30 \\
\hline
10,230
\end{array}
$$

Multiply 600 by the top number.
Remember to add two zeros on the right side before multiplying to hold the place value of the hundreds. Continue multiplying the top number by 6.

$$
\begin{array}{r}
\overset{2}{3}41 \\
\times\qquad 600 \\
\hline
204,600
\end{array}
$$

### Step 4
Add the products.
```
  11
  2387
  10,230
+204,600
 217,217
```

### Step 5
Replace the decimal in the answer.

To determine where to put the decimal point, count how many digits are to the right of both of the original decimals. There are 3 digits to the right of each decimal, so that is 6 digits in total.

Move the decimal 6 digits to the left of the sum.
217,217. → 0.217217

## 84. 3.11

### Step 1
Line up the decimals by place value.
```
 4.61
-1.50
```

### Step 2
Subtract the decimals from right to left.

- Hundredths: $1 - 0 = 1$
- Tenths: $6 - 5 = 1$
- Ones: $4 - 1 = 3$

### Step 3
Place the decimal in the same place as the decimals in the question.
```
 4.61
-1.50
 3.11
```
The difference between 4.61 and 1.50 is 3.11.

## 85. 4.24

### Step 1
Line up the decimals based on the place values of the digits.
```
 6.34
-2.10
```

### Step 2
Subtract the numbers from right to left.

Subtract the hundredths.
$4 - 0 = 4$

Subtract the tenths.
$3 - 1 = 2$

Subtract the ones.
$6 - 2 = 4$

### Step 3
Place the decimal in the same place as the decimal numbers being subtracted.
```
 6.34
-2.10
 4.24
```
The difference between 6.34 and 2.10 is 4.24.

## 86. 3.99

### Step 1
Line up the decimals by place value.
```
 2.41
+1.58
```

### Step 2
Add the decimals from right to left.
The ones can be calculated as $2 + 1 = 3$.
The tens can be calculated as $4 + 5 = 9$.
The hundreds can be calculated as $1 + 8 = 9$.

### Step 3
Place the decimal in the same place as the decimals being added.
```
 2.41
+1.58
 3.99
```
Therefore, the sum of 2.41 and 1.58 is 3.99.

## 87. 8.87

### Step 1
Line up the decimals by place value.
```
 5.86
+3.01
```

### Step 2
Add the decimals from right to left.

- Ones: $6 + 1 = 7$
- Tens: $8 + 0 = 8$
- Hundreds: $5 + 3 = 8$

### Step 3
Place the decimal in the same place as the decimals being added.
```
 5.86
+3.01
 8.87
```
Therefore, the sum of 3.01 and 5.86 is 8.87.

## 88. C

### Step 1

Determine what the problem is asking.
The problem is to determine the total cost of all 7 television sets.

### Step 2

Identify the information that is given.

- The cost of one television is $3,149.98.
- The number of televisions is 7.
- The keyword used is **of**.

### Step 3

Decide on the strategy or operation to use.
The keyword **of** implies multiplication.

### Step 4

Apply the strategy or operation.
Place the multiplicand over the multiplier with the digits lined up in vertical columns. Multiply the decimal numbers following the same process as multiplying whole numbers.

$$
\begin{array}{r}
314{,}998 \quad \text{(2 decimal places)} \\
\times \; 7 \phantom{0000000} \\
\hline
2{,}204{,}986
\end{array}
$$

Since there are two digits behind the decimal in the multiplicand, there will be two digits after the decimal in the product.
2,204,986 → 22,049.86
The total cost of all 7 television sets is $22,049.86.

# EXERCISE #2—NUMBER AND OPERATIONS IN BASE TEN

89. In the number 43,750, the value of the digit 4 is
   - A. 400,000
   - B. 40,000
   - C. 4,000
   - D. 400

90. To divide the number 578.542 by $10^3$, a person would have to move the decimal
   - A. three places to the right
   - B. three places to the left
   - C. four places to the right
   - D. four places to the left

91. If the value of 2 370 × 0.1 = 237, what is the value of 2 370 × 0.01?
   - A. 2.37
   - B. 23.7
   - C. 237
   - D. 237,000

92. How many zeros does the product of 900 and 10 have?
   - A. 3
   - B. 4
   - C. 5
   - D. 10

93. If a loaf of bread costs $3.49, how much would 1,000 loaves of bread cost?
   - A. $349.00
   - B. $3,490.00
   - C. $34,900.00
   - D. $349,000.00

94. Written as an exponential expression, the number 1,000,000 is
   - A. $6^{10}$
   - B. $8^{10}$
   - C. $10^6$
   - D. $10^8$

95. In the number 852.847, the value of the digit 7 is
   - A. 0.007
   - B. 0.7
   - C. 7.0
   - D. 70.00

**96.** Written in words, what is the number 162.570?

**97.** The expanded notation $100 + 1 + \dfrac{1}{100} + \dfrac{1}{1,000}$ represented in decimal form is _____.

**98.** Which of the following decimal numbers is greater than 0.700?
    **A.** 0.6                              **B.** 0.07
    **C.** 7.00                              **D.** 0.60

**99.** Which of the following lists of numbers orders the decimals 643.449, 643.441, 643.446, and 643.444 from **least** to **greatest**?
    **A.** 643.441, 643.449, 643.446, 643.444         **B.** 643.446, 643.441, 643.669, 643.444
    **C.** 643.441, 643.444, 643.446, 643.449         **D.** 643.449, 643.446, 643.444, 643.441

*Use the following information to answer the next question.*

Tasha, Annie, and Molly went shopping for new shoes. Tasha spent $33.75, Annie spent $35.48, and Molly spent $34.15.

100. If each amount of money is rounded to the nearest tenth, which two girls spent a total of $68.00?

101. What is the number 47.096 rounded to the nearest hundredth?

102. When rounded to the nearest whole number, what is the number 246.910 written as?

103. What is the product of 43 × 17?
    A. 344
    B. 371
    C. 711
    D. 731

104. If Dallin eats 12 almonds each day, how many almonds will he eat in 33 days?
    A. 333
    B. 396
    C. 412
    D. 426

105. The garden market has 67 bags of cucumbers for sale. In each bag, there are 44 cucumbers. How many cucumbers are there in total?
    A. 536
    B. 2,728
    C. 2,948
    D. 4,856

106. What is 4 multiplied by 2,863?
    A. 5,689
    B. 9,623
    C. 10,734
    D. 11,452

107. What is the product of 457 × 84?
    A. 37,388
    B. 38,388
    C. 39,399
    D. 40,000

*Use the following information to answer the next question.*

Blair has 693 stickers in his sticker collection. He wants to divide them into groups of 3 to paste into his sticker book.

108. Which of the following area models represents Blair's equation?

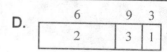

A.
| | 200 | 30 | 1 |
|---|---|---|---|
| 3 | 600 | 90 | 3 |

B.
| | 600 | 90 | 3 |
|---|---|---|---|
| 3 | 200 | 30 | 1 |

C.
| | 2 | 3 | 1 |
|---|---|---|---|
| | 6 | 9 | 3 |

D.
| | 6 | 9 | 3 |
|---|---|---|---|
| | 2 | 3 | 1 |

109. What is the quotient of 684 ÷ 15?
  A. 44
  B. 48
  C. 45R9
  D. 49R5

110. The solution to the expression 1,482 ÷ 2 is _____.

*Use the following information to answer the next question.*

Ivan had 1,243 marbles that he packaged in small pouches to sell at a flea market. Each pouch contained 11 marbles.

111. How many pouches did Ivan need to package all his marbles?
  A. 111
  B. 113
  C. 114
  D. 115

112. When 5,475 is divided by 73, the quotient is
  A. 65
  B. 74
  C. 75
  D. 78

113. The number 78.542 is multiplied by 4. In the product, the decimal is placed
  A. two places to the left
  B. three places to the left
  C. four places to the right
  D. five places to the right

114. What is the result of 63.42 ÷ 4.2?
  A. 14.9
  B. 15.1
  C. 15.8
  D. 16.0

*Use the following information to answer the next question.*

The total mass of 8 doughnuts is 655.2 g.

115. What is the mass of each individual doughnut?
  A. 8.19 g
  B. 80.7 g
  C. 81.9 g
  D. 647.2 g

*Use the following information to answer the next question.*

Rosa bought 4.6 m of red ribbon for a project she was working on. She went back to the store the next day and bought 1.75 m of white ribbon for the same project.

116. How much ribbon did Rosa buy in total? _____ m

117. Jerry and his grandma went shopping for some new clothes. The cost of the new clothes was $47.37.

How much money was left after Jerry's grandma paid for the clothes with three twenty dollar bills?

A. $12.37

B. $12.63

C. $12.72

D. $13.73

118. What is the product of 0.221 × 0.411?

# EXERCISE #2—NUMBER AND OPERATIONS IN BASE TEN
## ANSWERS AND SOLUTIONS

| | | | |
|---|---|---|---|
| 89. B | 97. 101.011 | 105. C | 113. B |
| 90. B | 98. C | 106. D | 114. B |
| 91. B | 99. C | 107. B | 115. C |
| 92. A | 100. See solution | 108. A | 116. 6.35 |
| 93. B | 101. See solution | 109. C | 117. B |
| 94. C | 102. See solution | 110. 741 | 118. 0.090831 |
| 95. A | 103. D | 111. B | |
| 96. See solution | 104. B | 112. C | |

## 89. B

**Step 1**

Make a place value chart.

| Thousands | | Ones | | |
|---|---|---|---|---|
| T | O | H | T | O |
| 4 | 3 | 7 | 5 | 0 |

**Step 2**

Identify the value of the digit 4.

The digit 4 is in the ten thousands place.

$4 \times 10,000 = 40,000$

In the number 43,750, the value of the digit 4 is 40,000.

## 90. B

To divide a number by 10, move the decimal one place to the left. To divide by $10^2$, move the decimal two places to the left. Therefore, to divide a number by $10^3$, move the decimal three places to the left.

## 91. B

When multiplying 2,370 by 0.01, you are multiplying by $\frac{1}{100}$ or dividing by 100.

The value of $2\,370 \times 0.01 =$

$2\,370 \times \frac{1}{100} = \frac{237}{10} = 23.7$

Another way to solve this problem is by moving the decimal point two decimal places to the left. Because there are two decimal places in the question(0.01), you move the decimal point two places to the left of the whole number (2,370). Therefore, $2\,370 \times 0.01 = 23.7$.

## 92. A

The product of two numbers is the number that results from multiplying them.

The number 900 has 2 zeros, and the number 10 has 1 zero.
$900 \times 10 = 9,000$

The product of 900 and 10 has 3 zeros.

## 93. B

One loaf of bread costs $3.49.

Therefore, 1,000 loaves of bread would cost:

$10 \times 3.49 = 3\,490$

1,000 loaves of bread would cost $3,490.00.

Remember, when multiplying a whole number by 1,000, move the decimal three places to the right.

## 94. C

To write 1,000,000 as a number with an exponent, you need to count the number of zeros. There are six zeros in 1,000,000, so your exponent will be 6.

When writing a positive power of 10 as an exponent, the base is always 10.

Therefore, 1,000,000 can be written as $10^6$.

## 95. A

**Step 1**

Place the number in a place value chart.

| H | T | O | . | Tth | Hth | Thth |
|---|---|---|---|---|---|---|
| 8 | 5 | 2 | . | 8 | 4 | 7 |

**Step 2**

Identify the place value of the digit 7 in 852.847.
Since the digit 7 is the third digit to the right of
the decimal point, it is in the thousandths place.
The place value of 7 is seven thousandths or
0.007.

**96.**

**Step 1**

Determine the whole number.
The whole number part of the decimal number
is 162, which is written as one hundred
sixty-two.
Since 162.570 is a decimal number, the word
*and* is written after the whole number. It is
written as one hundred sixty-two and.

**Step 2**

Determine the decimal.
The digits to the right of the decimal are written
as a fraction.

- The numerator is the group of digits to the
  right of the decimal, 570, and it is written as
  five hundred seventy.
- Since there are three digits to the right of the
  decimal, the denominator is 1,000, which is
  written as thousandths.
- The fraction part of the number is written as
  five hundred seventy-thousandths.

Putting the two parts together, the number
162.570 is written in words as one hundred
sixty-two and five hundred
seventy-thousandths.

**97. 101.011**

**Step 1**

Understand the fractions in the expanded
notation.
Decimals are parts of a whole, which can also
be expressed as a fraction. The denominator
shows the place value positions.

A number over 10 $\left(\dfrac{?}{10}\right)$ is in the tenths place

value, over 100 $\left(\dfrac{?}{100}\right)$ is the hundredths, and

over 1,000 $\left(\dfrac{?}{1,000}\right)$ is the thousandths.

The numerator tells you how many are in the
place value.

**Step 2**

Use a place value chart to help you see the
different place values represented in the
expanded notation.
Since there are no tens and no tenths, you need
to place a zero (place holder) in the tens position
and the tenths position to hold their positions.

| H | T | O | . | Tth | Hth | Thth |
|---|---|---|---|-----|-----|------|
| 1 | 0 | 1 | . | 0 | 1 | 1 |

The expanded notation

$100 + 1 + \dfrac{1}{100} + \dfrac{1}{1,000}$ can be represented by

the decimal 101.011.

**98. C**

**Step 1**

Determine the equivalent decimals for each
alternative.
Since 0.700 has a digit in the hundredths place,
each of the decimals must have a digit in the
hundredths place in order to be equivalent.
$0.07 \rightarrow 0.070$
$0.6 \rightarrow 0.600$
$7.00 \rightarrow 7.000$
$0.60 \rightarrow 0.600$

### Step 2

Compare the numbers.

Start from the left side, and compare the numbers in the greatest place value.

The decimal 7.000 is greater than 0.700.

The decimals 0.6 and 0.60 are equivalent, and they both have a number less than 0.700 in the tenths place value. Therefore, they are both less than 0.700.

The only given decimal number greater than 0.700 is 7.000

| Ones | | | . | Parts of a Whole | | |
|---|---|---|---|---|---|---|
| H | T | O | . | Tth | Hth | Thth |
| | | 0 | . | 7 | 0 | 0 |
| | | 0 | . | 6 | 0 | 0 |
| | | 7 | . | 0 | 0 | 0 |
| | | 0 | . | 6 | 0 | 0 |

### 99.  C

#### Step 1

Put the decimals into a place value chart.

| Ones | | | . | Parts of a Whole | | |
|---|---|---|---|---|---|---|
| H | T | O | . | Tth | Hth | Thth |
| 6 | 4 | 3 | . | 4 | 4 | 9 |
| 6 | 4 | 3 | . | 4 | 4 | 1 |
| 6 | 4 | 3 | . | 4 | 4 | 6 |
| 6 | 4 | 3 | . | 4 | 4 | 4 |

#### Step 2

Starting at the greatest place value, compare the decimals from left to right.

The digits in the hundreds, tens, ones, tenths, and hundredths positions all have the same value. Therefore, use the single digit in the thousandths position to determine the value of each decimal number.

$1 < 4 < 6 < 9$

In order from least to greatest value, the numbers are 643.441, 643.444, 643.446, and 643.449.

### 100.

#### Step 1

Round each decimal number to the nearest tenth.

- Since 5 = 5, 33.75 → 33.8.
- Since 8 > 5, 35.48 → 35.5.
- Since 5 = 5, 34.15 → 34.2.

#### Step 2

Since amounts of money must always be written with two digits to the right of the decimal, add a zero to the end of each rounded amount.

- 33.8 → $33.80
- 35.5 → $35.50
- 34.2 → $34.20

#### Step 3

Add the amounts to determine which two add up to $68.00.

- $33.80 + $35.50 = $69.30
- $35.50 + $34.20 = $69.70
- $33.80 + $34.20 = $68.00

If the amounts are rounded to the nearest tenth, the two girls who spent a total of $68.00 were Tasha ($33.75 rounded to $33.80) and Molly ($34.15 rounded to $34.20).

### 101.

#### Step 1

Identify the digit in the hundredths place.

| T | O | . | Tth | Hth | Thth |
|---|---|---|---|---|---|
| 4 | 7 | . | 0 | 9 | 6 |

The 9 is in the hundredths place.

#### Step 2

Round the number to the nearest hundredth.

Since the digit to the right of 9 hundredths is greater than 5(6 > 5), round the 9 hundredths up to 10 hundredths and drop the 6 thousandths.

When the 9 hundredths are rounded up to 10 hundredths, the place values will change. There will be 0 hundredths and 1 tenth in the rounded number.

| T | O | . | Tth | Hth |
|---|---|---|---|---|
| 4 | 7 | . | 1 | 0 |

47.096 → 47.10

**102.**

**Step 1**

Identify the digit in the ones place, the nearest whole number.

| Ones | | | . | Parts of a Whole | | |
|---|---|---|---|---|---|---|
| H | T | O | . | Tth | Hth | Thth |
| 2 | 4 | 6 | . | 9 | 1 | 0 |

The 6 is in the ones position.

**Step 2**

Since the 9 in the tenths position is greater than 5, the 6 ones are rounded up to 7 ones and all the digits to the right of the decimal are dropped. 246.910 → 247

**103. D**

**Step 1**

Multiply the 7 in the ones position by the 43.

$$\begin{array}{r} \overset{2}{43} \\ \times\ 7 \\ \hline 301 \end{array}$$

**Step 2**

Multiply the 10 (the 1 in the 17 is actually 10) by the 43.

$$\begin{array}{r} 43 \\ \times\ 10 \\ \hline 430 \end{array}$$

**Step 3**

Add the two products.
301 + 430 = 731

**104. B**

**Step 1**

Determine the equation that will find the number of almonds that will be eaten.

Dallin eats 12 almonds in one day.

This means the number of almonds that Dallin will eat in 33 days is equal to the value of the expression 12 × 33.

**Step 2**

Determine the product.

Multiply the ones digits first, then multiply the tens digits. Put a zero first when multiplying the tens because you are finished multiplying the ones.

$$\begin{array}{r} 12 \\ \times\ 33 \\ \hline 36 \\ +360 \\ \hline 396 \end{array}$$

Therefore, Dallin will eat 396 almonds in 33 days.

**105. C**

**Step 1**

Determine what the problem is asking.

There are 67 bags of 44 cucumbers.

This means that there are 67 groups of 44.

You need to multiply to find the answer.

$$\begin{array}{r} 67 \\ \times\ 44 \end{array}$$

**Step 2**

Multiply 67 by the ones digit of 44.

$$\begin{array}{r} \overset{2}{67} \\ \times\ 4 \\ \hline 268 \end{array}$$

**Step 3**

Multiply 67 by the tens of 44.

$$\begin{array}{r} \overset{2}{67} \\ \times\ 40 \\ \hline 2,680 \end{array}$$

**Step 4**

Add the two products.

$$\begin{array}{r} \overset{1}{268} \\ +2,680 \\ \hline 2,948 \end{array}$$

There are 2,948 cucumbers in total.

## 106. D

### Step 1

Multiply the one-digit number by the ones.

$4 \times 3 = 12$

Place the 2 under the ones place value, and carry over the 1 to the top of the tens place.

$$\begin{array}{r} \overset{1}{2863} \\ \times \quad 4 \\ \hline 2 \end{array}$$

### Step 2

Multiply the one-digit number by the tens. Do not forget to add the 1 that was carried over from the ones.

$4 \times 6 = 24$

$24 + 1 = 25$

Place the 5 under the tens place, and carry over the 2 to the top of the hundreds place.

$$\begin{array}{r} \overset{21}{2863} \\ \times \quad 4 \\ \hline 52 \end{array}$$

### Step 3

Multiply the one-digit number by the hundreds. Do not forget to add the 2 that was carried over from the tens.

$4 \times 8 = 32$

$32 + 2 = 34$

Place the 4 under the hundreds place, and carry over the 3 to the top of the thousands place.

$$\begin{array}{r} \overset{321}{2863} \\ \times \quad 4 \\ \hline 452 \end{array}$$

### Step 4

Multiply the one-digit number by the thousands. Do not forget to add the 3 that was carried over from the hundreds.

$4 \times 2 = 8$

$8 + 3 = 11$

Place the 1 under the thousands place.

There are no more numbers to be multiplied, so write the other 1 beside the 1 that was just placed under the thousands place.

$$\begin{array}{r} \overset{321}{2863} \\ \times \quad 4 \\ \hline 11,452 \end{array}$$

## 107. B

### Step 1

Estimate the product.

Round both numbers to the highest place value.

$84 \quad \rightarrow 80$

$457 \quad \rightarrow 500$

$500 \times 80 = 40,000$

### Step 2

Multiply the ones. Regroup where necessary.

$$\begin{array}{r} 457 \\ \times 4 \\ \hline 1,828 \end{array}$$

### Step 3

Multiply the tens. Regroup where necessary.

$$\begin{array}{r} 457 \\ \times 80 \\ \hline 36,560 \end{array}$$

When multiplying by the tens position, it is important to remember that even though it may seem that you are only multiplying by a single digit, you are really multiplying by 10. In the previous example, you are multiplying 8 tens, which is equal to 80. A zero must be added before multiplying to hold the place value of the tens position.

### Step 4

Add the products together.

$1,828 + 36,560 = 38,388$

### Step 5

Compare the estimated product to the calculated the product, and determine the reasonableness of the answer.

The calculated answer of 38,388 is close to the estimated answer of 40,000; therefore, the answer of 38,388 is reasonable.

## 108. A

### Step 1

Write the larger number in expanded notation. Split the larger number into hundreds, tens, and ones.

$693 = 600 + 90 + 3$

     Number and Operations in Base Ten

**Step 2**

Draw the area model.

Write the smaller number along the width of the rectangle. Write the ones, tens, and hundreds of the larger number inside the rectangle.

This area model represents 693 ÷ 3.

| | 200 | 30 | 1 |
|---|---|---|---|
| 3 | 600 | 90 | 3 |

If you need help, this is how the quotients are found:

600 ÷ 3 = 200
90 ÷ 3 = 30
3 ÷ 3 = 1

All of the individual quotients are written on top of the area being divided.

**Step 3**

To find the quotient of 693 ÷ 3, add the individual quotients from the expanded area.

200 + 30 + 1 = 231
693 ÷ 3 = 231

**109. C**

**Step 1**

Change the question into a long division equation.

15)684

**Step 2**

Determine the quotient.

The number 15 cannot go into 6, but it goes into 68 four times.

Multiply 15 by 4, and write the product below the 68 in the division equation. Subtract the two numbers, and write the difference below.

Bring down the 4, and determine how many times 15 goes into 84.

```
      4
15)684
   −60↓
     84
```

The number 15 goes into 84 five times. Multiply 15 by 5, and write the product below the 84. Subtract the two numbers, and write the difference below. Since 15 cannot go into 9, the remainder is 9.

```
     45
15)684
   −60↓
    714
     84
    −75
      9
```

684 ÷ 15 = 45R9

**110. 741**

**Step 1**

Set up the division equation.

Write the divisor (2) in front of the division bracket and the dividend (1,482) below the division bracket.

divisor)dividend
2)1,482

**Step 2**

Determine if the first digit in the dividend can be divided by the divisor. If not, use the first two digits of the dividend.

The first digit in the dividend (1) is smaller than 2 (the divisor). Use the first two digits of the dividend (14).

## Step 3

Determine how many times the divisor can go into the first number or numbers of the dividend. Write the number of equal groups in the quotient area of the formula above the first digit (or the second digit if the first was too small to be divided).

In this example, 2 can go into 14 seven times. Write 7 above the 14 of the dividend.

Multiply the 2 by the 7, and write the product (14) below the dividend.

```
    7
2)1,482
 - 14
    0
```

## Step 4

Subtract the two numbers.

$14 - 14 = 0$

Bring down the number 8. The dividend is now 8.

```
     7
2  )1,482
  - 14↓
     8
```

## Step 5

Repeat the previous steps until it is no longer possible to divide. The answer will be above the dividend.

```
      741
2  )1,482
  - 14↓↓
      8↓
    - 8↓
      2
    - 2
      0
```

The quotient is 741.

## 111. B

### Step 1

Set up the division equation.

Write the divisor (11) in front of the division bracket and the dividend (1,243) below the division bracket.

divisor)dividend
11)1,243

## Step 2

Divide 11 into 12.

Since 11 can go into 12 one time, place a 1 on top of the division bracket.

Multiply 11 by 1 to get 11.

Place the 11 under the 12, and subtract the two numbers.

$12 - 11 = 1$

Drop down the 4.

```
      1
11)1,243
  - 11
    14
```

## Step 3

Divide 11 into 14.

Since 11 can go into 14 one time, place a 1 on top of the division bracket.

Multiply 11 by 1 to get 11.

Place the 11 under the 14, and subtract the two numbers.

$14 - 11 = 3$

Drop down the 3.

```
     11
11)1,243
  - 11
    14
  - 11
    33
```

**Step 4**

Divide 11 into 33.

Since 11 goes into 33 three times, place a 3 on top of the division bracket.

Multiply 11 by 3 to get 33.

Place the 33 under the 33, and subtract the two numbers.

33 − 33 = 0

There are no remainders. The division statement is complete.

```
        113
11)1,243
   − 11
      14
    − 11
      33
    − 33
       0
```

Since 1,243 ÷ 11 = 113, Ivan needs 113 pouches to package all his marbles.

## 112. C

Use long division to solve this problem, as shown.

```
       75
73)5475
  −511
    365
   −365
      0
```

When 5,475 is divided by 73, the quotient is 75.

## 113. B

When a decimal number is multiplied, the decimal place is determined by how many digits are present after the decimal in both of the numbers being multiplied. In this case, there are three digits after the decimal in the number being multiplied; therefore, there will be three digits after the decimal in the product. The decimal will be placed three places to the left.

## 114. B

**Step 1**

Make the divisor a whole number.

The divisor 4.2 can be turned into a whole number by moving the decimal point one place to the right. The number then becomes 42.

**Step 2**

Move the decimal point in the dividend the same number of places as in the divisor.

Since the decimal point in the divisor was moved one place to the right, the decimal point in the dividend must also be moved one place to the right. Therefore, 63.42 becomes 634.2.

**Step 3**

Use long division to divide the two numbers.

```
      15.1
42)634.2
  −42
    214
  −210
     42
   −42
      0
```

**Step 4**

Place the decimal point in the answer exactly as it appears in the dividend.

When 63.42 is divided by 4.2, the result is 15.1.

## 115. C

To determine the mass of each doughnut, divide the total mass (655.2) by the number of doughnuts (8).

The mass of each doughnut will be equal to the value of the expression 655.2 ÷ 8.

Use long division.

```
     81.9
8)655.2
  64
  15
   8
  72
  72
   0
```

655.2 ÷ 8 = 81.9

The mass of each individual doughnut is 81.9 g.

## 116. 6.35

Rosa bought 6.35 m of ribbon in total.

Since 4.6 is a decimal in the tenths and 1.75 is a decimal in the hundredths, you can add a 0 to the right of the 6 in 4.6 to read as 4.60.

Add the two decimal numbers.

4.60 + 1.75 = 6.35

## 117. B

Jerry's grandma had $12.63 left after she paid for the clothes.

Three twenty dollar bills is equal to $60.00.
$60.00 − $47.37 = $12.63

## 118. 0.090831

**Step 1**

Remove the decimal point.

The zeros before the decimal point can be removed as well because having a zero in front does not change the value of the number.

221 × 411

**Step 2**

Line the numbers up based on place value.

$$\begin{array}{r} 221 \\ \times\ 411 \end{array}$$

**Step 3**

Multiply the two whole numbers together.

Multiply 1 by 221.

$$\begin{array}{r} 221 \\ \times\ 1 \\ \hline 221 \end{array}$$

Multiply 10 by 221.

Remember to add a zero on the right side before multiplying to hold the place value of the tens.

Continue multiplying the top number by 1.

$$\begin{array}{r} 221 \\ \times\ 10 \\ \hline 2{,}210 \end{array}$$

Multiply 400 by 221.

Remember to add two zeros on the right side before multiplying to hold the place value of the hundreds.

Continue multiplying the top number by 4.

$$\begin{array}{r} 221 \\ \times\ 400 \\ \hline 88{,}400 \end{array}$$

**Step 4**

Add the products together.

$$\begin{array}{r} 221 \\ 2{,}210 \\ {}^{1} \\ +\,88{,}400 \\ \hline 90{,}831 \end{array}$$

**Step 5**

Put the decimal back into the product.

Count the number of digits to the right of each of the original decimals. Both decimal numbers have three digits to the right of the decimal point. Added together, the new decimal should have six digits after the decimal point.

Because the product has only five digits in it, you need to place a zero in front of the 9 so that there are six digits after the decimal point.

0.221 × 0.411 = 0.090831

# NOTES

Number and Operations—Fractions

# NUMBER AND OPERATIONS—FRACTIONS

## Table of Correlations

| Standard | | Concepts | Exercise #1 | Exercise #2 |
|---|---|---|---|---|
| **5.NF** | Number and Operations—Fractions | | | |
| *5.NF.1* | *Add and subtract fractions with unlike denominators (including mixed numbers) by replacing given fractions with equivalent fractions in such a way as to produce an equivalent sum or difference of fractions with like denominators.* | Adding Fractions with Unlike Denominators | 119, 120 | 164 |
| | | Subtracting Fractions with Unlike Denominators | 121, 122 | 165 |
| | | Representing the Addition of Fractions with Unlike Denominators | 123, 124 | 166 |
| | | Representing the Subtraction of Fractions with Unlike Denominators | 125 | 167 |
| | | Writing Fractions with a Common Denominator | 126, 127 | 168 |
| *5.NF.2* | *Solve word problems involving addition and subtraction of fractions referring to the same whole, including cases of unlike denominators.* | Representing the Addition of Fractions with Unlike Denominators | 123, 124 | 166 |
| | | Representing the Subtraction of Fractions with Unlike Denominators | 125 | 167 |
| | | Solving Problems Involving the Addition of Fractions with Unlike Denominators | 128 | 175 |
| | | Solving Problems Involving the Subtraction of Fractions with Unlike Denominators | 133, 134 | 174 |
| | | Rounding Fractions to the Nearest Half or Whole Number | 135, 136, 137 | 173 |
| | | Estimating Sums of Fractions | 129, 130 | 169, 170 |
| | | Estimating Differences of Fractions | 131, 132 | 171, 172 |
| *5.NF.3* | *Interpret a fraction as division of the numerator by the denominator (a/b = a ÷ b). Solve word problems involving division of whole numbers leading to answers in the form of fractions or mixed numbers.* | Understanding Fractions as the Division of Whole Numbers | 138, 139 | 176, 177 |
| | | Understanding the Relationship between Whole Numbers and Fractions | | |
| *5.NF. 4A* | *Apply and extend previous understandings of multiplication to multiply a fraction or whole number by a fraction. Interpret the product (a/b) × q as a parts of a partition of q into b equal parts; equivalently, as the result of a sequence...* | Multiplying a Fraction by a Whole Number Using Repeated Addition | 140, 141 | 178 |
| | | Multiplying Whole Numbers by Fractions | 142, 143 | 179 |
| | | Multiplying Fractions by Fractions | 144, 145 | 180 |
| *5.NF. 4B* | *Apply and extend previous understandings of multiplication to multiply a fraction or whole number by a fraction. Find the area of a rectangle with fractional side lengths by tiling it with unit squares of the appropriate unit fraction side...* | Multiplying Fractions Using an Area Model | 146, 147 | 181 |
| | | Measure and Record Areas of Rectangles | 148, 149 | 182 |

| 5.NF. 5A | Interpret multiplication as scaling (resizing), by: Comparing the size of a product to the size of one factor on the basis of the size of the other factor, without performing the indicated multiplication. | Using Multiplication to Make Comparisons | 150, 151 | 183 |
|---|---|---|---|---|
| 5.NF. 5B | Interpret multiplication as scaling (resizing), by: Explaining why multiplying a given number by a fraction greater than 1 results in a product greater than the given number (recognizing multiplication by whole numbers greater than 1 as a... | Multiplying a Fraction by a Whole Number Using Repeated Addition | 140, 141 | 178 |
| | | Multiplying Whole Numbers by Fractions | 142, 143 | 179 |
| | | Multiplying Fractions by Fractions | 144, 145 | 180 |
| | | Creating Equivalent Fractions | 152, 153 | 184, 185 |
| 5.NF.6 | Solve real world problems involving multiplication of fractions and mixed numbers. | Multiplying Mixed Numbers | 154, 155 | 186 |
| | | Solving Problems Involving the Multiplication of Fractions | 156, 157 | 187 |
| 5.NF. 7A | Apply and extend previous understandings of division to divide unit fractions by whole numbers and whole numbers by unit fractions. Interpret division of a unit fraction by a non-zero whole number, and compute such quotients. | Dividing Fractions by a Whole Number | 158 | 188 |
| 5.NF. 7B | Apply and extend previous understandings of division to divide unit fractions by whole numbers and whole numbers by unit fractions. Interpret division of a whole number by a unit fraction, and compute such quotients. | Dividing Whole Numbers by Unit Fractions | 159 | 189 |
| 5.NF. 7C | Apply and extend previous understandings of division to divide unit fractions by whole numbers and whole numbers by unit fractions. Solve real world problems involving division of unit fractions by non-zero whole numbers and division of... | Solving Problems That Involve Dividing a Unit Fraction by a Whole Number | 160, 161 | 190 |
| | | Solving Problems by Dividing Whole Numbers by Unit Fractions | 162, 163 | 191 |

**5.NF.1** *Add and subtract fractions with unlike denominators (including mixed numbers) by replacing given fractions with equivalent fractions in such a way as to produce an equivalent sum or difference of fractions with like denominators.*

## ADDING FRACTIONS WITH UNLIKE DENOMINATORS

To add fractions with different denominators, follow these steps:

1. Write the fractions with the lowest common denominator (LCD).
2. Add the numerators of the fractions while keeping the denominators the same.
3. Reduce the resulting fraction to lowest terms.

*Example*

Add $\frac{1}{4}$ and $\frac{2}{3}$.

*Solution*

**Step 1**

Write the fractions with the lowest common denominator (LCD).

Write the multiples of each denominator until a common one appears.

- Multiples of 3:3, 6, 9, 12, 15
- Multiples of 4:4, 8, 12, 16, 20

The lowest common denominator for 3 and 4 is 12.

Use the LCD to create new equivalent fractions with a denominator of 12.

Multiply the numerator and the denominator by the same factor.

$$\frac{1 \times 3}{4 \times 3} = \frac{3}{12}, \frac{2 \times 4}{3 \times 4} = \frac{8}{12}$$

**Step 2**

Add the numerators of the fractions while keeping the denominators the same.

$$\frac{3+8}{12} = \frac{11}{12}$$

**Step 3**

Reduce the resulting fraction to lowest terms.

The fraction is in lowest terms.

$$\frac{1}{4} + \frac{2}{3} = \frac{11}{12}$$

---

## SUBTRACTING FRACTIONS WITH UNLIKE DENOMINATORS

To subtract fractions with different denominators, follow these steps:

1. Write the fractions with the lowest common denominator (LCD).
2. Subtract the numerators of the fractions while keeping the denominators the same.
3. Reduce the resulting fraction to lowest terms.

*Example*

Solve $\frac{2}{3} - \frac{1}{4}$.

*Solution*

### Step 1
Write the fractions with the lowest common denominator (LCD).
Write the multiples of each denominator until a common one appears.

- Multiples of 3:  3, 6, 9, 12, 15
- Multiples of 4:  4, 8, 12, 16, 20

The lowest common denominator for 3 and 4 is 12.
Use the LCD to create new equivalent fractions with a denominator of 12.
$$\frac{2 \times 4}{3 \times 4} = \frac{8}{12}, \frac{1 \times 3}{4 \times 3} = \frac{3}{12}$$

### Step 2
Subtract the numerators of the fractions while keeping the denominators the same.
$$\frac{8 - 3}{12} = \frac{5}{12}$$

### Step 3
Reduce the resulting fraction to lowest terms.
The fraction is in lowest terms.
$$\frac{2}{3} - \frac{1}{4} = \frac{5}{12}$$

---

*Example*

When $\frac{2}{8}$ is subtracted from $\frac{3}{5}$, what is the difference?

*Solution*

### Step 1
Write the fractions with the lowest common denominator (LCD).
Write the multiples of each denominator until a common one appears.

- Multiples of 8:  8, 16, 24, 32, 40
- Multiples of 5:  5, 10, 15, 20, 25, 30, 35, 40

The lowest common denominator for 8 and 5 is 40.
Use the LCD to create new equivalent fractions with a denominator of 40.
$$\frac{3 \times 8}{5 \times 8} = \frac{24}{40}$$

$$\frac{2 \times 5}{8 \times 5} = \frac{10}{40}$$

### Step 2
Subtract the numerators of the fractions while keeping the denominators the same.
$$\frac{24 - 10}{40} = \frac{14}{40}$$

**Step 3**

Reduce the resulting fraction to lowest terms.

$$\frac{14}{40} = \frac{7}{20}$$

Therefore, $\frac{3}{5} - \frac{2}{8} = \frac{7}{20}$.

---

# REPRESENTING THE ADDITION OF FRACTIONS WITH UNLIKE DENOMINATORS

Fractions show how many parts are compared to the whole. The denominator represents the whole. The numerator represents the number of parts.

Fractions with unlike denominators cannot be added until they have like denominators. Follow these steps to represent the addition of fractions with unlike denominators:

1. Find the lowest common denominator (LCD) for the two fractions. Make sure to multiply the numerator by the same number as the denominator.
2. Draw a grid using the factors of the common denominator.
3. Color in the number of parts equivalent to each of the numerators.
4. Add the numerators of the fractions while keeping the denominators the same.

*Example*

Solve the expression $\frac{1}{2} + \frac{1}{4}$ by drawing a representation.

*Solution*

**Step 1**

Draw two grids.

Draw a grid for each of the fractions based on the denominator.

- $\frac{1}{2} \rightarrow$

- $\frac{1}{4} \rightarrow$

**Step 2**

Shade in the parts equivalent to the numerator for each fraction.

- The numerator for the fraction $\frac{1}{2}$ is 1.

- The numerator for the fraction $\frac{1}{4}$ is 1.

## Step 3

Create a common denominator.

To create a common denominator, make $\frac{1}{2}$ into $\frac{2}{4}$.

 →

The expression is now $\frac{2}{4} + \frac{1}{4}$.

## Step 4

Shade in the parts for each numerator

Draw a 2 × 2 grid.

Shade in $\frac{2}{4}$ and $\frac{1}{4}$.

## Step 5

Add the total number of shaded parts.

There are two parts with lines and one part with dots. This equals a total of three shaded parts.

$$\frac{2}{4} + \frac{1}{4} = \frac{3}{4}$$
$$\frac{1}{2} + \frac{1}{4} = \frac{3}{4}$$

---

*Example*

Solve the expression $\frac{1}{3} + \frac{2}{4}$ by drawing a representation.

*Solution*

### Step 1

Find the lowest common denominator for 3 and 4 by making a list of the factors of each number.

- Factors of 3 include 3, 6, 9, 12, and 15.
- Factors of 4 include 4, 8, 12, and 16.

The LCD for the two fractions is 12.

$$\frac{1 \times 4}{3 \times 4} = \frac{4}{12}$$
$$\frac{2 \times 3}{4 \times 3} = \frac{6}{12}$$

## Step 2
The lowest common denominator is 12, so draw a grid with 12 squares.

## Step 3
Shade in the parts equivalent to each numerator
The numerators are 4 and 6.  Use a different shade for each numerator.

## Step 4
Add the total number of colored parts.
There are four parts with lines and six parts with dots.  This equals a total of 10 shaded parts.

$$\frac{4}{12} + \frac{6}{12} = \frac{10}{12}$$
$$\frac{1}{3} + \frac{2}{4} = \frac{10}{12}$$

# REPRESENTING THE SUBTRACTION OF FRACTIONS WITH UNLIKE DENOMINATORS

Fractions show how many parts are being compared to the whole.  The denominator represents the whole, and the numerator represents the number of parts.  The subtraction of fractions can be shown using diagrams.

To subtract fractions with unlike denominators, follow these steps:

1. Find the lowest common denominator (LCD), and rewrite the fractions with it.
2. Draw a grid based on the factors of the denominator.
3. Color in the parts equivalent to the first numerator.
4. Cross out the shaded parts equivalent to the second numerator.
5. Count the total number of remaining shaded parts.

## Example

Solve the equation $\frac{2}{3} - \frac{1}{5} = ?$ by creating representations.

## Solution

### Step 1

Find the lowest common denominator (LCD), and rewrite the fractions.

To find the lowest common denominator, write out the multiples for each of the denominators until there is one they share.

- Multiples of 3 include 3, 6, 9, 12, 15,...
- Multiples of 5 include 5, 10, 15,...

The LCD is 15.

$$\frac{2 \times 5}{3 \times 5} = \frac{10}{15}$$

$$\frac{1 \times 3}{5 \times 3} = \frac{3}{15}$$

The new equation becomes $\frac{10}{15} - \frac{3}{15} = $ .

### Step 2

Draw a grid based on the factors of the denominator.

The denominator is 15.

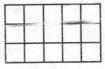

### Step 3

Color in the parts equivalent to the first numerator.

The first numerator is 10. Color in 10 parts.

### Step 4

Cross out the shaded parts equivalent to the second numerator.

The second numerator is 3. Cross out three of the shaded parts.

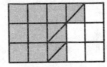

### Step 5

Count the total number of remaining shaded parts.

$10 - 3 = 7$

There are 7 remaining parts.

$$\frac{10}{15} - \frac{3}{15} = \frac{7}{15}$$

# WRITING FRACTIONS WITH A COMMON DENOMINATOR

It is hard to add, subtract, or compare fractions with different denominators. One way to handle the problem is to rewrite the fractions so they have the same denominator. This strategy is called finding a **common denominator**.

To write fractions with common denominators, follow these steps:

1. Choose a common denominator.
2. Rewrite the first fraction.
3. Rewrite the second fraction.

It is often easiest to choose the lowest common denominator (LCD) when you rewrite the fractions.

*Example*

Write the fractions $\frac{1}{3}$ and $\frac{2}{5}$ with a common denominator.

*Solution*

**Step 1**

Choose a common denominator.

The denominator of $\frac{1}{3}$ is 3. The denominator of $\frac{2}{5}$ is 5. Find a number that is a multiple of both 3 and 5 by looking at the multiples of each number:

- Some multiples of 3 are 3, 6, 9, 12, and 15.
- Some multiples of 5 are 5, 10, 15, and 20.

The number 15 is the lowest multiple of both 3 and 5. Use this as the common denominator.

**Step 2**

Rewrite the first fraction with a denominator of 15.

$$\frac{1}{3} = \frac{?}{15}$$

To go from a denominator of 3 to a denominator of 15, you need to multiply by 5. Multiply the numerator and denominator by 5.

$$\frac{1}{3} = \frac{1 \times 5}{3 \times 5} = \frac{5}{15}$$

**Step 3**

Rewrite the second fraction with a denominator of 15.

$$\frac{2}{5} = \frac{?}{15}$$

To go from a denominator of 5 to a denominator of 15, you need to multiply by 3. Multiply the numerator and denominator by 3.

$$\frac{2}{5} = \frac{2 \times 3}{5 \times 3} = \frac{6}{15}$$

Written with a common denominator, the fractions $\frac{1}{3}$ and $\frac{2}{5}$ are equal to $\frac{5}{15}$ and $\frac{6}{15}$.

---

*5.NF.2*   *Solve word problems involving addition and subtraction of fractions referring to the same whole, including cases of unlike denominators.*

## SOLVING PROBLEMS INVOLVING THE ADDITION OF FRACTIONS WITH UNLIKE DENOMINATORS

The first step to solving word problems is to determine the operation. Addition problems often have the following key words:

- Sum
- Total
- Altogether
- More than

Once you have determined that the word problem is an addition problem, follow these steps:

1. Identify the important information.
2. Set up the addition equation.
3. Determine the multiples of all the given fractions. The least common multiple will be used to create new fractions.
4. Create equivalent (equal) fractions with the denominator from step 3.
5. Leave the denominators the same, and add the numerators together. Make sure the fraction is in simplest form.

*Example*

James owns $\frac{3}{5}$ of an acre of land, and his brother Art owns $\frac{1}{2}$ of an acre.

How much land do the brothers own altogether?

*Solution*

**Step 1**
Identify the key words and important information.
The key word *altogether* means addition.

James owns $\frac{3}{5}$ of an acre of land. Art owns $\frac{1}{2}$ of an acre of land.

**Step 2**
Write the addition equation.
$$\frac{3}{5} + \frac{1}{2} = \square$$

**Step 3**
Determine the multiples for each denominator. Remember that the least common multiple will be used to create new fractions.

- Multiples of 2 are 2, 4, 6, 8, and 10.
- Multiples of 5 are 5 and 10.

The least common multiple is 10.

**Step 4**

Create equivalent fractions with the least common multiple.

Since 10 is the least common multiple, it will be used to create equivalent fractions. Remember that what you do to the denominator must be done to the numerator.

$$\frac{1}{2} = \frac{1 \times 5}{2 \times 5} = \frac{5}{10}$$

$$\frac{3}{5} = \frac{3 \times 2}{5 \times 2} = \frac{6}{10}$$

**Step 5**

Add the fractions.

$$\frac{5}{10} + \frac{6}{10} = \frac{11}{10}$$

The fraction cannot be simplified. Altogether, the brothers own $\frac{11}{10}$ of an acre of land.

---

# SOLVING PROBLEMS INVOLVING THE SUBTRACTION OF FRACTIONS WITH UNLIKE DENOMINATORS

To solve word problems involving the subtraction of fractions, look for the following key words:

- Difference
- Less than
- Take away
- Taken from
- Have left

Once you have determined that the word problem is a subtraction problem, follow these steps:

1. Identify the important information.
2. Determine the multiples of all the given fractions. The least common multiple will be used to create new fractions.
3. Create equivalent (equal) fractions with the denominator from step 2.
4. Leave the denominator the same, and subtract the numerators. Make sure the fraction is in simplest form.

*Example*

Chanel has to complete $\frac{5}{6}$ of her homework for Monday. By Saturday night, she had completed $\frac{1}{4}$ of her homework.

How much homework does Chanel have left to do?

*Solution*

**Step 1**

Identify the important information and key words.

The key word in the problem is *left*. This indicates subtraction.

The important information is that Chanel has to have a total of $\frac{5}{6}$ of her homework completed for

Monday. She has already completed $\frac{1}{4}$. To determine how much homework she has left, you must

subtract the two fractions.

## Step 2

Write out the multiples of both denominators. Remember that the first common multiple will be used to create new fractions.

- The multiples of 4 are 4, 8, and 12.
- The multiples of 6 are 6 and 12.

The first common multiple is 12.

## Step 3

Create equivalent fractions with the first common multiple.

To create new fractions with a denominator of 12, remember that what you do to the denominator must be done to the numerator.

$$\frac{5}{6} = \frac{5 \times 2}{6 \times 2} = \frac{10}{12}$$

$$\frac{1}{4} = \frac{1 \times 3}{4 \times 3} = \frac{3}{12}$$

## Step 4

Subtract the fractions.

Leave the denominators the same, and subtract only the numerators.

$$10 - 3 = 7$$

$$\frac{10}{12} - \frac{3}{12} = \frac{7}{12}$$

Chanel has $\frac{7}{12}$ of her homework left.

---

# ROUNDING FRACTIONS TO THE NEAREST HALF OR WHOLE NUMBER

When you are working with fractions, it is sometimes helpful to be able to round them. It is easier to work with whole or half numbers than with fractions like $\frac{17}{19}$ or $1\frac{3}{8}$. If you want to round a fraction to the nearest whole or half number, there are three strategies you can use:

- Draw a picture.
- Make a number line.
- Use your number sense.

# DRAWING A PICTURE

If you draw a picture of a fraction, you can then look at it to see which whole or half number it is closest to.

*Example*

Look at the fractions $2\frac{1}{8}$, $2\frac{3}{8}$, and $2\frac{7}{8}$.

| Fraction | Picture | Rounded Fraction |
|---|---|---|
| $2\frac{1}{8}$ | | The third circle is almost empty, so you can round it down 2. |
| $2\frac{3}{8}$ | | The third circle is about half full, so you can round to $2\frac{1}{2}$. |
| $2\frac{7}{8}$ | | The third circle is almost full, so you can round up to 3. |

# MAKING A NUMBER LINE

Putting a fraction on a number line is another way to help you round it to the nearest whole or half number.

*Example*

Look at the fractions $4\frac{1}{9}$, $4\frac{5}{9}$, and $4\frac{8}{9}$.

| Fraction | Number Line | Rounded Fraction |
|---|---|---|
| $4\frac{1}{9}$ | | The fraction $4\frac{1}{9}$ is closer to 4 than 5, so you can round it down to 4. |
| $4\frac{5}{9}$ | | The fraction $4\frac{5}{9}$ is about halfway between 4 and 5, so you can round it to $4\frac{1}{2}$. |
| $4\frac{8}{9}$ | | The fraction $4\frac{8}{9}$ is closer to 5 than 4, so you can round it up to 5. |

## USING YOUR NUMBER SENSE

Another strategy for rounding fractions is to compare the numerator and the denominator.

*Example*

Look at the fractions $5\frac{3}{20}$, $5\frac{9}{20}$, and $5\frac{19}{20}$.

| Fraction | Comparison | Rounded Fraction |
|---|---|---|
| $5\frac{3}{20}$ | The numerator is much smaller than the denominator, so $\frac{3}{20}$ is a very small fraction. | The fraction $5\frac{3}{20}$ is closer to 5 than 6, so round it down to 5. |
| $5\frac{9}{20}$ | The denominator is 20. Half of 20 is 10. The numerator is close to 10, so $\frac{9}{20}$ is almost the same as $\frac{1}{2}$. | The fraction $5\frac{9}{20}$ is about halfway between 5 and 6, so you can round it to $5\frac{1}{2}$. |
| $5\frac{19}{20}$ | The numerator is almost as big as the denominator. This means that $\frac{19}{20}$ is almost equal to a whole. | The fraction $5\frac{19}{20}$ is closer to 6 than 5, so you can round it up to 6. |

## ESTIMATING SUMS OF FRACTIONS

When you do not need an exact answer, you can estimate to find the sum of fractions. To find the sum of fractions, follow these steps:

1. Round each fraction to the nearest half or whole.
2. Add the rounded fractions.

When you want to round fractions, you can use your number sense to know what to round the fraction to. For example, you can round $3\frac{1}{50}$ to 3 because $\frac{1}{50}$ is so small. Or, you can round $6\frac{14}{15}$ to 7 because $\frac{14}{15}$ is almost a whole.

Another way to round fractions is by using representations. For example, if you need to round $\frac{3}{8}$, you can draw a picture.

The picture shows that $\frac{3}{8}$ is pretty close to $\frac{1}{2}$.

*Example*

Estimate the sum of $3\frac{1}{50} + 2\frac{3}{8}$.

*Solution*

**Step 1**

Round each fraction to the nearest half or whole.

$3\frac{1}{50} \rightarrow 3$

$2\frac{3}{8} \rightarrow 2\frac{1}{2}$

**Step 2**

Add the rounded fractions.

$3 + 2\frac{1}{2} = 5\frac{1}{2}$

The sum of $3\frac{1}{50}$ and $2\frac{3}{8}$ is about $5\frac{1}{2}$.

## ESTIMATING DIFFERENCES OF FRACTIONS

When you do not need an exact answer, you can estimate to find the difference of two fractions. To estimate the difference of two fractions, take the following steps:

1. Round each fraction to the nearest half or whole.
2. Subtract the rounded fractions.

When you want to round fractions, you can use your number sense to know what to round the fraction to.

For example, you can round $1\frac{1}{10}$ to 1 because $\frac{1}{10}$ is so small. Or, you can round $3\frac{19}{20}$ to 4 because $\frac{19}{20}$ is almost a whole.

Another way to round fractions is by drawing a picture. For example, if you draw $\frac{7}{12}$, you can see that it is pretty close to $\frac{1}{2}$.

*Example*

Estimate the difference of $3\frac{19}{20} - 1\frac{7}{12}$.

*Solution*

**Step 1**

Round each fraction to the nearest half or whole.

$3\frac{19}{20} \rightarrow 4$

$1\frac{7}{12} \rightarrow 1\frac{1}{2}$

**Step 2**

Subtract the rounded fractions.

$4 - 1\frac{1}{2} = 2\frac{1}{2}$

The difference between $3\frac{19}{20}$ and $1\frac{7}{12}$ is about $2\frac{1}{2}$.

---

*5.NF.3*    *Interpret a fraction as division of the numerator by the denominator (a/b = a ÷ b). Solve word problems involving division of whole numbers leading to answers in the form of fractions or mixed numbers.*

## UNDERSTANDING FRACTIONS AS THE DIVISION OF WHOLE NUMBERS

You can use fractions as another way to represent the division of whole numbers. For example, $1 \div 3 = \frac{1}{3}$. When you are solving division problems involving whole numbers, the quotient may be a fraction.

To solve these types of problems, use the following steps:

1. Write the division problem as a fraction.
2. Determine the greatest common factor.
3. Simplify the fraction.

*Example*

If you have 2 brownies and 4 people want to share them, the division problem will state 2 ÷ 4, which means 2 brownies divided by 4 people. The division equation can be written as the fraction $\frac{2}{4}$.

To determine how much brownie each person will get, simplify the fraction. To simplify a fraction, find the greatest common factor.

The factors of 2 are 1 and 2. The factors of 4 are 1, 2, and 4.

The greatest common factor is 2. Divide both the numerator and the denominator by 2.

$\frac{2 \div 2}{4 \div 2} = \frac{1}{2}$

Therefore, each person will get $\frac{1}{2}$ a brownie.

---

## Example

Kevin ordered a pizza for himself and 6 friends to share. There were 6 slices of pizza in total. However, 2 more people joined Kevin and his friends.

How much pizza did each person get?

## Solution

**Step 1**

Write the division problem as a fraction.

The division problem is 6 ÷ 9, which means 9 people (Kevin plus the original 6 friends plus the 2 more who showed up) dividing 6 pieces of pizza.

$\frac{6}{9}$

**Step 2**

Determine the greatest common factor.

The factors of 9 are 1, 3, and 9. The factors of 6 are 1, 2, 3, and 6.

The greatest common factor is 3.

**Step 3**

Simplify the fraction.

$\frac{6 \div 3}{9 \div 3} = \frac{2}{3}$

$6 \div 9 = \frac{2}{3}$

Therefore, each person got $\frac{2}{3}$ of a piece of pizza.

---

# UNDERSTANDING THE RELATIONSHIP BETWEEN WHOLE NUMBERS AND FRACTIONS

You can write division statements by using the division symbol or by representing the division as a fraction.

For example, 2 divided by 3 can be written as 2 ÷ 3 or as $\frac{2}{3}$.

When you write division as a fraction, the dividend becomes the numerator of the fraction and the divisor becomes the denominator.

## Example

To show the division statement 3 ÷ 4, you can use the fraction $\frac{3}{4}$. Both represent 3 being divided into 4 equal parts. The numerator is always divided by the denominator.

---

## Example

To show the division statement 5 ÷ 9, you can use the fraction $\frac{5}{9}$. Both represent 5 being divided into 9 equal parts. The numerator is always divided by the denominator.

---

*5.NF.4A   Apply and extend previous understandings of multiplication to multiply a fraction or whole number by a fraction.  Interpret the product (a/b) × q as a parts of a partition of q into b equal parts; equivalently, as the result of a sequence...*

## MULTIPLYING A FRACTION BY A WHOLE NUMBER USING REPEATED ADDITION

When multiplying a fraction by a whole number using repeated addition, the whole number will tell you how many fractions to add together.  For example, to multiply $\frac{1}{4}$ × 3 by using repeated addition, add $\frac{1}{4}$ three times.

$$\frac{1}{4} + \frac{1}{4} + \frac{1}{4}$$

When you add fractions with like denominators, remember to keep the denominators the same and add together all the numerators.

$$\frac{1}{4} + \frac{1}{4} + \frac{1}{4} = \frac{3}{4}$$

*Example*

> Determine the product of $\frac{1}{3}$ × 5 = □ using repeated addition.

*Solution*

**Step 1**
Rewrite the multiplication equation as addition.

The whole number tells you how many fractions to add together.  You should add $\frac{1}{3}$ five times.

$$\frac{1}{3} + \frac{1}{3} + \frac{1}{3} + \frac{1}{3} + \frac{1}{3} = \square$$

**Step 2**
Solve the addition equation.
The denominator remains the same (3).  Add all the numerators together, and place the sum over the denominator.

$$1 + 1 + 1 + 1 + 1 = 5$$
$$\frac{1}{3} + \frac{1}{3} + \frac{1}{3} + \frac{1}{3} + \frac{1}{3} = \frac{5}{3}$$

## MULTIPLYING WHOLE NUMBERS BY FRACTIONS

Fractions can be shown with simple pictures.  You can divide a shape into equal parts to represent the denominator, and you can represent the numerator by shading in a number of sections.

The given diagram represents the fraction $\frac{4}{6}$.

Multiplying fractions can be represented using an area model.  An area model is a rectangle where the length is one factor, the width is the other factor, and the product is the area.

To multiply fractions by whole numbers using an area model, follow these steps:

1. Draw enough rectangles to represent the whole number, and color each of the rectangles entirely.
2. Multiply each of the rectangles by the fraction by dividing each of the wholes into the number of parts represented by the denominator.
3. Determine the product.

*Example*

Use an area model to solve $4 \times \dfrac{2}{3}$.

*Solution*

**Step 1**

Draw rectangles to represent the whole number.

Because the whole number is 4, there needs to be 4 whole rectangles.

Draw 4 whole rectangles, and shade them entirely.

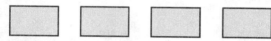

**Step 2**

Multiply each of the rectangles by $\dfrac{2}{3}$.

Divide each rectangle into 3 horizontal strips, which is equal to the value of the denominator. Shade 2 horizontal strips darker, which is equal to the value of the numerator.

**Step 3**

Determine the product.

The darker shaded sections represent the product.

In total, 2 sections are overlapping out of 3 sections in each rectangle.

$2 + 2 + 2 + 2 = 8$

Place the number 8 over the denominator (3).

$$4 \times \dfrac{2}{3} = \dfrac{8}{3}$$

---

## MULTIPLYING FRACTIONS BY FRACTIONS

A fraction consists of a numerator and a denominator. When multiplying fractions, you do not need a common denominator.

To multiply fractions, multiply the numerator of the first fraction by the numerator of the second fraction and the denominator of the first fraction by the denominator of the second fraction.

*Example*

Calculate $\frac{2}{5} \times \frac{2}{3}$.

*Solution*

Multiply numerator by numerator and denominator by denominator.

$$\frac{2}{5} \times \frac{2}{3} = \frac{2 \times 2}{5 \times 3}$$

$$= \frac{4}{15}$$

---

*Example*

When $\frac{1}{2}$ is multiplied by $\frac{3}{7}$, what is the product?

*Solution*

Multiply numerator by numerator and denominator by denominator.

$$\frac{1}{2} \times \frac{3}{7} = \frac{1 \times 3}{2 \times 7}$$

$$= \frac{3}{14}$$

---

**5.NF.4B** *Apply and extend previous understandings of multiplication to multiply a fraction or whole number by a fraction. Find the area of a rectangle with fractional side lengths by tiling it with unit squares of the appropriate unit fraction side...*

## MULTIPLYING FRACTIONS USING AN AREA MODEL

Fractions can be shown with simple pictures. A shape can divided into equal parts to represent the denominator and the numerator can be represented by shading in a number of sections. For example, $\frac{4}{6}$ can be shown as follows:

The process of multiplying fractions can be modeled using an area model. An area model is a rectangular model that illustrates that the area inside the rectangle is a product of two dimensions: its length and its width. When two drawn fractions overlap in an area model, the overlapping section results in the product.

To multiply fractions using an area model, follow these steps:

1. Model the multiplicand.
2. Add the multiplier to the rectangle.
3. Determine the product.

*Example*

Use an area model to solve $\frac{1}{4} \times \frac{2}{3}$.

*Solution*

### Step 1

Model the multiplicand.

Draw a rectangle divided into 4 vertical strips, which is equal to the value of the denominator. Shade 1 strip, which is equal to the value of the numerator.

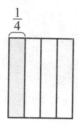

### Step 2

Add the multiplier to the rectangle.

Divide the rectangle into 3 horizontal strips, which is equal to the value of the denominator. Shade 2 horizontal strips, which is equal to the value of the numerator.

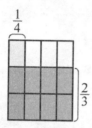

### Step 3

Determine the product.

The overlapping (blue) sections represent the product.

In total, 2 sections are overlapping out of 12 sections.

$$\frac{2}{12} = \frac{1}{6}$$

$$\frac{2}{12} = \frac{2 \div 2}{12 \div 2} = \frac{1}{6}$$

$$\frac{1}{4} \times \frac{2}{3} = \frac{1}{6}$$

---

# MEASURE AND RECORD AREAS OF RECTANGLES

**Area** is how much space a shape covers. The area of a shape is expressed as the number of square units, such as square **inches** ($in^2$), square **yards** ($yd^2$), square **centimeters** ($cm^2$), square **meters** ($m^2$).

For example, one square inch, or $1\ in^2$, has a width of 1 in and a length of 1 in. This area is written as $1\ in^2$ to show the two dimensions. You read $in^2$ as *square inches* or *inches squared*.

To find the area of a rectangle, multiply the length by the width.

Area = length × width

$\quad A = l \times w$

$\quad A = \text{units}^2$

*Example*

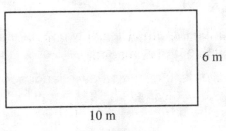

*A rectangle*

Find the **area** of the given rectangle.  Be sure to include the correct unit of measure in your answer.

*Solution*

$\quad A = l \times w$

$\quad A = 10\ \text{m} \times 6\ \text{m}$

$\quad A = 60\ \text{m}^2$

---

*Example*

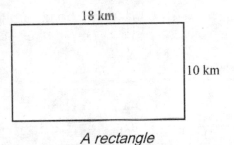

*A rectangle*

Find the **area** of the given rectangle.  Be sure to include the correct unit of measure in your answer.

*Solution*

$\quad A = l \times w$

$\quad A = 18\ \text{km} \times 10\ \text{km}$

$\quad A = 180\ \text{km}^2$

---

*5.NF.5A    Interpret multiplication as scaling (resizing), by:  Comparing the size of a product to the size of one factor on the basis of the size of the other factor, without performing the indicated multiplication.*

## USING MULTIPLICATION TO MAKE COMPARISONS

When you multiply, you are comparing the quantities of two amounts.  For example, in the equation 3 × 5 = 15, you know that 15 is equal to 3 sets of 5 or 5 sets of 3.

To describe these relationships in words, use comparative language and say "five times more than" or "three times as many as."  So, instead of saying that 15 is equal to 3 sets of 5, you will say that 15 is 3 times as many as 5 or 3 times more than 5.

*Example*

In this picture, there are 3 gumballs on the left and 18 gumballs on the right.

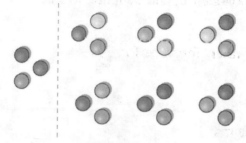

You can see that there are 6 times as many gumballs in the picture on the right.  Therefore, you have identified the comparative relationship in the picture:  18 is 6 times as many as 3.
3 × 6 = 18

---

*Example*

Don is 9 years old, and his uncle Clint is 27 years old.

In words, describe the given comparative relationship by telling how many times older Clint is than Don.

*Solution*

Because 9 × 3 = 27, Clint is 3 times older than Don.

---

*5.NF.5B    Interpret multiplication as scaling (resizing), by:  Explaining why multiplying a given number by a fraction greater than 1 results in a product greater than the given number (recognizing multiplication by whole numbers greater than 1 as a...*

## CREATING EQUIVALENT FRACTIONS

Fractions are made up of two parts:  a numerator and a denominator.

It is possible to create more fractions that are equal to the first fraction by multiplying or dividing both the numerator and denominator by the same value.  When the numerator and denominator are different but are proportionally related to the first fraction, they are known as **equivalent fractions**.

Look at the following two diagrams. In the first diagram, 6 of 9 rectangles are shaded. In the second diagram, 2 of 3 of the rows are shaded. Each drawing shows the same amount shaded. Therefore, they are equivalent fractions.

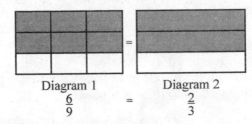

Diagram 1          Diagram 2
$\frac{6}{9}$          =          $\frac{2}{3}$

Two methods used for making equivalent fractions are division and multiplication.

To make an equivalent fraction by dividing, follow these steps:

1. Find common factors of both terms.
2. Divide the numerator and denominator by the common factor.

*Example*

Use division to create two equivalent fractions for $\frac{8}{12}$.

*Solution*

### Step 1
Find common factors of both terms.
Use divisibility rules to find factors that divide evenly into the numerator and denominator of the fraction.

- Factors of 8: 1, 2, 4, 8
- Factors of 12: 1, 2, 3, 4, 6, 12

Common factors of the numerator and denominator are 2 and 4.

### Step 2
Divide the numerator and denominator by the factor 2.

$$\frac{8 \div 2}{12 \div 2} = \frac{4}{6}$$

$\frac{4}{6}$ is an equivalent fraction to $\frac{8}{12}$.

### Step 3
Divide the numerator and denominator by the factor 4.

$$\frac{8 \div 4}{12 \div 4} = \frac{2}{3}$$

$\frac{2}{3}$ is an equivalent fraction to $\frac{8}{12}$.

$\frac{2}{3}$ and $\frac{4}{6}$ are equivalent to $\frac{8}{12}$.

To make an equivalent fraction by multiplying, follow these steps:

1. Choose any number to be the factor.
2. Multiply the numerator and denominator by the factor.

*Example*

Use multiplication to create two equivalent fractions for $\frac{3}{4}$.

*Solution*

**Step 1**
Choose any number to be the factors.
3 and 4 will be the factors.

**Step 2**
Multiply the numerator and denominator by these factors.
$$\frac{3 \times 3}{4 \times 3} = \frac{9}{12}$$
$\frac{9}{12}$ is an equivalent fraction.

$$\frac{3 \times 4}{4 \times 4} = \frac{12}{16}$$
$\frac{12}{16}$ is an equivalent fraction.

$\frac{9}{12}$ and $\frac{12}{16}$ are equivalent to $\frac{3}{4}$.

---

*5.NF.6    Solve real world problems involving multiplication of fractions and mixed numbers.*

## MULTIPLYING MIXED NUMBERS

A **mixed number** consists of a combination of a whole number and a proper fraction. To multiply mixed numbers, change the mixed numbers into improper fractions. Then, multiply the numerator by the numerator and the denominator by the denominator. Finally, reduce the product to lowest terms, and change it back to a mixed number, if necessary.

When you have a mixed number in the form $a\frac{b}{c}$, the improper fraction becomes $\frac{a \times c + b}{c}$.

*Example*

Simplify $4\frac{2}{3} \times 2\frac{4}{7}$.

*Solution*

**Step 1**
Change the mixed numbers into improper fractions.
$$\frac{4 \times 3 + 2}{3} \times \frac{2 \times 7 + 4}{7} = \frac{14}{3} \times \frac{18}{7}$$

**Step 2**

Multiply numerator by numerator and denominator by denominator.

$$\frac{14}{3} \times \frac{18}{7} = \frac{14 \times 18}{3 \times 7} = \frac{252}{21}$$

**Step 3**

Reduce the fraction to lowest terms.

Divide 252 and 21 by their greatest common factor, which is 21.

$$\frac{252 \div 21}{21 \div 21} = \frac{12}{1} = 12$$

Expressed in lowest terms, the product of $4\frac{2}{3}$ and $2\frac{4}{7}$ is 12.

---

*Example*

Simplify $2\frac{4}{6} \times 3\frac{3}{5}$.

*Solution*

**Step 1**

Change the mixed numbers to improper fractions.

$$\frac{2 \times 6 + 4}{6} \times \frac{3 \times 5 + 3}{5} = \frac{16}{6} \times \frac{18}{5}$$

**Step 2**

Multiply numerator by numerator and denominator by denominator.

$$\frac{16}{6} \times \frac{18}{5} = \frac{16 \times 18}{6 \times 5} = \frac{288}{30}$$

**Step 3**

Reduce the fraction to lowest terms.

Since the greatest common factor of 288 and 30 is 6, divide each of them by it.

$$\frac{288 \div 6}{30 \div 6} = \frac{48}{5}$$

**Step 4**

Change the reduced improper fraction to a mixed number.

Numerator of improper fraction ÷ Denominator = Quotient + $\frac{\text{Remainder}}{\text{Denominator}}$.

$48 \div 5 = 9$, remainder 3

The product of $2\frac{4}{6}$ and $3\frac{3}{5}$ is $9\frac{3}{5}$.

---

When you are solving word problems, look for keywords that tell you what operation to perform. Some multiplication keywords are *of, times, product, double,* and *triple.*

*Example*

Following his favorite recipe, Barry uses $2\frac{1}{4}$ cups of flour to make one cake. He wants to make 5 cakes.

How much flour will he need?

*Solution*

**Step 1**
Change the mixed numbers to improper fractions.
$$\frac{2 \times 4 + 1}{4} \times \frac{5}{1} = \frac{9}{4} \times \frac{5}{1}$$

**Step 2**
Multiply the numerator by the numerator and the denominator by the denominator.
$$\frac{9}{4} \times \frac{5}{1} = \frac{9 \times 5}{4 \times 1} = \frac{45}{4}$$

**Step 3**
Reduce the fraction to lowest terms.

Since the only common factor of 45 and 4 is 1, the improper fraction is already in lowest terms.

**Step 4**
Change the reduced improper fraction to a mixed number.

$$\text{Numerator of improper fraction} \div \text{Denominator} = \text{Quotient} + \frac{\text{Remainder}}{\text{Denominator}}.$$

$45 \div 4 = 11$, remainder 1

Raman needs $11\frac{1}{4}$ cups of flour to make five cakes.

---

## SOLVING PROBLEMS INVOLVING THE MULTIPLICATION OF FRACTIONS

Keywords in problems can tell you what operation to perform in order to solve the problem. The following keywords tell you that you need to multiply:

- Of
- Triple
- Times
- Double
- Product

For example, if a problem asks you to find $\frac{2}{3}$ of $\frac{1}{5}$, it is asking you to solve $\frac{2}{3} \times \frac{1}{5}$.

To solve problems involving fractions, follow these steps:

1. Identify the important information. Look for keywords that tell you to multiply.
2. Determine the number sentence that represents the problem.
3. Multiply the numerator by the numerator and the denominator by the denominator.

*Example*

Joey, Tamar, Elaine, and Travis are working on a school project. Together they must decorate $\frac{1}{2}$ of the bulletin board in their classroom. They agree that they will each be responsible for $\frac{1}{4}$ of their part of the board.

What fraction of the entire bulletin board will each student in the group end up decorating?

*Solution*

**Step 1**

Identify the important information. The following information is important for this question:

- Joey, Tamar, Elaine, and Travis are decorating $\frac{1}{2}$ of the bulletin board.

- Each of them will decorate $\frac{1}{4}$ of $\frac{1}{2}$ of the bulletin board.

- The keyword "of" means this problem can be solved by multiplying.

**Step 2**

Determine the number sentence that represents the problem.

$\frac{1}{4} \times \frac{1}{2}$

**Step 3**

Multiply the numerator by the numerator and the denominator by the denominator.

$\frac{1}{4} \times \frac{1}{2}$

$= \frac{1 \times 1}{4 \times 2}$

$= \frac{1}{8}$

Each student in the group will end up decorating $\frac{1}{8}$ of the bulletin board.

*5.NF.7A    Apply and extend previous understandings of division to divide unit fractions by whole numbers and whole numbers by unit fractions. Interpret division of a unit fraction by a non-zero whole number, and compute such quotients.*

## DIVIDING FRACTIONS BY A WHOLE NUMBER

Fractions and mixed numbers can be divided together like any other numbers.

Division questions involving fractions require the question to be changed into a multiplication question by taking the **reciprocal** of the term after the division sign.

To divide a fraction by a whole number, it is necessary to change the whole number into a fraction.

*Example*

What is the solution to the problem $\frac{1}{6} \div 4$?

*Solution*

### Step 1
Create a reciprocal fraction from the whole number.

Change the whole number 4 into a fraction by giving it a denominator of 1: $\frac{4}{1}$.

The reciprocal of $\frac{4}{1}$ is $\frac{1}{4}$.

### Step 2
Multiply the first fraction by the reciprocal of the second fraction.
Multiply numerator by numerator and denominator by denominator.

$$\frac{1}{6} \times \frac{1}{4} = \frac{1 \times 1}{6 \times 4} = \frac{1}{24}$$

The fraction cannot be reduced.

$$\frac{1}{6} \div 4 = \frac{1}{24}$$

---

*5.NF.7B    Apply and extend previous understandings of division to divide unit fractions by whole numbers and whole numbers by unit fractions. Interpret division of a whole number by a unit fraction, and compute such quotients.*

## DIVIDING WHOLE NUMBERS BY UNIT FRACTIONS

You may already know how to add, subtract, and multiply fractions. However, you may not know that it is also possible to divide by fractions. For example, if you want to divide $3 \div \frac{1}{4}$, flip $\frac{1}{4}$ upside down to make $\frac{4}{1}$. Then, you can multiply $3 \times \frac{4}{1}$ to find the answer.

$$\begin{aligned} 3 \div \frac{1}{4} &= 3 \times \frac{4}{1} \\ &= 3 \times 4 \\ &= 12 \end{aligned}$$

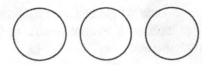

To show why this is true, imagine 3 wholes.

Now, divide the 3 wholes into quarters.

When you count the quarters, you find that there are 12 equal parts.

So, $3 \div \dfrac{1}{4} = 12$.

When you divide by a fraction, you can always flip the divisor upside down and multiply.

When you divide by a fraction with a numerator of 1, you can multiply the dividend by the denominator of the divisor. In the previous example, 3 was the dividend and 4 was the denominator of the divisor, so $3 \times 4 = 12$.

*Example*

Solve $5 \div \dfrac{1}{7}$.

*Solution*

**Method 1**

The divisor has a numerator of 1. Multiply the dividend by the denominator of the divisor.

The dividend is 5. The denominator of the divisor is 7.

$$5 \div \frac{1}{7} = 5 \times 7$$
$$= 35$$

**Method 2**

Flip the divisor upside down, and multiply.

$$5 \div \frac{1}{7} = 5 \times \frac{7}{1}$$
$$= 5 \times 7$$
$$= 35$$

*5.NF.7C  Apply and extend previous understandings of division to divide unit fractions by whole numbers and whole numbers by unit fractions. Solve real world problems involving division of unit fractions by non–zero whole numbers and division of...*

## SOLVING PROBLEMS THAT INVOLVE DIVIDING A UNIT FRACTION BY A WHOLE NUMBER

Fractions and mixed numbers can be divided together like any other numbers.

Division questions involving fractions require that the question be changed into a multiplication question by taking the reciprocal of the term after the division sign. The reciprocal is found by reversing the numerator and the denominator of a fraction.

To divide a fraction by a whole number, it is necessary to change the whole number into a fraction. To change a whole number into a fraction, use the whole number as the numerator and use 1 as the denominator. For instance, $4 = \frac{4}{1}$.

*Example*

Katrina brings $\frac{1}{6}$ of her birthday cake to school to share it with 4 friends.

What fraction of cake will each friend get?

*Solution*

**Step 1**

Create a reciprocal fraction from the whole number.

Change the whole number 4 into a fraction by giving it a denominator of 1.

$\frac{4}{1}$

The reciprocal of $\frac{4}{1}$ is $\frac{1}{4}$.

**Step 2**

Multiply the first fraction by the reciprocal of the second fraction.

Multiply numerator by numerator and denominator by denominator.

$$\frac{1}{6} \times \frac{1}{4} = \frac{1 \times 1}{6 \times 4}$$

$$= \frac{1}{24}$$

The fraction cannot be reduced.

Therefore, $\frac{1}{6} \div 4 = \frac{1}{24}$.

Each friend will get $\frac{1}{24}$ of cake.

## SOLVING PROBLEMS BY DIVIDING WHOLE NUMBERS BY UNIT FRACTIONS

Whenever you have a word problem, you need to read it carefully to see what the problem is asking you to do. The kind of situation in the problem can help you decide which operation to use. Keywords can also tell you what operation to perform in order to solve the problem.

The following keywords tell you that you need to divide:

- Per
- Out of
- Split
- Each
- Groups
- Quotient

For example, if a problem asks you to split 4 into groups of $\frac{1}{5}$, it is asking you to solve $4 \div \frac{1}{5}$.

To solve problems involving whole numbers and unit fractions, follow these steps:

1. Identify the important information. Look for keywords that tell you to divide.
2. Determine the number sentence that represents the problem.
3. Perform the division.

*Example*

Janelle is planning a pizza party. She has enough money to buy 3 pizzas and decides to divide the pizza slices into eighths.

How many pizza slices will Janelle have for her party?

*Solution*

**Step 1**

Identify the important information.

The following information is important for this question:

- Janelle will have 3 pizzas.

- Each pizza will be divided into eighths. Eighths is the same as $\frac{1}{8}$.

- The keyword *each* tells you to divide.

**Step 2**

Determine the number sentence that represents the problem.

$3 \div \frac{1}{8}$

**Step 3**

Perform the division.

$3 \div \frac{1}{8}$

$= 3 \times \frac{8}{1}$

$= 3 \times 8$

$= 24$

Janelle will have 24 pizza slices for her party.

# EXERCISE #1—NUMBER AND OPERATIONS—FRACTIONS

**119.** Solve $\frac{1}{5} + \frac{3}{4}$.

**120.** Solve $\frac{5}{7} + \frac{4}{5}$.

$\frac{3}{4}$ $\frac{1}{2}$

**121.** Solve $\frac{5}{6} - \frac{3}{12}$.

**122.** Solve $\frac{5}{7} - \frac{2}{5}$.

*Use the following information to answer the next question.*

Amy represents the fraction problem $\frac{1}{2} + \frac{1}{3}$ visually.

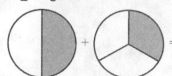

123. Which of the following representations can **best** help Amy add $\frac{1}{2} + \frac{1}{3}$?

A.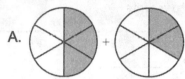

B.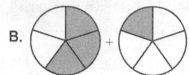

C.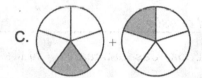

D.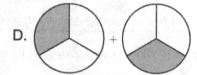

124. Which of the following pictures shows the answer to $\frac{2}{3} + \frac{1}{6}$?

A.

B.

C.

D.

125. Which of the following diagrams represents the solution to the equation $\frac{4}{5} - \frac{1}{3} = \square$?

A.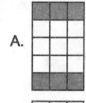

B.

C.

D.

126. Written with the lowest common denominator, $\frac{1}{2}$ and $\frac{2}{3}$ are equal to the fractions

A. $\frac{1}{6}$ and $\frac{2}{6}$

B. $\frac{3}{6}$ and $\frac{4}{6}$

C. $\frac{1}{12}$ and $\frac{2}{12}$

D. $\frac{6}{12}$ and $\frac{8}{12}$

*Use the following information to answer the next question.*

Alice wants to write $\frac{3}{5}$ and $\frac{7}{10}$ with common denominators. She knows that 10 can be a common denominator, so she does not have to rewrite $\frac{7}{10}$. She only needs to rewrite $\frac{3}{5}$.

127. When Alice writes $\frac{3}{5}$ with a denominator of 10, the numerator will be _____.

*Use the following information to answer the next question.*

Jasdeep and Marco are taking turns reading to each other from a book. Jasdeep reads $\frac{3}{8}$ of the book, and Marco reads $\frac{1}{4}$ of the book.

128. What fraction of the book did the two students read to each other in total?

A. $\frac{4}{8}$

B. $\frac{5}{8}$

C. $\frac{4}{12}$

D. $\frac{5}{12}$

129. The **best** estimate for $2\frac{1}{8} + 2\frac{18}{20}$ is

A. 3

B. $3\frac{1}{2}$

C. $4\frac{1}{2}$

D. 5

130. The **best** estimate for $\frac{6}{10} + 2\frac{95}{100}$ is

A. 2

B. 3

C. $3\frac{1}{2}$

D. $4\frac{1}{2}$

131. What is the **best** estimate of the solution to the expression $9\frac{1}{6} - 1\frac{7}{8}$?

   A. $6\frac{1}{2}$

   B. 7

   C. 8

   D. $8\frac{1}{2}$

132. The **best** estimate of the solution to the expression $6\frac{5}{9} - 4\frac{1}{12}$ is

   A. 1

   B. $1\frac{1}{2}$

   C. 2

   D. $2\frac{1}{2}$

*Use the following information to answer the next question.*

Jason has a bag of chips that is $\frac{2}{3}$ full. He eats $\frac{1}{4}$ of the bag.

133. How much of the bag of chips is left?

   A. $\frac{1}{7}$

   B. $\frac{5}{7}$

   C. $\frac{1}{12}$

   D. $\frac{5}{12}$

*Use the following information to answer the next question.*

Kayla has $\frac{3}{5}$ of a can of paint. She uses $\frac{1}{3}$ of the can to paint one of the walls in her bedroom.

134. How much of the can of paint is left?

   A. $\frac{3}{4}$

   B. $\frac{4}{8}$

   C. $\frac{3}{12}$

   D. $\frac{4}{15}$

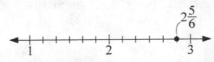

*Use the following information to answer the next question.*

Christine wants to round $2\frac{5}{6}$ to the nearest half or whole number. She decides to make a number line to help her.

135. Which number should Christine round $2\frac{5}{6}$ to?

A. $3\frac{1}{2}$

B. 3

C. 2

D. $2\frac{1}{2}$

136. What is $2\frac{3}{10}$ rounded to the nearest half or whole number?

A. $3\frac{1}{2}$

B. 3

C. $2\frac{1}{2}$

D. 2

137. What is $3\frac{5}{100}$ rounded to the nearest half or whole number?

A. 3

B. $3\frac{1}{2}$

C. 4

D. $4\frac{1}{2}$

*Use the following information to answer the next question.*

Jolene brought 4 brownies to school. She decided to share them with her two best friends.

138. How many brownies does each of the 3 girls get?

A. $1\frac{1}{4}$

B. $1\frac{1}{3}$

C. $3\frac{1}{4}$

D. $4\frac{1}{3}$

*Use the following information to answer the next question.*

Marty, Trevor, and Leena are doing a report together. They need to read 2 pages from their science book then explain them to their class. They decide to split the reading evenly between them.

139. Expressed as a fraction, how much of a page does each student need to read?

A. $\dfrac{2}{3}$

B. $\dfrac{3}{2}$

C. $\dfrac{2}{5}$

D. $\dfrac{3}{5}$

140. Which of the following expressions shows $\dfrac{2}{5} \times 4$ as repeated addition?

A. $\dfrac{2}{5} + 4$

B. $\dfrac{2}{5} + \dfrac{2}{5}$

C. $\dfrac{2}{5} + \dfrac{2}{5} + 4$

D. $\dfrac{2}{5} + \dfrac{2}{5} + \dfrac{2}{5} + \dfrac{2}{5}$

141. Which of the following expressions is equal to $\dfrac{1}{6} + \dfrac{1}{6} + \dfrac{1}{6}$?

A. $\dfrac{1}{6} + 3$

B. $\dfrac{1}{6} \times 3$

C. $\dfrac{3}{6} + 3$

D. $\dfrac{3}{6} \times 3$

*Use the following information to answer the next question.*

An area model is given.

142. Which of the following number sentences represents this area model?

A. $\dfrac{3}{4} \times 1$

B. $\dfrac{3}{8} \times 1$

C. $\dfrac{1}{4} \times 2$

D. $\dfrac{1}{8} \times 2$

*Use the following information to answer the next question.*

Aaliyah drew four area models but forgot to label them with the right multiplication sentences.

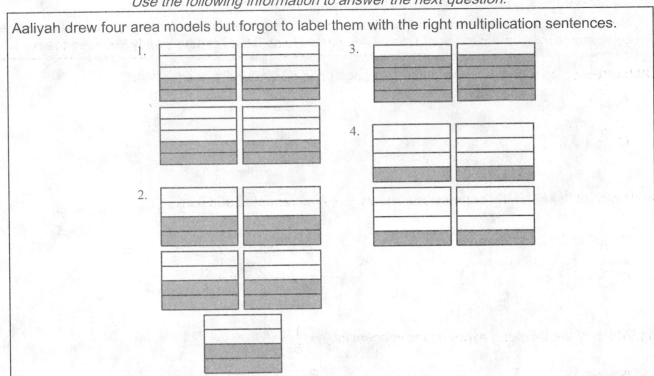

**143.** Which of the given area models shows the solution to $\frac{2}{5} \times 4$?

    A. 1                           B. 2

    C. 3                           D. 4

**144.** What is the product of $\frac{1}{8} \times \frac{3}{5}$?

    A. $\frac{4}{13}$                      B. $\frac{3}{13}$

    C. $\frac{4}{40}$                      D. $\frac{3}{40}$

**145.** What is the product of $\frac{2}{7} \times \frac{3}{5}$?

    A. $\frac{5}{35}$                      B. $\frac{6}{35}$

    C. $\frac{5}{12}$                      D. $\frac{6}{12}$

Copyright Protected

146. Which of the following area models represents the solution to the expression $\frac{5}{6} \times \frac{2}{5}$?

A.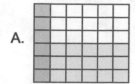

B.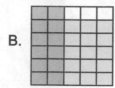

C.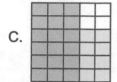

D.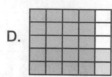

*Use the following information to answer the next question.*

An area model diagram is shaded as shown.

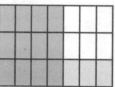

147. What is the solution to the expression represented by the given area model?

A. $\frac{15}{21}$

B. $\frac{8}{21}$

C. $\frac{7}{21}$

D. $\frac{4}{21}$

*Use the following information to answer the next question.*

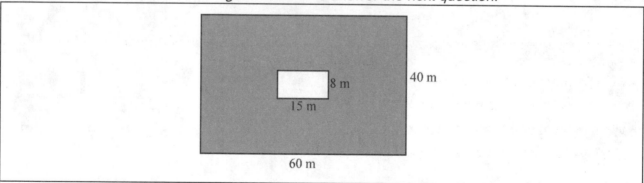

148. What is the area of the shaded part of the rectangle?

A. 2,200 m²

B. 2,280 m²

C. 2,300 m²

D. 2,400 m²

Exercise #1

Castle Rock Research

*Use the following information to answer the next question.*

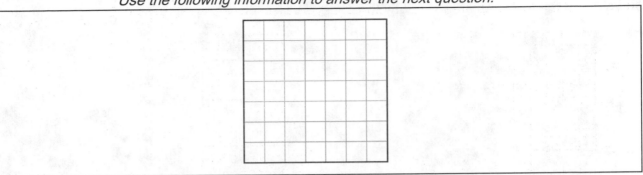

**149.** Find the area of the shape.

**150.** Which of the following statements describes the comparative relationship in the equation
$8 \times 6 = 48$?

    **A.** The number 6 is 8 times as many as 48.

    **B.** The number 48 is 6 times as many as 8.

    **C.** The number 48 is 8 times more than 8.

    **D.** The number 8 is 6 times more than 48.

**151.** Which of the following statements describes the comparative relationship in the equation
$5 \times 7 = 35$?

    **A.** Five is 7 times more than 35.

    **B.** Seven is 5 times as many as 35.

    **C.** Thirty-five is 7 times more than 5.

    **D.** Thirty-five is 5 times as many as 5.

152. Use multiplication to create two equivalent fractions for $\frac{1}{3}$.

153. Use multiplication and division to make equivalent fractions for $\frac{14}{21}$.

154. What is the value when $2\frac{1}{4}$ is multiplied by $2\frac{2}{3}$?

A. $2\frac{3}{7}$

B. $4\frac{1}{6}$

C. $4\frac{2}{7}$

D. 6

*Use the following information to answer the next question.*

Phillipa has $\frac{3}{4}$ of a regular deck of 52 cards.  One-third of these are red.

155. How many black cards does she have?
   A. 39

   C. 18

   B. 26

   D. 13

*Use the following information to answer the next question.*

Gavin surveys the Grade 5 students at his school about what they like to do for fun.  He finds that $\frac{3}{5}$ of the Grade 5 students play on a sports team, and $\frac{3}{4}$ of those students are on a soccer team.

156. What fraction of the Grade 5 students play on a soccer team?

   A. $\frac{4}{5}$

   B. $\frac{6}{9}$

   C. $\frac{9}{20}$

   D. $\frac{6}{25}$

*Use the following information to answer the next question.*

Manny, Taylor, and Heba are volunteering to make sandwiches for the food bank.  Together, they need to make $\frac{1}{2}$ of the total number of sandwiches the food bank needs for the week.  They agree they will each make $\frac{1}{3}$ of the sandwiches for which they are responsible.

157. What fraction of all the sandwiches will Manny, Taylor, and Heba each end up making?

   A. $\frac{1}{6}$

   B. $\frac{1}{2}$

   C. $\frac{2}{3}$

   D. $\frac{3}{4}$

158. What is the solution to the problem $\frac{1}{2} \div 8$?

   A. $\frac{1}{16}$

   B. $\frac{1}{14}$

   C. $\frac{1}{12}$

   D. $\frac{1}{10}$

159. The solution to the expression $4 \div \frac{1}{6}$ is _____.

*Use the following information to answer the next question.*

Joseph has a $\frac{1}{2}$ qt of juice. He pours it into 4 glasses.

160. How much juice is there in each glass?

A. $\frac{1}{3}$ qt

B. $\frac{1}{4}$ qt

C. $\frac{1}{6}$ qt

D. $\frac{1}{8}$ qt

*Use the following information to answer the next question.*

Manuel has $\frac{1}{5}$ m of ribbon. He is going to use it to make 3 bows for small gift bags.

161. How much ribbon will he use for each bow?

A. $\frac{1}{15}$ m

B. $\frac{1}{13}$ m

C. $\frac{1}{8}$ m

D. $\frac{1}{2}$ m

162. If Dr. Robertson spends $\frac{1}{4}$ of an hour with each of his patients, how many patients can he see in 9 h?

A. 20

B. 24

C. 32

D. 36

*Use the following information to answer the next question.*

Lydia is making friendship bracelets. Each bracelet is 8 in long. She puts one bead in every $\frac{1}{2}$ in of the bracelet.

163. How many beads does Lydia use to make one bracelet?

A. 4

B. 8

C. 12

D. 16

$\boxed{\frac{3}{4}\frac{1}{2}}$

# EXERCISE #1—NUMBER AND OPERATIONS—FRACTIONS
## ANSWERS AND SOLUTIONS

| | | | |
|---|---|---|---|
| 119. See solution | 131. B | 143. A | 155. B |
| 120. See solution | 132. D | 144. D | 156. C |
| 121. See solution | 133. D | 145. B | 157. A |
| 122. See solution | 134. D | 146. D | 158. A |
| 123. A | 135. B | 147. D | 159. 24 |
| 124. D | 136. C | 148. B | 160. D |
| 125. C | 137. A | 149. See solution | 161. A |
| 126. B | 138. B | 150. B | 162. D |
| 127. 6 | 139. A | 151. C | 163. D |
| 128. B | 140. D | 152. See solution | |
| 129. D | 141. B | 153. See solution | |
| 130. C | 142. C | 154. D | |

**119.**

**Step 1**
Find the lowest common denominator (LCD).
Write the multiples of each denominator until a common one appears.

- Multiples of 4 are 4, 8, 12, 16, 20.
- Multiples of 5 are 5, 10, 15, 20.

The LCD of 4 and 5 is 20.
Use the LCD to create new equivalent fractions with a denominator of 20.
Multiply the numerator and denominator of each fraction by the same factor.
$$\frac{1\times 4}{5\times 4}=\frac{4}{20}, \frac{3\times 5}{4\times 5}=\frac{15}{20}$$

**Step 2**
Add the numerators of the fractions while keeping the denominators the same.
$$\frac{4+15}{20}=\frac{19}{20}$$

**Step 3**
Reduce the resulting fraction to lowest terms.
The fraction is already in lowest terms.
$$\frac{1}{5}+\frac{3}{4}=\frac{19}{20}$$

**120.**

**Step 1**
Find the lowest common denominator.
Write multiples of each denominator until a common one appears.

- Multiples of 7 are 7, 14, 21, 28, and 35.
- Multiples of 5 are 5, 10, 15, 20, 25, 30, and 35.

The lowest common denominator (LCD) of 7 and 5 is 35.

**Step 2**
Use the LCD to create new equivalent fractions with a denominator of 35.
Multiply the numerator and denominator of each fraction by the same factor.
$$\frac{5\times 5}{7\times 5}=\frac{25}{35}$$
$$\frac{4\times 7}{5\times 7}=\frac{28}{35}$$

**Step 3**
Add the numerators of the fractions while keeping the denominator the same.
$$\frac{25}{35}+\frac{28}{35}=\frac{53}{35}$$

**Step 4**

Convert the improper fraction to a mixed fraction, and reduce to lowest terms.

$$\frac{53}{35} = 1\frac{18}{35}$$

The mixed fraction $1\frac{18}{35}$ is in lowest terms.

Therefore, $\frac{5}{7} + \frac{4}{5} = 1\frac{18}{35}$.

**121.**

**Step 1**

Write the fractions with the lowest common denominator (LCD).

Write the multiples of each denominator until a common one appears.

- Multiples of 6: 6, 12, 18, 24
- Multiples of 12: 12, 24

The lowest common denominator for 6 and 12 is 12.

Use the LCD to create new equivalent fractions with a denominator of 12.

$$\frac{5 \times 2}{6 \times 2} = \frac{10}{12}$$
$$\frac{3 \times 1}{12 \times 1} = \frac{3}{12}$$

**Step 2**

Subtract the numerators of the fractions while keeping the denominators the same.

$$\frac{10 - 3}{12} = \frac{7}{12}$$

**Step 3**

Reduce the resulting fraction to lowest terms. The fraction is already in lowest terms.

Therefore, $\frac{5}{6} - \frac{3}{12} = \frac{7}{12}$.

**122.**

**Step 1**

Write the fractions with the lowest common denominator (LCD).

Write the multiples of each denominator until a common one appears.

- Multiples of 7: 7, 14, 21, 28, 35
- Multiples of 5: 5, 10, 15, 20, 25, 30, 35

The LCD for 7 and 5 is 35.

Use the LCD to create new equivalent fractions with a denominator of 35.

$$\frac{5 \times 5}{7 \times 5} = \frac{25}{35}, \frac{2 \times 7}{5 \times 7} = \frac{14}{35}$$

**Step 2**

Subtract the numerators of the fractions while keeping the denominators the same.

$$\frac{25 - 14}{35} = \frac{11}{35}$$

**Step 3**

Reduce the resulting fraction to lowest terms. The fraction is already in lowest terms.

Therefore, $\frac{5}{7} - \frac{2}{5} = \frac{11}{35}$.

**123. A**

The given fraction circles have different-sized parts, so they cannot be added together. Find a way to split up the fraction circles in a different way so they both have the same size parts.

When you split the fraction circle representing $\frac{1}{2}$ into sixths, it becomes $\frac{3}{6}$.

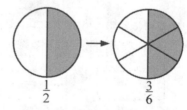

When you split the fraction circle representing $\frac{1}{3}$ into sixths, it becomes $\frac{2}{6}$.

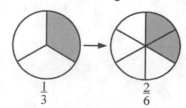

The equation now becomes $\frac{3}{6} + \frac{2}{6} = \square$.

If you want to find the answer, you can count up the total number of shaded parts. There are five shaded parts, so the answer is $\frac{5}{6}$.

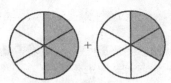

### 124. D

**Step 1**

Draw a picture of each fraction. Make your drawings exactly the same size.

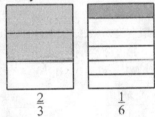

$$\frac{2}{3} \qquad \frac{1}{6}$$

**Step 2**

You cannot add because the fractions have different-sized pieces. Find a way to split up the fractions differently, so that they both have the same size pieces.

When you split $\frac{2}{3}$ like this, it becomes $\frac{4}{6}$.

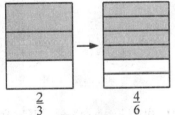

$$\frac{2}{3} \qquad \frac{4}{6}$$

**Step 3**

To add $\frac{4}{6} + \frac{1}{6}$, draw a picture of $\frac{4}{6}$ and then shade in $\frac{1}{6}$ more.

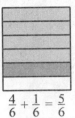

$$\frac{4}{6} + \frac{1}{6} = \frac{5}{6}$$

### 125. C

**Step 1**

Find the lowest common denominator (LCD), and rewrite the fractions.

To find the lowest common denominator, write out the multiples for each of the denominators until there is one they share.

- Multiples of 5 include 5, 10, and 15.
- Multiples of 3 include 3, 6, 9, 12, and 15.
- The lowest common denominator is 15.

**Step 2**

Rewrite the two fractions with the LCD.

$$\frac{4}{5} = \frac{4 \times 3}{5 \times 3} = \frac{12}{15}$$
$$\frac{1}{3} = \frac{1 \times 5}{3 \times 5} = \frac{5}{15}$$

The expression becomes $\frac{12}{15} - \frac{5}{15}$.

**Step 3**

Draw a grid based on the factors of the denominator.

The denominator is 15.

$5 \times 3 = 15$

## Step 4
Shade in the parts equivalent to the first numerator.

The first numerator is 12.  Shade in 12 parts.

## Step 5
Cross out the shaded parts equivalent to the second numerator.

The second numerator is 5.  Cross out 5 of the shaded parts.

## Step 6
Count the total number of remaining shaded parts.

There are 7 remaining shaded parts.

$$\frac{12}{15} - \frac{5}{15} = \frac{7}{15}$$

## 126.  B

### Step 1
Choose a common denominator.

The denominator of $\frac{1}{2}$ is 2.  The denominator of $\frac{2}{3}$ is 3.  Find a number that is a multiple of both 2 and 3:

- Multiples of 2 include 2, 4, 6, 8, and 10.
- Multiples of 3 include 3, 6, 9, 12, and 15.

The number 6 is the lowest common multiple of both 2 and 3.  Use this as the common denominator.

## Step 2
Write the first fraction with a denominator of 6.

$$\frac{1}{2} = \frac{?}{6}$$

To go from a denominator of 2 to a denominator of 6, you need to multiply by 3.  Multiply the numerator and denominator by 3.

$$\frac{1}{2} = \frac{1 \times 3}{2 \times 3} = \frac{3}{6}$$

## Step 3
Write the second fraction with a denominator of 6.

$$\frac{2}{3} = \frac{?}{6}$$

To go from a denominator of 3 to a denominator of 6, you need to multiply by 2.  Multiply the numerator and denominator by 2.

$$\frac{2}{3} = \frac{2 \times 2}{3 \times 2} = \frac{4}{6}$$

The fractions $\frac{1}{2}$ and $\frac{2}{3}$ are equal to $\frac{3}{6}$ and $\frac{4}{6}$.

## 127.  6

Rewrite $\frac{3}{5}$ with a denominator of 10.

$$\frac{3}{5} = \frac{?}{10}$$

To go from a denominator of 5 to a denominator of 10, you need to multiply by 2.  Multiply the numerator and denominator by 2.

$$\frac{3}{5} = \frac{3 \times 2}{5 \times 2} = \frac{6}{10}$$

The numerator of Alice's new fraction will be 6.

## 128.  B

### Step 1
Identify the important information.

Jasdeep read $\frac{3}{8}$ of the book, and Marco read $\frac{1}{4}$ of the book.  The question is asking for the total fraction of the book the two students read.

$$\boxed{\frac{3}{4} \quad \frac{1}{2}}$$

## Step 2
Create equivalent fractions.

Fractions must have the same denominator before they can be added together. Determine the lowest common multiple of the two denominators, and use it to create new fractions.

Multiples of 4 include 4, 8, 12, and 16. Multiples of 8 include 8, 16, and 24.

The lowest common multiple is 8. Use 8 as the denominator to create new fractions.

Remember that any operation done to the denominator must be done to the numerator.

$$\frac{1}{4} = \frac{1 \times 2}{4 \times 2} = \frac{2}{8}$$

The fraction $\frac{3}{8}$ already has a denominator of 8,

so it will remain the same.

## Step 3
Add the equivalent fractions.

$$\frac{2}{8} + \frac{3}{8} = \frac{5}{8}$$

### 129. D

#### Step 1
Round each fraction to the nearest half or whole.

- $2\frac{1}{8} \rightarrow 2$

- $2\frac{18}{20} \rightarrow 3$

#### Step 2
Add the rounded fractions.
$$2 + 3 = 5$$

The sum of $2\frac{1}{8}$ and $2\frac{18}{20}$ is about 5.

### 130. C

#### Step 1
Round each fraction to the nearest half or whole.

- $\frac{6}{10} \rightarrow \frac{1}{2}$

- $2\frac{95}{100} \rightarrow 3$

## Step 2
Add the rounded fractions.

$$\frac{1}{2} + 3 = 3\frac{1}{2}$$

The sum of $\frac{6}{10}$ and $2\frac{95}{100}$ is about $3\frac{1}{2}$.

### 131. B

#### Step 1
Round each fraction to the nearest half or whole.

- $9\frac{1}{6} \rightarrow 9$

- $1\frac{7}{8} \rightarrow 2$

#### Step 2
Subtract the rounded fractions.
$$9 - 2 = 7$$

The difference between $9\frac{1}{6}$ and $1\frac{7}{8}$ is about 7.

### 132. D

#### Step 1
Round each fraction to the nearest half or whole.

$$6\frac{5}{9} \rightarrow 6\frac{1}{2}$$

$$4\frac{1}{12} \rightarrow 4$$

#### Step 2
Subtract the rounded fractions.

$$6\frac{1}{2} - 4 = 2\frac{1}{2}$$

The difference between $6\frac{5}{9}$ and $4\frac{1}{12}$ is about

$2\frac{1}{2}$.

**133. D**

**Step 1**

Identify the important information.

The bag of chips is $\frac{2}{3}$ full.

Jason eats $\frac{1}{4}$ of the remaining chips.

To find out how much is left, subtract $\frac{1}{4}$ from $\frac{2}{3}$.

**Step 2**

Create equivalent fractions by using the first common multiple.

To determine common multiples, write out the multiples of both denominators.

- Multiples of 3 include 3, 6, 9, and 12.
- Multiples of 4 include 4, 8, and 12.

The first common multiple is 12. Change both fractions to have a denominator of 12.

$$\frac{2}{3} = \frac{2 \times 4}{3 \times 4} = \frac{8}{12}$$
$$\frac{1}{4} = \frac{1 \times 3}{4 \times 3} = \frac{3}{12}$$

**Step 3**

Subtract the equivalent fractions.
Subtract the numerators. The denominator remains the same.

$$\frac{8}{12} - \frac{3}{12} = \frac{5}{12}$$

There is $\frac{5}{12}$ of the bag of chips left over.

**134. D**

**Step 1**

Identify the important information.

Kayla starts out with $\frac{3}{5}$ of a can of paint.

She uses $\frac{1}{3}$ of the can.

The question is asking how much paint is left in the can.
You will need to use subtraction to solve this problem.

**Step 2**

Create equivalent fractions by using the first common multiple.

To determine common multiples, write out the multiples of both denominators.

Multiples of 3 are 3, 6, 9, 12, and 15.
Multiples of 5 are 5, 10, and 15.

The first common multiple is 15. Therefore, 15 will be used to create the equivalent fractions. What you do to the denominator, you must also do to the numerator.

$$\frac{1}{3} = \frac{1 \times 5}{3 \times 5} = \frac{5}{15}$$
$$\frac{3}{5} = \frac{3 \times 3}{5 \times 3} = \frac{9}{15}$$

**Step 3**

Subtract the equivalent fractions.
The denominator remains the same while you subtract the numerators.

$$\frac{9}{15} - \frac{5}{15} = \frac{4}{15}$$

There is $\frac{4}{15}$ of the can of paint left.

**135. B**

The fraction $2\frac{5}{6}$ is over halfway between 2 and 3, and it is closer to 3 than 2.

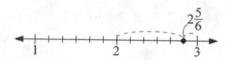

Christine should round $2\frac{5}{6}$ to 3.

## 136. C

**Method 1**
Draw a picture.

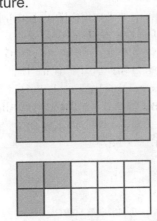

The third picture only needs to have two more squares filled to have $\frac{1}{2}$ the third square filled in, so you would round $2\frac{3}{10}$ up to $2\frac{5}{10}$, or its reduced form, $2\frac{1}{2}$.

**Method 2**
Make a number line.

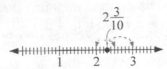

The fraction $2\frac{3}{10}$ is closer to 2.5 than 2, so round it up to 2.5.

**Method 3**
Use your number sense.
You know that 5 is half of 10. The fraction $2\frac{3}{10}$ is closer to $2\frac{5}{10}$ than it is to the number 2 or to the number 3. You can round $2\frac{3}{10}$ up to $2\frac{5}{10}$, or its reduced form, $2\frac{1}{2}$.

## 137. A

**Method 1**
Draw a picture.

The fourth square is almost empty, so round $3\frac{5}{100}$ down to 3.

**Method 2**
Make a number line.

The fraction $3\frac{5}{100}$ is closer to 3 than 4, so round it down to 3.

**Method 3**
Use your number sense.
Compare the numerator and the denominator. Compared to 100, 5 is very small. Therefore, $\frac{5}{100}$ is a very small fraction. Round $3\frac{5}{100}$ down to 3.

## 138. B

**Step 1**
Turn the division statement into a fraction.
There are 4 brownies being divided between 3 girls.
$4 \div 3$

This is the same as the fraction $\frac{4}{3}$.

**Step 2**
Reduce the fraction.
The fraction $\frac{4}{3}$ cannot be reduced, but you can write it as a mixed number.
$\frac{4}{3} = 1\frac{1}{3}$

Each girl gets $1\frac{1}{3}$ brownies.

**139.  A**

Turn the division statement into a fraction.

There are 2 pages being divided between 3 students.

$2 \div 3$

This is the same as the fraction $\frac{2}{3}$. The fraction $\frac{2}{3}$ cannot be reduced.

Each student needs to read $\frac{2}{3}$ of a page.

**140.  D**

**Step 1**
Decide how many times you need to add the fraction.

The expression $\frac{2}{5} \times 4$ means that there are 4 groups of $\frac{2}{5}$. You should add the fraction 4 times.

**Step 2**
Write the addition sentence.

$\frac{2}{5} + \frac{2}{5} + \frac{2}{5} + \frac{2}{5}$

If you want to solve the multiplication problem, you can add the fractions.

$$\frac{2}{5} \times 4 = \frac{2}{5} + \frac{2}{5} + \frac{2}{5} + \frac{2}{5}$$
$$= \frac{2+2+2+2}{5}$$
$$= \frac{8}{5}$$

**141.  B**

The fraction $\frac{1}{6}$ is added together 3 times.

This is the same as saying that there are 3 groups of $\frac{1}{6}$. You should multiply by 3.

Write the multiplication sentence.

$\frac{1}{6} \times 3$

If you want to solve the multiplication problem, you can add the fractions.

$$\frac{1}{6} \times 3 = \frac{1}{6} + \frac{1}{6} + \frac{1}{6}$$
$$= \frac{1+1+1}{6}$$
$$= \frac{3}{6}$$

**142.  C**

**Step 1**
Figure out the whole number.
The large rectangles represent the whole number.
There are 2 large rectangles, so the whole number is 2.

**Step 2**
Figure out the fraction that is multiplied by the whole number.

The denominator of the fraction is equal to the number of parts in which each rectangle is divided.  The denominator is 4 because each rectangle is divided into 4 parts.

$\frac{\phantom{1}}{4}$

The numerator of the fraction will be equal to the number of shaded parts.  The numerator is 1 because 1 part of each rectangle is shaded.

$\frac{1}{4}$

**Step 3**
Figure out the number sentence.
The expression represented by the area model is $\frac{1}{4} \times 2$.

To find the product, count the total number of shaded parts and put it over the denominator (4).

$$\frac{1}{4} \times 2 = \frac{2}{4}$$

## 143. A

The correct area model shows the multiplication of a whole number by a fraction.

### Step 1
Draw rectangles to represent the whole number.
The whole number is 4, so draw four whole rectangles.

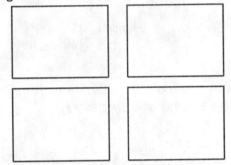

### Step 2
Multiply each of the rectangles by $\frac{2}{5}$.

The denominator is 5, so divide each rectangle into five horizontal strips. The numerator is 2, so shade two of the strips.

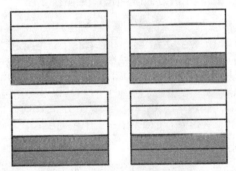

You can use the area model to find the product of $\frac{2}{5} \times 4$. The shaded sections represent the product.

In total, two sections out of five sections in each rectangle are shaded.
$2 + 2 + 2 + 2 = 8$
Place the number 8 over the denominator (5).
$$\frac{2}{5} \times 4 = \frac{8}{5}$$
This product is shown in area model 1.

## 144. D

Multiply numerator by numerator and denominator by denominator.
$$\frac{1}{8} \times \frac{3}{5}$$
$$= \frac{1 \times 3}{8 \times 5}$$
$$= \frac{3}{40}$$

## 145. B

Multiply numerator by numerator and denominator by denominator.
$$\frac{2}{7} \times \frac{3}{5} = \frac{2 \times 3}{7 \times 5}$$
$$= \frac{6}{35}$$

## 146. D

### Step 1
Model the multiplicand.
Draw a rectangle divided into six vertical strips, which is equal to the value of the denominator. Shade five strips, which is equal to the value of the numerator.

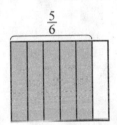

### Step 2
Add the multiplier to the rectangle.
Divide the rectangle into five horizontal strips, which is equal to the value of the denominator. Shade two horizontal strips, which is equal to the value of the numerator.

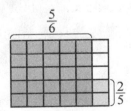

## 147. D

### Step 1

Determine the numerator.

Count up the number of tiles that overlap.

There are four tiles that overlap.

### Step 2

Determine the denominator.

Count up all the tiles in the area model.

There are 21 tiles in total.

### Step 3

Set up the fraction.

$\dfrac{4}{21}$

The solution to the expression represented by the area model is $\dfrac{4}{21}$.

## 148. B

### Step 1

Determine the area of the large rectangle by substituting the appropriate numbers for the length (60 m) and the width (40 m) in the area formula.

$A = l \times w$

$A = 60 \times 40$

$A = 2{,}400 \text{ m}^2$

### Step 2

Determine the area of the small (white) rectangle.

$A = l \times w$

$A = 15 \times 8$

$A = 120 \text{ m}^2$

### Step 3

Subtract the two areas to determine the area of the shaded part.

$2{,}400 \text{ m}^2 - 120 \text{ m}^2 = 2{,}280 \text{ m}^2$

The area of the shaded part of the rectangle is $2{,}280 \text{ m}^2$.

## 149.

### Step 1

Determine the side lengths.

Count the number of squares on the length and the width.

$s = 7$ units

### Step 2

Substitute the known values into the area formula, and solve.

Since both the length and width measure 7 units, use the area formula for a square.

$A = s^2$

$\quad = 7^2$

$\quad = 7 \times 7$

$\quad = 49 \text{ units}^2$

The area of the square is $49 \text{ units}^2$.

## 150. B

The equation $8 \times 6 = 48$ means that in 48 there are 8 sets of 6 or 6 sets of 8.

Another way to describe this relationship is to say that the number 48 is 6 times as many as 8 or 8 times as many as 6.

The statement that the number 48 is 6 times as many as 8 is the only statement that describes the comparative relationship in the equation $8 \times 6 = 48$.

## 151. C

The equation $5 \times 7 = 35$ means that there are 5 sets of 7 or 7 sets of 5 in 35.

Another way to describe this relationship is to say that 35 is 7 times more than 5 or 5 times more than 7.

The statement that 35 is 7 times more than 5 is the only given statement that describes the equation.

## 152.

### Step 1

Choose any two numbers to be the factors.

Let 2 and 3 be the factors.

### Step 2

Multiply the numerator and denominator by these factors.

$\dfrac{1 \times 2}{3 \times 2} = \dfrac{2}{6}$

$\dfrac{1 \times 3}{3 \times 3} = \dfrac{3}{9}$

Therefore, $\dfrac{2}{6}$ and $\dfrac{3}{9}$ are equivalent to $\dfrac{1}{3}$.

**153.**

**Step 1**
Create two equivalent fractions using multiplication.
Let 2 and 5 be the factors.
$$\frac{14 \times 2}{21 \times 2} = \frac{28}{42}$$
$$\frac{14 \times 5}{21 \times 5} = \frac{70}{105}$$
Therefore, $\frac{28}{42}$ and $\frac{70}{105}$ are equivalent to $\frac{14}{21}$.

**Step 2**
Identify the common factors of 14 and 21.
List the factors of 14 and 21.

- Factors of 14: 1, 2, 7, 14
- Factors of 21: 1, 3, 7, 21

The greatest common factor of the numerator and denominator is 7.

**Step 3**
Divide the numerator and denominator by 7.
$$\frac{14 \div 7}{21 \div 7} = \frac{2}{3}$$
Therefore, $\frac{2}{3}$ is equivalent to $\frac{14}{21}$.

**154. D**

**Step 1**
Change the mixed numbers into improper fractions.
$$2\frac{1}{4} \times 2\frac{2}{3} = \frac{2 \times 4 + 1}{4} \times \frac{2 \times 3 + 2}{3}$$
$$= \frac{9}{4} \times \frac{8}{3}$$

**Step 2**
Multiply numerator by numerator and denominator by denominator.
$$\frac{9}{4} \times \frac{8}{3} = \frac{72}{12}$$

**Step 3**
Reduce the fraction to lowest terms.
Divide 72 and 12 by their greatest common factor, which is 12.
$$\frac{72 \div 12}{12 \div 12} = \frac{6}{1} = 6$$
Therefore, $2\frac{1}{4} \times 2\frac{2}{3} = 6$.

**155. B**

**Step 1**
Determine the number of cards Phillipa has.
Since Phillipa has $\frac{3}{4}$ of 52 cards, multiply $\frac{3}{4}$ by 52.
Multiply numerator by numerator and denominator by denominator, and reduce the fraction to its lowest terms.
$$\frac{3}{4} \times \frac{52}{1} = \frac{3 \times 52}{4 \times 1} = \frac{156}{4} = 39$$
Phillipa has 39 cards.

**Step 2**
Determine the number of red cards she has.
Since $\frac{1}{3}$ of 39 cards are red, multiply $\frac{1}{3}$ by 39.
$$\frac{1}{3} \times \frac{39}{1} = \frac{1 \times 39}{3 \times 1} = \frac{39}{3} = 13$$
There are 13 red cards.

**Step 4**
Calculate how many black cards she has.
To calculate the number of black cards, subtract the number of red cards (13) from the total number of cards (39).
$$39 - 13 = 26$$

**156. C**

**Step 1**
Identify the important information.
- The fraction of students who play on a sports team is $\frac{3}{5}$.
- The fraction of students who play on a soccer team is $\frac{3}{4}$ of the students who play on a sports team.
- The keyword *of* tells you to multiply.

**Step 2**
Determine the number sentence that represents the problem.
$$\frac{3}{5} \times \frac{3}{4}$$

**Step 3**

Multiply the numerator by the numerator and the denominator by the denominator.

$$\frac{3}{5} \times \frac{3}{4} = \frac{3 \times 3}{5 \times 4}$$

$$= \frac{9}{20}$$

Out of all the Grade 5 students, $\frac{9}{20}$ play on a soccer team.

**157. A**

**Step 1**

Identify the important information.

Manny, Taylor, and Heba are making $\frac{1}{2}$ of the total number of sandwiches needed by the food bank, and each of them will make $\frac{1}{3}$ of $\frac{1}{2}$ of these sandwiches.

The keyword *of* tells you to multiply.

**Step 2**

Determine the number sentence that represents the problem.

$$\frac{1}{3} \times \frac{1}{2}$$

**Step 3**

Multiply the numerator by the numerator and the denominator by the denominator.

$$\frac{1}{3} \times \frac{1}{2} = \frac{1 \times 1}{3 \times 2}$$

$$= \frac{1}{6}$$

The fraction of sandwiches Manny, Taylor, and Heba will each have to make is $\frac{1}{6}$.

**158. A**

**Step 1**

Create a reciprocal fraction from the whole number.

Change the whole number 8 into a fraction by giving it a denominator of 1.

$$\frac{8}{1}$$

The reciprocal of $\frac{8}{1}$ is $\frac{1}{8}$.

**Step 2**

Multiply the first fraction by the reciprocal of the second fraction.

$$\frac{1}{2} \times \frac{1}{8}$$

Multiply the numerator by the numerator and the denominator by the denominator.

$$\frac{1}{2} \times \frac{1}{8} = \frac{1 \times 1}{8 \times 2} = \frac{1}{16}$$

The fraction cannot be reduced.

$$\frac{1}{2} \div 8 = \frac{1}{16}$$

**159. 24**

**Method 1**

The divisor has a numerator of 1. Multiply the dividend by the denominator of the divisor. The dividend is 4. The denominator of the divisor is 6.

$$4 \div \frac{1}{6} = 4 \times 6$$

$$= 24$$

**Method 2**

Flip the divisor upside down, and multiply.

$$4 \div \frac{1}{6} = 4 \times \frac{6}{1}$$

$$= 4 \times 6$$

$$= 24$$

**160. D**

**Step 1**

Write a division sentence.

$$\frac{1}{2} \div 4 =$$

**Step 2**

Write the division as a multiplication sentence. Change the whole number 4 into a fraction by giving it a denominator of 1.

$$\frac{4}{1}$$

The reciprocal of $\frac{4}{1}$ is $\frac{1}{4}$.

$$\frac{1}{2} \div 4 = \frac{1}{2} \div \frac{4}{1}$$

$$= \frac{1}{2} \times \frac{1}{4}$$

**Step 3**
Multiply numerator by numerator and denominator by denominator.
$$\frac{1}{2} \times \frac{1}{4} = \frac{1 \times 1}{2 \times 4}$$
$$= \frac{1}{8}$$

There is $\frac{1}{8}$ qt of juice in each cup.

## 161. A

**Step 1**
Write a division sentence.
$$\frac{1}{5} \div 3 =$$

**Step 2**
Write the division sentence as a multiplication sentence.
Change the whole number 3 into a fraction by giving it a denominator of 1.
$$\frac{3}{1}$$

The reciprocal of $\frac{3}{1}$ is $\frac{1}{3}$.

$$\frac{1}{5} \div 3 = \frac{1}{5} \div \frac{3}{1}$$
$$= \frac{1}{5} \times \frac{1}{3}$$

**Step 3**
Multiply numerator by numerator and denominator by denominator.
$$\frac{1}{5} \times \frac{1}{3} = \frac{1 \times 1}{5 \times 3}$$
$$= \frac{1}{15}$$

Each bow will be made of $\frac{1}{15}$ m of ribbon.

## 162. D

**Step 1**
Identify the important information. The following information is important for this question:
- Dr. Robertson has 9 h to see patients.
- He spends $\frac{1}{4}$ of an hour with each patient.
- The keyword *each* tells you to divide.

**Step 2**
Determine the number sentence that represents the problem.
$$9 \div \frac{1}{4}$$

**Step 3**
Perform the division.
$$9 \div \frac{1}{4} = 9 \times \frac{4}{1}$$
$$= 9 \times 4$$
$$= 36$$

Dr. Robertson will be able to see 36 patients in 9 h.

## 163. D

**Step 1**
Identify the important information.
Each bracelet is 8 in long, and one bead is used in every $\frac{1}{2}$ in of the bracelet. The keyword *per* tells you to divide.

**Step 2**
Determine the number sentence that represents the problem.
$$8 \div \frac{1}{2}$$

**Step 3**
Perform the division.
$$8 \div \frac{1}{2} = 8 \times \frac{2}{1}$$
$$= 8 \times 2$$
$$= 16$$

Lydia uses 16 beads for every bracelet.

# EXERCISE #2—NUMBER AND OPERATIONS—FRACTIONS

**164.** Solve $\dfrac{3}{4} + \dfrac{5}{6}$.

**165.** Solve $\dfrac{3}{7} - \dfrac{6}{11}$.

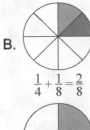

**166.** Which of the following circles shows the answer to the expression $\frac{1}{4} + \frac{1}{8}$?

A.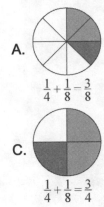

$\frac{1}{4} + \frac{1}{8} = \frac{3}{8}$

B.

$\frac{1}{4} + \frac{1}{8} = \frac{2}{8}$

C.

$\frac{1}{4} + \frac{1}{8} = \frac{3}{4}$

D.

$\frac{1}{4} + \frac{1}{8} = \frac{2}{4}$

**167.** Which of the following images shows the solution to the problem $\frac{1}{2} - \frac{1}{3}$?

A.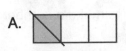

B.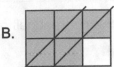

C.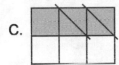

D.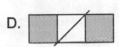

**168.** Which of the following numbers is a common denominator of the fractions $\frac{3}{4}$ and $\frac{5}{8}$?

A. 12

B. 20

C. 24

D. 36

**169.** The **best** estimate for $4\frac{4}{7} + 2\frac{5}{12}$ is

A. 5

B. 6

C. 7

D. 8

**170.** The **best** estimate for $\frac{17}{20} + 5\frac{45}{100}$ is

A. $5\frac{1}{2}$

B. $6\frac{1}{2}$

C. 7

D. 8

171. What is the **best** estimate of the solution to the expression $4\frac{1}{15} - 3\frac{9}{20}$?

A. 0

B. $\frac{1}{2}$

C. $1\frac{1}{2}$

D. 2

172. The **best** estimate of the difference of $7\frac{9}{10} - 4\frac{3}{7}$ is

A. 3

B. $3\frac{1}{2}$

C. 4

D. $4\frac{1}{2}$

*Use the following information to answer the next question.*

Lianna wants to round $1\frac{3}{5}$ to the nearest half or whole number. She decides to make a number line to help her.

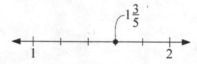

173. Which of the following numbers is closest to $1\frac{3}{5}$?

A. 1

B. $1\frac{1}{2}$

C. 2

D. $2\frac{1}{2}$

*Use the following information to answer the next question.*

Julie ordered some pizzas for her birthday party. At the end of the party, only $\frac{7}{12}$ of a pizza was left. The next morning, her brother ate an amount of pizza equal to $\frac{1}{2}$ of a full pizza for breakfast. Julie brought the rest of the pizza to school for her lunch.

174. How much pizza did Julie bring for her lunch?

A. $\frac{1}{12}$

B. $\frac{1}{10}$

C. $\frac{6}{10}$

D. $\frac{6}{12}$

*Use the following information to answer the next question.*

Kane and Kaia are saving money to buy a Mother's Day gift. Kane has saved $\frac{1}{2}$ of the money they need. Kaia has saved another $\frac{1}{6}$ of the money.

175. What fraction of the money have Kane and Kaia already saved?

A. $\frac{2}{4}$　　　　　　　　　　　　B. $\frac{2}{3}$

C. $\frac{2}{6}$　　　　　　　　　　　　D. $\frac{2}{8}$

*Use the following information to answer the next question.*

Jesse had a pizza birthday party, and 16 of his friends came. He ordered 4 pizzas for his friends to share.

176. How much pizza did each friend receive?

A. $\frac{1}{2}$　　　　　　　　　　　　B. $\frac{1}{4}$

C. $\frac{1}{6}$　　　　　　　　　　　　D. $\frac{1}{8}$

*Use the following information to answer the next question.*

Mrs. Koper handed out large sheets of paper for her Grade 1 students to color on. She had 12 sheets of paper and 24 students.

177. What portion of paper did each student receive?

A. $\frac{1}{2}$　　　　　　　　　　　　B. $\frac{1}{4}$

C. $\frac{1}{12}$　　　　　　　　　　　D. $\frac{1}{24}$

178. What is the product of $\frac{1}{4} \times 3$?

A. $\frac{6}{4}$　　　　　　　　　　　　B. $\frac{3}{4}$

C. $\frac{3}{12}$　　　　　　　　　　　D. $\frac{1}{12}$

*Use the following information to answer the next question.*

An area model is shown.

179. Which of the following number sentences represents this area model?

A. $3 \times \dfrac{1}{3}$

B. $4 \times \dfrac{1}{3}$

C. $3 \times \dfrac{3}{4}$

D. $4 \times \dfrac{3}{4}$

180. What is the product of $\dfrac{3}{4} \times \dfrac{5}{8}$?

A. $\dfrac{15}{32}$

B. $\dfrac{15}{24}$

C. $\dfrac{8}{12}$

D. $\dfrac{8}{10}$

181. Which of the following area models represents the solution to $\dfrac{3}{5} \times \dfrac{1}{2}$?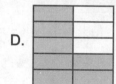

A.

B.

C.

D.

$\frac{3}{4}$ $\frac{1}{2}$

*Use the following information to answer the next question.*

Shayla drew the given rectangle on centimeter grid paper. Each square of the grid paper represents 1 cm$^2$.

**182.** What is the area of Shayla's rectangle?

- A. 50 cm$^2$
- B. 78 cm$^2$
- C. 98 cm$^2$
- D. 158 cm$^2$

*Use the following information to answer the next question.*

Annie has 9 pencils in her pencil case. Frederic has twice as many pencils.

**183.** How many pencils does Frederic have? _____

**184.** Use division to create two equivalent fractions for $\frac{12}{16}$.

**185.** Use multiplication and division to make equivalent fractions for $\frac{15}{25}$.

*Use the following information to answer the next question.*

There are 365 days in any year that is not a leap year.

**186.** To the nearest whole number, how many days are there in $2\frac{1}{2}$ years if there are no leap years?

A. 910                                    B. 913

C. 915                                    D. 921

*Use the following information to answer the next question.*

In the school band, $\frac{1}{6}$ of the members play string instruments, and $\frac{5}{8}$ of the students who play string instruments play the violin.

**187.** What is the fraction of students in the school band who play the violin?

A. $\frac{5}{48}$                         B. $\frac{6}{36}$

C. $\frac{6}{14}$                         D. $\frac{19}{24}$

**188.** What is the solution to the division problem $\frac{1}{6} \div 3$?

A. $\frac{1}{18}$                         B. $\frac{1}{20}$

C. $\frac{1}{22}$                         D. $\frac{1}{24}$

$$\boxed{\frac{3}{4} \ \frac{1}{2}}$$

**189.** What is $3 \div \frac{1}{5}$?

A. $\frac{3}{5}$ 

B. $\frac{5}{3}$

C. 12 

D. 15

*Use the following information to answer the next question.*

Thomas brings over $\frac{1}{2}$ of his marble collection. He divides these marbles equally among 3 friends.

**190.** What fraction of Thomas's entire marble collection did each friend get?

A. $\frac{6}{1}$ 

B. $\frac{1}{6}$

C. $\frac{1}{5}$ 

D. $\frac{5}{1}$

*Use the following information to answer the next question.*

Rebecca is lost on a desert island. She has 6 cans of soup. She is trying to make her food last longer, so she plans to eat $\frac{1}{3}$ of a can of soup each day.

**191.** How many days will her soup last?

A. 12 

B. 18

C. 24 

D. 30

# EXERCISE #2—NUMBER AND OPERATIONS—FRACTIONS
## ANSWERS AND SOLUTIONS

| | | | |
|---|---|---|---|
| 164. See solution | 171. B | 178. B | 185. See solution |
| 165. See solution | 172. B | 179. C | 186. B |
| 166. A | 173. B | 180. A | 187. A |
| 167. C | 174. A | 181. B | 188. A |
| 168. C | 175. B | 182. C | 189. D |
| 169. C | 176. B | 183. 18 | 190. B |
| 170. B | 177. A | 184. See solution | 191. B |

**164.**

**Step 1**
Find the lowest common denominator (**LCD**).
Write the multiples of each denominator until a common one appears.

- Multiples of 4 are 4, 8, 12…
- Multiples of 6 are 6, 12, 18…

The **LCD** for 4 and 6 is 12.
Use the **LCD** to create new equivalent fractions with a denominator of 12.
Multiply the numerator and denominator of each fraction by the same factor.

$$\frac{3 \times 3}{4 \times 3} = \frac{9}{12}, \frac{5 \times 2}{6 \times 2} = \frac{10}{12}$$

**Step 2**
Add the numerators of the fractions while keeping the denominator the same.

$$\frac{9 + 10}{12} = \frac{19}{12}$$

**Step 3**
Convert the improper fraction to a mixed fraction.

$$\frac{19}{12} = 1\frac{7}{12}$$

Reduce the resulting fraction to lowest terms. The fraction is in lowest terms.

Therefore, $\frac{3}{4} + \frac{5}{6} = 1\frac{7}{12}$.

**165.**

**Step 1**
Write the fractions with the lowest common denominator (LCD).
Write the multiples of each denominator until a common one appears.

- Multiples of 7: 7, 14, 21, 28, 35, 42, 49, 70, 77
- Multiples of 11: 11, 22, 33, 44, 55, 66, 77

The lowest common denominator for 7 and 11 is 77.
Use the LCD to create new equivalent fractions with a denominator of 77.

$$\frac{3 \times 11}{7 \times 11} = \frac{33}{77}, \frac{6 \times 7}{11 \times 7} = \frac{42}{77}$$

**Step 2**
Subtract the numerators of the fractions while keeping the denominators the same.

$$\frac{33 - 42}{77} = -\frac{9}{77}$$

**Step 3**
Reduce the resulting fraction to lowest terms.
The fraction is already in lowest terms.

Therefore, $\frac{3}{7} - \frac{6}{11} = -\frac{9}{77}$.

## 166. A

### Step 1

Draw a circle showing each fraction. Make your drawings exactly the same size.

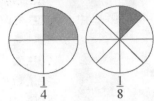

$\frac{1}{4}$ $\frac{1}{8}$

### Step 2

You cannot add the two fractions because the pieces are different sizes. Fractions must have the same denominator before they can be added.

You must find a way to split the fractions so they have the same-size pieces.

Divide the circle into 8 pieces. Now, the fraction $\frac{1}{4}$ is split and becomes $\frac{2}{8}$.

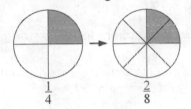

$\frac{1}{4}$ $\frac{2}{8}$

### Step 3

To add $\frac{2}{8} + \frac{1}{8}$, draw a circle that is divided into 8 pieces. Shade $\frac{2}{8}$, then shade $\frac{1}{8}$ more.

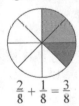

$\frac{2}{8} + \frac{1}{8} = \frac{3}{8}$

## 167. C

### Step 1

Draw a picture of each fraction.

Make the drawings exactly the same size.

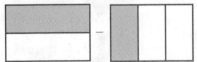

You cannot subtract because the pieces of the fractions are different sizes.

### Step 2

Find another way to split up the fractions so they both have pieces that are the same size.

- Split $\frac{1}{2}$ so it becomes $\frac{3}{6}$.

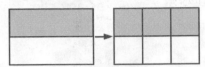

- Split $\frac{1}{3}$ so it becomes $\frac{2}{6}$.

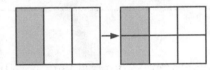

### Step 3

Subtract $\frac{1}{2} - \frac{1}{3}$.

The fraction $\frac{1}{2}$ is the same as $\frac{3}{6}$, and $\frac{1}{3}$ is the same as $\frac{2}{6}$. This means you can subtract $\frac{3}{6} - \frac{2}{6}$.

Look at the picture of $\frac{3}{6}$. To take $\frac{2}{6}$ away, cross off 2 of the 3 shaded squares. Only 1 square is left.

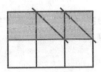

This means that $\frac{1}{2} - \frac{1}{3} = \frac{1}{6}$.

## 168. C

The denominator of $\frac{3}{4}$ is 4. The denominator of $\frac{5}{8}$ is 8. List the multiples of 4 and 8.

- Multiples of 4 include 4, 8, 12, 16, 20, 24, 28, 32, and 36.
- Multiples of 8 include 8, 16, 24, 32, and 40.
- The common multiples are 8, 16, 24, and 32.

Any of these numbers can be used as a common denominator of the fractions $\frac{3}{4}$ and $\frac{5}{8}$. The only one of these common denominators that is given as an option is 24.

**169. C**

**Step 1**
Round each fraction to the nearest half or whole.

- $4\frac{4}{7} \to 4\frac{1}{2}$
- $2\frac{5}{12} \to 2\frac{1}{2}$

**Step 2**
Add the rounded fractions.

$4\frac{1}{2} + 2\frac{1}{2} = 7$

The sum of $4\frac{4}{7}$ and $2\frac{5}{12}$ is about 7.

**170. B**

**Step 1**
Round each fraction to the nearest half or whole.

- $\frac{17}{20} \to 1$
- $5\frac{45}{100} \to 5\frac{1}{2}$

**Step 2**
Add the rounded fractions.

$1 + 5\frac{1}{2} = 6\frac{1}{2}$

The sum of $\frac{17}{20}$ and $5\frac{45}{100}$ is about $6\frac{1}{2}$.

**171. B**

**Step 1**
Round each fraction to the nearest half or whole.

$4\frac{1}{15} \to 4$

$3\frac{9}{20} \to 3\frac{1}{2}$

**Step 2**
Subtract the rounded fractions.

$4 - 3\frac{1}{2} = \frac{1}{2}$

The difference between $4\frac{1}{15}$ and $3\frac{9}{20}$ is about $\frac{1}{2}$.

**172. B**

**Step 1**
Round each fraction to the nearest half or whole.

- $7\frac{9}{10} \to 8$
- $4\frac{3}{7} \to 4\frac{1}{2}$

**Step 2**
Subtract the rounded fractions.

$8 - 4\frac{1}{2} = 3\frac{1}{2}$

The difference between $7\frac{9}{10}$ and $4\frac{3}{7}$ is about $3\frac{1}{2}$.

**173. B**

The fraction $1\frac{3}{5}$ is just over halfway between 1 and 2, and it is closer to $1\frac{1}{2}$ than it is to 2.

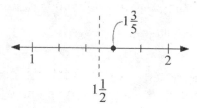

Lianna should round it to $1\frac{1}{2}$.

**174. A**

**Step 1**
Identify the important information.

At the end of the party, $\frac{7}{12}$ of a pizza was left

over. Then, Julie's brother ate $\frac{1}{2}$ of a pizza.

The question is asking how much pizza is left. To find this number, subtract the two fractions.

**Step 2**
Determine the multiples of both denominators. The lowest common multiple will be used to create new fractions.
Find the lowest common multiple of 2 and 12:

- Multiples of 2 include 2, 4, 6, 8, 10, and 12.
- Multiples of 12 include 12, 24, and 36.

The lowest common multiple is 12.

**Step 3**
Create equivalent fractions using the lowest common multiple as the denominator.
Since the given fractions have different denominators, create equivalent fractions so that they can be subtracted. The denominator will be 12.
Remember that any operation performed on the denominator must also be performed on the numerator.
$$\frac{1}{2} = \frac{1 \times 6}{2 \times 6} = \frac{6}{12}$$

The fraction $\frac{7}{12}$ already has a denominator of

12, so it will stay the same.

**Step 4**
Subtract the equivalent fractions, and reduce. Keep the denominators the same while subtracting only the numerators.
$$\frac{7}{12} - \frac{6}{12} = \frac{1}{12}$$

Julie brought $\frac{1}{12}$ of a pizza for lunch.

**175. B**

**Step 1**
Identify the important information.

Kane has saved $\frac{1}{2}$ of the money.

Kaia has saved $\frac{1}{6}$ of the money.

The question is asking how much they have saved in total, so you need to add the two fractions together.

**Step 2**
Create equivalent fractions.
Only fractions with the same denominator can be added together. To create equivalent fractions, you must find the lowest common multiple of the two denominators and use it to create new fractions.

- Multiples of 2 are 2, 4, 6, and 8.
- Multiples of 6 are 6, 12, and 18.

The lowest common multiple is 6. Use 6 as the denominator for the new fractions. Remember that the operations performed on the denominator must also be done to the numerator.
$$\frac{1}{2} = \frac{1 \times 3}{2 \times 3} = \frac{3}{6}$$

Since $\frac{1}{6}$ already has a denominator of 6, It

remains the same.

**Step 3**
Add the fractions.
The denominator remains the same while you add the numerators.
$$\frac{3}{6} + \frac{1}{6} = \frac{4}{6}$$

Simplify the fraction.
$$\frac{4}{6} = \frac{4 \div 2}{6 \div 2} = \frac{2}{3}$$

Altogether, Kane and Kaia have saved $\frac{2}{3}$ of

the money.

**176. B**

**Step 1**
Turn the division statement into a fraction.
There are 4 pizzas being divided between 16 people.
4 ÷ 16

This is the same as the fraction $\frac{4}{16}$.

**Step 2**
Reduce the fraction, if possible.
The numbers 4 and 16 can both be divided by 4.
$$\frac{4}{16} = \frac{4 \div 4}{16 \div 4} = \frac{1}{4}$$

Each person received $\frac{1}{4}$ of a pizza.

**177. A**

**Step 1**
Turn the division statement into a fraction.
There are 12 pieces of paper being divided among 24 students.
12 ÷ 24

This is the same as the fraction $\frac{12}{24}$.

**Step 2**
Reduce the fraction if possible.
$$\frac{12}{24} = \frac{1}{2}$$

Each student received $\frac{1}{2}$ a piece of paper.

**178. B**

**Step 1**
Rewrite the equation as an addition equation.
The whole number shows how many times to add the fraction. The whole number is 3.
Therefore, add one-fourth 3 times.
$$\frac{1}{4} + \frac{1}{4} + \frac{1}{4} = \square$$

**Step 2**
Add the fractions.
Add the numerators while keeping the denominator the same.
$$1 + 1 + 1 = 3$$
$$\frac{1}{4} + \frac{1}{4} + \frac{1}{4} = \frac{3}{4}$$
$$\frac{1}{4} \times 3 = \frac{3}{4}$$

**179. C**

**Step 1**
Figure out the whole number.
Each large rectangle represents the whole number.
There are 3 large rectangles, so the whole number is 3.

**Step 2**
Figure out the fraction that is multiplied by the whole number.
The denominator of the fraction is equal to the number of parts each rectangle is divided into. The denominator is 4 since each rectangle is divided into 4 parts.
The numerator of the fraction will be equal to the number of shaded parts. The numerator is 3 since 3 parts of each rectangle are shaded.

**Step 3**
Figure out the number sentence.
The expression represented by the area model is $3 \times \frac{3}{4}$.

To find the product, count the total number of shaded parts and put this number over the denominator (4).
$$3 \times \frac{3}{4} = \frac{9}{4}$$

**180. A**

Multiply numerator by numerator and denominator by denominator.
$$\frac{3}{4} \times \frac{5}{8}$$
$$= \frac{3 \times 5}{4 \times 8}$$
$$= \frac{15}{32}$$

## 181. B

### Step 1
Model the multiplicand.

Draw a rectangle divided into 5 vertical strips, which is equal to the value of the denominator. Shade 3 strips, which is equal to the value of the numerator.

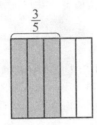

### Step 2
Add the multiplier to the rectangle.

Divide the rectangle into 2 horizontal strips, which is equal to the value of the denominator. Shade 1 horizontal strip, which is equal to the value of the numerator.

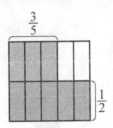

## 182. C

Choice C is correct. The area of Shayla's rectangle is 98 cm².

Area is the amount of surface of a shape, measured in square units. You could use one of these strategies to solve this problem:

- add the number of squares in each row:
  $14 + 14 + 14 + 14 + 14 + 14 + 14 = 98$
- count by sevens for 14 counts:
  7, 14, 21, 28, 35, 42, 49, 56, 63, 70, 77, 84, 91, 98
- multiply the number of squares in each row by the number of rows:
  $14 \times 7 = 98$

## 183. 18

The phrase *twice as many* means the same thing as two times as many.

Multiply the number of pencils that Annie has by 2.
$9 \times 2 = 18$

Frederic has 18 pencils.

## 184.

### Step 1
Find common factors.
List the factors of 12 and 16.

- Factors of 12: 1, 2, 3, 4, 6, 12
- Factors of 16: 1, 2, 4, 8, 16

The common factors of the numerator and denominator are 2 and 4.

### Step 2
Divide the numerator and denominator by the factor 2.
$$\frac{12 \div 2}{16 \div 2} = \frac{6}{8}$$

### Step 3
Divide the numerator and denominator by the factor 4.
$$\frac{12 \div 4}{16 \div 4} = \frac{3}{4}$$

### Step 4
Write the equivalent fractions.

Therefore, $\frac{6}{8}$ and $\frac{3}{4}$ are equivalent to $\frac{12}{16}$.

## 185.

### Step 1
Create two equivalent fractions using multiplication.
Choose any two numbers to be the factors.
Let 2 and 5 be the factors.

### Step 2
Multiply the numerator and denominator by the factors 2 and 5.
$$\frac{15 \times 2}{25 \times 2} = \frac{30}{50}$$
$$\frac{15 \times 5}{25 \times 5} = \frac{75}{125}$$

Therefore, $\frac{30}{50}$ and $\frac{75}{125}$ are equivalent to $\frac{15}{25}$.

**Step 3**

Identify the common factors of 15 and 25.
List the factors of 15 and 25.

- Factors of 15:  1, 3, 5, 15
- Factors of 25:  1, 5, 25

The greatest common factor is 5.

**Step 4**

Divide the numerator and denominator by 5.

$$\frac{15 \div 5}{25 \div 5} = \frac{3}{5}$$

Therefore, $\frac{3}{5}$ is equivalent to $\frac{15}{25}$.

**186.  B**

**Step 1**

Calculate the number of days in $2\frac{1}{2}$ years.

To calculate the number of days in $2\frac{1}{2}$ years, multiply $2\frac{1}{2}$ by 365.

Number of days = $2\frac{1}{2} \times 365$

**Step 2**

Change the mixed number into an improper fraction.

$$2\frac{1}{2} \times 365 = \frac{2 \times 2 + 1}{2} \times 365$$

$$= \frac{5}{2} \times 365$$

**Step 3**

Multiply numerator by numerator and denominator by denominator.

$$\frac{5}{2} \times \frac{365}{1} = \frac{5 \times 365}{2 \times 1} = \frac{1,825}{2}$$

**Step 4**

Convert the improper fraction into a mixed number.

$$\frac{1,825}{2} = 912\frac{1}{2}$$

To the nearest whole number, there are 913 days in $2\frac{1}{2}$ years.

**187.  A**

**Step 1**

Identify the important information.

- In the school band, $\frac{1}{6}$ of the students play string instruments.

- Of the $\frac{1}{6}$ of the students who play string instruments, $\frac{5}{8}$ play the violin.

- The keyword "of" means you need to multiply.

**Step 2**

Determine the number sentence that represents the problem.

$$\frac{1}{6} \times \frac{5}{8}$$

**Step 3**

Multiply the numerator by the numerator and the denominator by the denominator.

$$\frac{1}{6} \times \frac{5}{8}$$

$$= \frac{1 \times 5}{6 \times 8}$$

$$= \frac{5}{48}$$

The fraction of students in the school band who play the violin is $\frac{5}{48}$.

**188.  A**

**Step 1**

Create a reciprocal fraction from the whole number.

Change the whole number 3 into a fraction by giving it a denominator of 1.

$$\frac{3}{1}$$

The reciprocal of $\frac{1}{3}$ is $\frac{3}{1}$.

**Step 2**

Multiply the first fraction by the reciprocal of the second fraction.

Multiply numerator by numerator and denominator by denominator.

$$\frac{1}{6} \times \frac{1}{3} = \frac{1 \times 1}{6 \times 3} = \frac{1}{18}$$

The fraction cannot be reduced. Therefore, $\frac{1}{6} \div 3 = \frac{1}{18}$.

**189. D**

**Method 1**

The divisor has a numerator of 1, so you can multiply the dividend by the denominator of the divisor.

The dividend is 3. The denominator of the divisor is 5.

$$3 \div \frac{1}{5} = 3 \times 5$$
$$= 15$$

**Method 2**

Flip the divisor upside down, and multiply.

$$3 \div \frac{1}{5} = 3 \times \frac{5}{1}$$
$$= 3 \times 5$$
$$= 15$$

**190. B**

**Step 1**

Write a division sentence.

$$\frac{1}{2} \div 3$$

**Step 2**

Write the division as a multiplication sentence. Change the whole number 3 into a fraction by giving it a denominator of 1.

$$\frac{3}{1}$$

The reciprocal of $\frac{3}{1}$ is $\frac{1}{3}$.

$$\frac{1}{2} \div 3 = \frac{1}{2} \div \frac{3}{1}$$
$$= \frac{1}{2} \times \frac{1}{3}$$

**Step 3**

Multiply numerator by numerator and denominator by denominator.

$$\frac{1}{2} \times \frac{1}{3} = \frac{1 \times 1}{2 \times 3}$$
$$= \frac{1}{6}$$

Each friend gets $\frac{1}{6}$ of the marble collection.

**191. B**

**Step 1**

Identify the important information. The following information is important for this question:

- Rebecca has 6 cans of soup.

- She eats $\frac{1}{3}$ of a can each day.

- The keyword *each* tells you to divide.

**Step 2**

Determine the number sentence that represents the problem.

$$6 \div \frac{1}{3}$$

**Step 3**

Perform the division.

$$6 \div \frac{1}{3} = 6 \times \frac{3}{1}$$
$$= 6 \times 3$$
$$= 18$$

Rebecca's soup will last for 18 days.

# NOTES

# Measurement and Data

# MEASUREMENT AND DATA

## Table of Correlations

| Standard | | Concepts | Exercise #1 | Exercise #2 |
|---|---|---|---|---|
| **5.MD** | Measurement and Data | | | |
| 5.MD.1 | Convert among different-sized standard measurement units within a given measurement system, and use these conversions in solving multi–step, real world problems. | Converting between Milliliters and Liters | 192, 193 | 226 |
| | | Solving Length Problems | 194, 195 | 227 |
| | | Solving Problems Involving Mass | 196, 197 | 228 |
| | | Converting between Customary Units of Length | 198, 199 | 229 |
| | | Converting between Customary Units of Mass | 200, 201 | 230 |
| | | Converting Customary Units of Capacity | 202, 203 | 231 |
| | | Converting Metric Units of Mass | 204, 205 | 232 |
| | | Converting Metric Units of Length | 206, 207 | 233 |
| 5.MD.2 | Make a line plot to display a data set of measurements in fractions of a unit (1/2, 1/4, 1/8). Use operations on fractions for this grade to solve problems involving information presented in line plots. | Calculating the Mean | 208, 209 | 234 |
| | | Organizing Collected Data using Line Plots | 210, 211 | 235 |
| | | Finding the Range of a Set of Data | 212, 213 | 236 |
| | | Calculating the Mode | 214, 215 | 237 |
| | | Finding the Median | 216, 217 | 238 |
| 5.MD. 3A | Recognize volume as an attribute of solid figures and understand concepts of volume measurement. A cube with side length 1 unit, called a "unit cube," is said to have "one cubic unit" of volume, and can be used to measure... | Calculating the Volume of a Given 3-D Object by Filling it with Cubes | 218, 219 | 239 |
| 5.MD. 3B | Recognize volume as an attribute of solid figures and understand concepts of volume measurement. A solid figure which can be packed without gaps or overlaps using n unit cubes is said to have a volume of n cubic units. | Calculating the Volume of a Given 3-D Object by Filling it with Cubes | 218, 219 | 239 |
| 5.MD.4 | Measure volumes by counting unit cubes, using cubic cm, cubic in, cubic ft, and improvised units. | Calculating the Volume of a Given 3-D Object by Filling it with Cubes | 218, 219 | 239 |
| 5.MD. 5A | Find the volume of a right rectangular prism with whole-number side lengths by packing it with unit cubes, and show that the volume is the same as would be found by multiplying the edge lengths, equivalently by multiplying the height by... | Calculating the Volume of a Given 3-D Object by Filling it with Cubes | 218, 219 | 239 |
| | | Developing a Volume Formula | | |
| 5.MD. 5B | Relate volume to the operations of multiplication and addition and solve real world and mathematical problems involving volume. Apply the formulas $V=l \times w \times h$ and $V=b \times h$ for rectangular prisms to find volumes of right rectangular... | Solving Problems Involving Volume of Rectangular Prisms | 220, 221 | 240 |
| | | Finding the Volume of a Rectangular Prism | 222, 223 | 241 |

| 5.MD. 5C | Relate volume to the operations of multiplication and addition and solve real world and mathematical problems involving volume. Recognize volume as additive. Find volumes of solid figures composed of two non–overlapping... | Calculating the Volume of Two Solid Figures | 224, 225 | 242 |

**5.MD.1** *Convert among different-sized standard measurement units within a given measurement system, and use these conversions in solving multi–step, real world problems.*

## CONVERTING BETWEEN MILLILITERS AND LITERS

You may need to compare or order objects by capacities measured in different units. For example, one object may be measured in liters, while another is measured in milliliters. To compare different units, you need to convert all the measurements into the same unit.

To convert measurements, you need to know the relationship between milliliters and liters. There are 1,000 milliliters in 1 liter. That means that 1 milliliter is one-thousandth of a liter.

| 1,000 milliliters→ | 1 liter |
|---|---|
| 1 milliliter→ | $\frac{1}{1,000}$ liter |

## CHANGING LITERS INTO MILLILITERS

When you change from the larger unit, liters, to the smaller unit, milliliters, the number of milliliters will be larger than the number of liters. That means you should multiply the number of liters by 1,000 to find the number of equal milliliters.

*Example*

How many milliliters are in 4 L?

*Solution*

Larger unit to smaller unit → think multiplication.

Since 1 L = 1,000 mL, then 4 L will be equal to four times as many milliliters.
4 L × 1,000 = 4,000 mL
    4 L = 4,000 mL
A quick way to multiply by 1,000 is to add three zeros to the end of the number.

---

## CHANGING MILLILITERS INTO LITERS

When you change from the smaller unit, milliliters, to the larger unit, liters, the number of liters will be smaller than the number of milliliters. That means you should divide the number of milliliters by 1,000 to find the number of equal liters.

*Example*

How many liters are in 3,550 milliliters?

*Solution*

Smaller unit to larger unit → think division.

Since 1,000 mL = 1 L, you need to divide 3,550 mL by 1,000 to solve the problem.
3,550 mL ÷ 1,000 = 3.55 L
    3,550 mL = 3.55 L
A quick way to divide by 1,000 is to move the decimal point three places to the left.

---

## SOLVING LENGTH PROBLEMS

When you solve problems involving length, the units of measure must be the same. If they are not the same, you must convert them before solving the problem.

The given chart is a review of measurement relationships that will help you when you convert units.

| Unit | Equivalent Unit |
|------|-----------------|
| 1 cm | 10 mm |
| 1 m | 100 cm |
| 1 km | 1,000 m |

When you convert a large unit into a smaller unit, the answer will be a larger number.
large unit → smaller unit = larger number

To convert a large unit to a smaller unit, use multiplication.

For example, to convert 5 meters into centimeters, multiply 5 m by 100.
5 × 100 = 500
    5 m = 500 cm

When you convert a small unit to a larger unit, the answer will be a smaller number.
small unit → larger unit = smaller number

When you convert from a small unit to a larger unit, use division.

For example, to convert 4,000 meters to kilometers, divide 4,000 m by 1,000.
4,000 ÷ 1,000 = 4
        4,000 m = 4 km

### Example

Lucy's parents are putting new trim on her bedroom wall. The bedroom wall measures 2 m in length. They have 300 cm of trim to use.

Once the wall is completely trimmed, how many meters of trim will be left over?

### Solution

**Step 1**
Convert the 300 cm of trim into meters.

Because you are converting a small unit (centimeters) to a larger unit (meters), use division.
100 cm ÷ 100 = 1 m
300 cm ÷ 100 = 3 m

Lucy's parents have 3 m of trim to use.

**Step 2**
Determine how many meters of trim will be left over.

Subtract 3 m of trim from 2 m of wall.
3 m – 2 m = 1 m

Once the new trim is on Lucy's bedroom wall, there will be 1 m of trim left over.

## SOLVING PROBLEMS INVOLVING MASS

To solve problems that involve mass, you need to make sure that all the units are the same before comparing them.

To convert measurements, you need to know the relationship between grams and kilograms. There are 1,000 g in 1 kg. That means that one gram is one thousandth of a kilogram.

When you change from a larger unit, such as kilograms, to a smaller unit, such as grams, the number of grams will be larger than the number of kilograms. That means you should multiply the number of kilograms by 1,000 to find the number of equal grams.

When you change from a smaller unit, such as grams, to a larger unit, such as kilograms, the number of kilograms will be smaller than the number of grams. That means you should divide the number of grams by 1,000 to find the number of equal kilograms.

*Example*

Mike bought a bag of sugar and a bag of flour. The bag of sugar was marked as weighing 4 kg, and the flour was marked as weighing 3,000 g.

Determine how much less the bag of flour weighs in kilograms.

*Solution*

**Step 1**

Identify the important information.

The bag of sugar has a mass of 4 kg, and the bag of flour has a mass of 3,000 g.

**Step 2**

Determine which operation to use.

The words *how much less* indicate subtraction, because they are asking for the difference between the two masses.

**Step 3**

Convert grams into kilograms.
        1,000 g = 1 kg
3,000 g ÷ 1,000 = 3 kg

The bag of flour weighs 3 kg.

**Step 4**

Find the difference in weight between the sugar and flour.
4 kg – 3 kg = 1 kg

The flour weighs 1 kg less than the sugar.

---

# CONVERTING BETWEEN CUSTOMARY UNITS OF LENGTH

From smallest to largest, the common customary units of length are inches (in), feet (ft), yards (yd), and miles (mi).

In order to convert between customary units of length, you need to understand the relationship between each unit.

| Relationships between Customary Units of Length | | |
|---|---|---|
| 1 mi = 1,760 yd | 1 yd = 3 ft | 1 ft = 12 in |
| 1 mi = 5,280 ft | 1 yd = 3 ft | |

To convert customary units of length, follow these steps:

1. Identify the units involved, and choose the correct conversion ratio by remembering or referring to the table.
2. Use the conversion ratio to convert the units.

To convert from a larger unit to a smaller unit, multiply by the conversion ratio. For example, to convert from yards to feet, multiply by 3 because there are 3 ft in 1 yd.

*Example*
How many inches are in 6 ft?

*Solution*

**Step 1**
Choose the correct conversion ratio.
1 ft:12 in

**Step 2**
Use the ratio to convert the feet into inches.
When converting from a larger to a smaller unit, use multiplication.
6 × 12 = 72
There are 72 in in 6 ft.

To convert from a smaller unit to a larger unit, divide by the conversion ratio. For example, to convert from feet to yards, divide by 3 because there are 3 ft in 1 yd.

*Example*
How many yards are in 180 in?

*Solution*

**Step 1**
Choose the correct conversion ratio.
1 yd:36 in

**Step 2**
Use the ratio to convert inches into yards.
When converting from a smaller unit (inches) to a larger unit (yards), divide by the conversion ratio.
180 ÷ 36 = 5
There are 5 yd in 180 in.

## CONVERTING BETWEEN CUSTOMARY UNITS OF MASS

In the **customary system**, mass is measured in tons, pounds, and ounces. The given table shows the relationships among these units.

| Unit | Conversion |
|---------|---------------|
| 1 ton | 2,000 pounds |
| 1 pound | 16 ounces |

To convert from a smaller unit to a larger unit, divide by the conversion. To convert from a larger unit to a smaller unit, multiply by the conversion.

*Example*

Becky learned that the Florida panther is an endangered species in the state of Arkansas. She also learned that a male Florida panther weighs 150 lb.

How much does this animal weigh in ounces?

*Solution*

To convert pounds to ounces, use the conversion that in 1 lb, there are 16 oz.

Multiply the total number of pounds by 16 oz.

150 × 16 = 2,400 oz

Therefore, the Florida panther weighs 2,400 oz.

## CONVERTING CUSTOMARY UNITS OF CAPACITY

Capacity is the amount of liquid a container can hold.

These are the standard units for capacity written from smallest to largest:

- Ounces (oz)
- Cups (c)
- Pints (pt)
- Quarts (qt)
- Gallons (gal)

This conversion chart shows how one unit compares to another.

| Unit | Conversion |
|------|------------|
| 1 gal | 4 qt |
| 1 qt | 2 pt |
| 1 pt | 2 c |
| 1 c | 8 oz |

You can compare units of capacity to each other by converting between them. When you are converting a larger unit into a smaller unit, you will use division. When you are converting a smaller unit into a larger unit, you will use multiplication.

*Example*

How many cups equal 10 quarts?

*Solution*

**Step 1**
Choose the correct conversion ratios.
1 qt = 2 pt
1 pt = 2 c

**Step 2**

Convert quarts to cups.

First, convert quarts to pints. Multiply 10 by 2 to convert 10 quarts to 20 pints.

Next, convert pints to cups. Multiply 20 by 2 to convert 20 pints to 40 cups.

10 quarts is equal to 40 cups.

## CONVERTING METRIC UNITS OF MASS

In the metric system, mass is measured in milligrams, grams, and kilograms. Sometimes, you will need to compare objects by their mass. These objects will not always be measured using the same unit, so you will need to convert the units of measurement.

This table shows how each unit of mass relates to the other.

| Unit | Conversion |
|------|------------|
| 1 g  | 1,000 mg   |
| 1 kg | 1,000 g    |

## CONVERTING SMALLER UNITS TO LARGER UNITS

When you are converting a smaller unit into a larger unit of mass, you will always use division. For example, when converting grams into kilograms, the number of kilograms will be smaller than the number of grams.

*Example*

How many kilograms are in 5,000 g?

*Solution*

To solve this problem, convert 5,000 g to kilograms (kg).

Since the conversion is from a smaller unit to a larger unit (grams to kilograms), use division.

Since 1,000 g = 1 kg, divide 5,000 g by 1,000.
5,000 g ÷ 1,000 = 5 kg

There are 5 kg in 5,000 g.

# CONVERTING LARGER UNITS TO SMALLER UNITS

When you are converting a larger unit into a smaller unit of mass, you will always use multiplication. For example, when converting grams into milligrams, the number of grams will be smaller than the number of milligrams.

*Example*

How many milligrams are there in 3 g?

*Solution*

To solve this problem, convert 3 g to milligrams (mg).

Since the conversion is from a larger unit to a smaller unit (grams to milligrams), use multiplication.

Since 1 g = 1,000 mg, then 3 g will be equal to three times as many milligrams.
3 g × 1,000 = 3,000 mg

There are 3,000 mg in 3 g.

---

# CONVERTING METRIC UNITS OF LENGTH

The most common units of length, listed from smallest to largest, are as follows:

- Millimeters (mm)
- Centimeters (cm)
- Meters (m)
- Kilometers (km)

Sometimes, you will need to compare objects by their lengths. These objects will not always be measured in the same units, so you may need to convert the units of measurement. The given table shows how these units of length are related.

| Unit | Conversion |
| --- | --- |
| 1 cm | 10 mm |
| 1 m | 100 cm |
| 1 m | 1,000 mm |
| 1 km | 1,000 m |

# CONVERTING SMALLER UNITS TO LARGER UNITS

When you are converting a smaller unit of length into a larger unit, you will always use division. For example, when converting centimeters into meters, the number of meters will be smaller than the number of centimeters.

*Example*

How many meters are in 200 cm?

*Solution*

Convert 200 cm into meters.

When converting a smaller unit into a larger unit (centimeters to meters), use division. Since 100 cm = 1 m, divide 200 cm by 100 to solve the problem.
200 cm ÷ 100 = 2 m

Therefore, 2 m is equal to 200 cm.

---

# CONVERTING LARGER UNITS TO SMALLER UNITS

When you are converting a larger unit of length into a smaller unit, you will always use multiplication. For example, when converting kilometers into meters, the number of kilometers will be smaller than the number of meters.

*Example*

How many millimeters are there in 5 cm?

*Solution*

Convert 5 cm to millimeters.

When converting a larger unit into a smaller unit (centimeters to millimeters), use multiplication. Since 1 cm = 10 mm, 5 cm will be equal to 5 times as many millimeters.
5 cm × 10 mm = 50 mm

Therefore, 5 cm is equal to 50 mm.

---

*5.MD.2    Make a line plot to display a data set of measurements in fractions of a unit (1/2, 1/4, 1/8). Use operations on fractions for this grade to solve problems involving information presented in line plots.*

## CALCULATING THE MEAN

The **mean** of a set of values is the average of the set of values. The easiest way to calculate the mean is to find the sum of all the values in the set and then divide the sum by the number of values.

*Example*

Mr. Johnson recorded the ages of five of his students in the given chart. What is the mean of the students' ages?

| Student | Age |
|---------|-----|
| Katie | 10 |
| Billy | 9 |
| Jim | 15 |
| Kathy | 12 |
| Mike | 14 |

To determine the mean, or average, of the ages, first add the ages of the five students.

$$10 + 9 + 15 + 12 + 14 = 60$$

Then, divide the sum (60) by the number of values (ages), which is 5.

$$60 \div 5 = 12$$

The mean of the students' ages is 12.

## ORGANIZING COLLECTED DATA USING LINE PLOTS

A **line plot** is a sketch of data in which a check mark, "X", or other symbol is drawn above a number line. It shows how often each result occurs.

To organize collected data on a line plot, follow these steps:

• Draw a horizontal line segment. Label all the possible outcomes under the line segment.
• Use a symbol to represent each time the outcome occurred.

*Example*

Bill performed a probability experiment with a die. He rolled the die 60 times and recorded the results.

**Results of 60 Die Rolls**

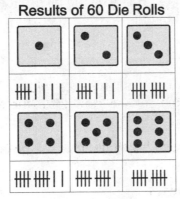

Draw a **line plot** showing Bill's results.

*Solution*

**Step 1**

Create your line plot.

Draw a horizontal line. Write all the possible outcomes under the line.

Give your line plot a title.

**Results of 60 Die Rolls**

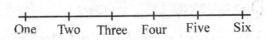

One   Two   Three   Four   Five   Six

**Step 2**

Use a symbol to represent each time the outcome occurred.

In this case, draw Xs above the line to show Bill's results. Since he rolled one 9 times, you should make 9 Xs above the one heading. Record the number of times Bill rolled each number on the line plot.

**Results of 60 Die Rolls**

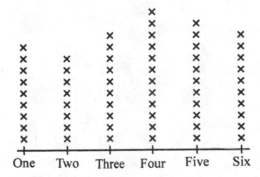

One   Two   Three   Four   Five   Six

# FINDING THE RANGE OF A SET OF DATA

You can organize data to find the range.  **Range** is the difference between the highest number and the lowest number in a set of data.  A **set of data** is a group of numbers or values.  The set is usually given within curly brackets { }.

To find the range of a set of data, follow these steps:

1.  Place the numbers in order from the lowest to the highest.
2.  Subtract the lowest value from the highest value.

*Example*

Calculate the range of the data set {14, 2, 16, 8, 3, 11, 14}.

*Solution*

**Step 1**
Place the numbers in order.
{2, 3, 8, 11, 14, 14, 16}

**Step 2**
Subtract the lowest value from the greatest value.
16 – 2 = 14
The range is 14.

---

# CALCULATING THE MODE

The **mode** is the value in a set of data that occurs most often.  A set of data can have one mode, more than one mode, or no mode at all.  If a set of data has only one mode, one number occurs more often than the other numbers.  If there is more than one mode, more than one number occurs the same number of times.  Finally, if there is no mode, all the numbers occur the same number of times.

To find the mode of a set of numbers, follow these steps:

1.  Place the values in order from least to greatest.
2.  Determine which numbers occur most often, if any.

*Example*

Carlos recorded the ages of children entering a toy store.  He collected the following data:
7, 3, 4, 8, 5, 6, 3

Identify the mode from the data set.

*Solution*

**Step 1**
Arrange the numbers in order from least to greatest.
3, 3, 4, 5, 6, 7, 8

**Step 2**
Identify the number that appears most often.
The number 3 appears more often than any other number in the data set.  This data set has one mode.
The mode of this data set is 3.

---

*Example*

The marks obtained by 10students on a mathematics test are 76, 78, 94, 82, 84, 88, 85, 88, 92, and 76.

What is the mode of the students' marks?

*Solution*

**Step 1**
Arrange the numbers in order from least to greatest.

76, 76, 78, 82, 84, 85, 88, 88, 92, 94

**Step 2**
Identify the numbers that appear most often in the data set.
The numbers 76 and 88 each appear twice. This data set has two modes.

The modes are 76 and 88.

---

## FINDING THE MEDIAN

The **median** is the number in the middle of a set of data.

For example, the data set 1, 4, 6, 8, 11 has five numbers. The median is 6 because it is exactly in the middle. Half of the numbers are greater than 6, and half of the numbers are less than 6.

Sometimes, a data set does not have a number that is exactly in the middle. In the data set 3, 4, 6, 9, the numbers 4 and 6 are both in the middle. To find the median, you need to find out which number is exactly between the two middle numbers.

To do this, add up the two middle numbers, and then divide by 2.
$(4 + 6) \div 2$
$= 10 \div 2$
$= 5$

The median in this data set is 5. Half of the numbers in the set are greater than 5, and half of the numbers in the set are less than 5.

To find the median of a data set, follow these steps:

1. Put the numbers in order from least to greatest.
2. Find the middle number or numbers.
3. If two numbers are in the middle, add them together, and then divide by 2.

*Example*

Find the median of the data set 5, 12, 2, 7, 10, 9.

*Solution*

**Step 1**
Order the numbers from least to greatest.
2, 5, 7, 9, 10, 12

**Step 2**
Find the numbers in the middle.

The numbers 7 and 9 are both in the middle of the data set.

**Step 3**

Find the median.

Add 7 and 9 together, and then divide by 2.

$(7 + 9) \div 2 = 16 \div 2$

$\qquad\qquad\qquad = 8$

The median is 8.

---

*5.MD.3A*  *Recognize volume as an attribute of solid figures and understand concepts of volume measurement. A cube with side length 1 unit, called a "unit cube," is said to have "one cubic unit" of volume, and can be used to measure...*

## CALCULATING THE VOLUME OF A GIVEN 3-D OBJECT BY FILLING IT WITH CUBES

**Volume** is the amount of space a three-dimensional figure holds. You can find the volume of a 3-D figure by counting the number of cubic units needed to fill the space in the figure. The volume is recorded as a number with the words *cubic units* after the number.

*Example*

Mike looked at the shape of the given box. He used cubes to build a model of the box.

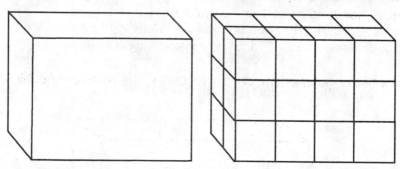

Calculate the **volume** of Mike's box.

*Solution*

To solve this problem, count all the cubes used in the model. Count the cube even if you cannot see it.

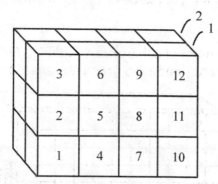

One way to do this is to count all the cubes used to make the front face. You can see all 12 of these cubes. You can also see that there is another group of cubes behind the front face. Even though you cannot see all the cubes, there will be the same number as in the front face. There will be 12 cubes in this group as well. 12 + 12 = 24 or 12 × 2 = 24

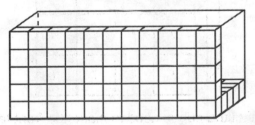

Mike used 24 cubes to build the model of the box. The volume of the box is 24 cubic units.

---

*5.MD.5A   Find the volume of a right rectangular prism with whole-number side lengths by packing it with unit cubes, and show that the volume is the same as would be found by multiplying the edge lengths, equivalently by multiplying the height by...*

## DEVELOPING A VOLUME FORMULA

**Volume** is the amount of space that a 3-D figure holds. Volume is measured in cubic units (units$^3$). A cubic unit is a cube with equal side lengths of 1 unit on all six sides.

= 1 cubic unit

To find the **volume** of a **rectangular prism**, start by counting the number of cubic units needed to fill the base of the prism.

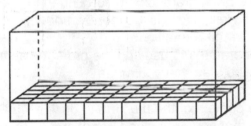

Another way to do this is to find the area of the base of the prism. Use the formula for determining area

Length × Width = Area

The next step is to determine the number of cubic units needed to fill the prism. To do this, it is necessary to know how many layers of cubes are needed to reach the top of the prism.

When the height of the prism is known (the number of layers of cubes needed), multiply the area by the height.

Area × Height = Volume

Another way to express this formula is Length × Width × Height = Volume

The volume of the rectangular prism shown is 275 units$^3$.

11 × 5 × 5 = 275 units$^3$

*5.MD.5B  Relate volume to the operations of multiplication and addition and solve real world and mathematical problems involving volume.  Apply the formulas V=l×w×h and V=b×h for rectangular prisms to find volumes of right rectangular...*

## SOLVING PROBLEMS INVOLVING VOLUME OF RECTANGULAR PRISMS

To calculate the volume of a rectangular prism, use the formula $V_{rectangular\ prism} = lwh$, where *l* represents the length, *w* represents the width, and *h* represents the height of the rectangular prism.

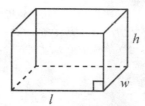

You can use this knowledge to help you solve a wide variety of real-world problems.  Whenever you have a problem that involves finding the volume of rectangular prisms, follow this four-step problem-solving process:

1.  Read the question carefully, and determine what is being asked.
    Pay special attention to the numbers and values that are given, and look for keywords.  Sometimes you may want to draw a picture or diagram to help you understand the problem more clearly.
    Decide what kind of answer you will give.  (Is it a money amount?  A volume?  A quantity?) Decide if your answer will be a big number or a small one.
2.  Make a plan.  Decide which operations to use and the order to use them in.
3.  Solve the problem.  Carry out the plan that you made.
4.  Decide if your answer is reasonable.
    You can use estimation or the context of the problem to decide if an answer is reasonable.  You can also think about the operation that you are using.  For example, if you are multiplying, you know that your answer will be greater than the numbers you are multiplying.  If your answer is less, then it is not reasonable.  Once you have made sure your answer is reasonable, give your answer as a sentence.

*Example*

Christine uses the given measurements to calculate the volumes of a box of cereal and a box of popcorn.

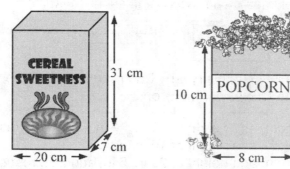

What is the difference between the volume of the box of cereal and the volume of the box of popcorn?

*Solution*

**Step 1**

Determine what is being asked.

The cereal box is 20 cm by 7 cm by 31 cm. The popcorn box is 10 cm by 8 cm by 5 cm.

You need to use this information to find the difference in volume between the two boxes.

Your answer will be given in units cubed because it will be a volume. Also, because it is the difference between the two volumes, it has to be less than the volume of the larger container.

**Step 2**

Make a plan.

First, find the volume of each container. Use the formula for volume, $V = lwh$.

Next, find the difference. Subtract the volume of the smaller container from the volume of the larger container.

**Step 3**

Solve the problem.

Calculate the volume of each container.

$$V_{cereal} = lwh$$
$$= 20 \times 7 \times 31$$
$$= 4{,}340 \text{ cm}^3$$
$$V_{popcorn} = lwh$$
$$= 10 \times 8 \times 5$$
$$= 400 \text{ cm}^3$$

Find the difference.

$$4{,}340 - 400 = 3{,}940 \text{ cm}^3$$

**Step 4**

Decide if your answer is reasonable.

Your answer is in cubic centimeters and is smaller than the volume of the larger container, which is what you predicted in step 1.

You can also use estimation to check your answer.

For the cereal container, round 31 to 30 and then multiply by 7.

$20 \times 30 = 600$
$600 \times 7 = 4{,}200$

For the popcorn box, round 8 up to 10 and then multiply by 5.

$10 \times 10 = 100$
$100 \times 5 = 500$

The difference between the estimated volumes is $4{,}200 - 500 = 3{,}700$. This is very close to the answer you calculated, so it is a reasonable answer.

The difference between the volumes of the two containers is $3{,}940 \text{ cm}^3$.

---

*Example*

Theo is using three containers in a chemistry lab. Each container has the shape of a rectangular prism. The containers have the following dimensions:

- Container 1 has a length, width, and height of 15 in, 10 in, and 12 in, respectively.
- Container 2 has a length, width, and height of 10 in each.
- Container 3 has a length, width, and height of 20 in, 5 in, and 2 in, respectively.

When their volumes are arranged from least to greatest, what is the order of the given containers?

*Solution*

### Step 1
Determine what is being asked.

You are given the dimensions of three containers, and you are asked to order them.

Your answer will be a list of the containers with the smallest one first and the largest one last.

### Step 2
Make a plan.

First, find the volume of each container. Use the formula for finding the volume of rectangular prisms, $V = lwh$.

Next, order the containers from smallest to largest.

### Step 3
Solve the problem.

Find the volume of each container.

$$V_{container\ 1} = lwh$$
$$= 15 \times 10 \times 12$$
$$= 1,800\ in^3$$
$$V_{container\ 2} = lwh$$
$$= 10 \times 10 \times 10$$
$$= 1,000\ in^3$$
$$V_{container\ 3} = lwh$$
$$= 20 \times 5 \times 2$$
$$= 200\ in^3$$

Place the containers in order.

The order is container 3 (200 $in^3$), container 2 (1,000 $in^3$), and container 1 (1,800 $in^3$).

### Step 4
Decide if your answer is reasonable.

Your answer is the list of containers with the smallest first and the largest last, which is what you predicted in step 1.

You can also use the dimensions of the containers to estimate the order. Container 1 has the largest dimensions and container 3 has the smallest, so it makes sense that the order is 3, 2, 1. Therefore, your answer is reasonable.

The order of the given containers is container 3, container 2, and container 1.

---

## FINDING THE VOLUME OF A RECTANGULAR PRISM

**Volume** measures the amount of space an object takes up.

A formula to find the volume of a prism is $V = A_{base} \times h$.

Remember that a prism gets its name from its base. For example, a rectangular prism has a rectangular base.

The volume of a rectangular prism is found by taking the area of the base of the rectangle ($l \times w$) multiplied by the height. The formula for calculating volume can be written as follows:

$$V = A_{base} \times h$$
$$= (l \times w) \times h$$
$$= l \times w \times h$$

Always remember to include the unit in your answer. When calculating volume, you are multiplying three dimensions, so the answer is always expressed in cubic units (unit$^3$).

*Example*

A rectangular prism is given.

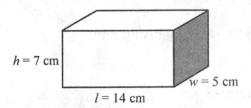

$h = 7$ cm    $w = 5$ cm    $l = 14$ cm

Calculate the volume of the given rectangular prism.

*Solution*

**Step 1**
Write the formula for calculating volume.
$V = l \times w \times h$

**Step 2**
Substitute the given dimensions into the formula.
$V = 14 \times 5 \times 7$
$V = 490$ cm$^3$
Remember to include the unit when you write your answer.
The volume of the rectangular prism is 490 cm$^3$.

---

*Example*

A rectangular prism has a length of 9 in, a width of 4 in, and a height of 5 in.

What is the volume of the prism?

*Solution*

**Step 1**
Write the formula for calculating volume.
$V = l \times w \times h$

**Step 2**
Substitute the given dimensions into the formula.
$V = l \times w \times h$
$= 9 \times 4 \times 5$
$= 180$ in$^3$
Remember to include the unit when you write your answer.
The volume of the rectangular prism is 180 in$^3$.

*5.MD.5C   Relate volume to the operations of multiplication and addition and solve real world and
mathematical problems involving volume.  Recognize volume as additive.  Find volumes of
solid figures composed of two non–overlapping...*

## CALCULATING THE VOLUME OF TWO SOLID FIGURES

The volume of a prism is the amount of space the prism takes up.  When you have a solid figure made
up of two rectangular prisms placed together without intersecting, you can calculate the volume of each
figure and then add the two volumes together.

*Example*

The given figure is made up of two rectangular prisms.

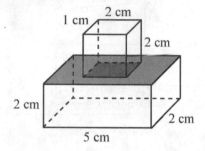

Calculate the volume of the given figure.

*Solution*

Substitute the known measurements into the volume formula $V = l \times w \times h$. Express your answer in
cubic units.

**Step 1**
Calculate the volume of the larger prism.
$V = l \times w \times h$
$V = (5) \times (2) \times (2)$
$V = 20 \text{ cm}^3$

**Step 2**
Calculate the volume of the smaller prism.
$V = l \times w \times h$
$V = (2) \times (1) \times (2)$
$V = 4 \text{ cm}^3$

**Step 3**
Add the volumes.
$20 + 4 = 24$
The total volume of the given figure is $24 \text{ cm}^3$.

# EXERCISE #1—MEASUREMENT AND DATA

192. List the following capacities in order from the least volume to greatest volume.

0.9 L, 2,300 mL, 2.5 L, 1,059 mL, 1.25 L

*Use the following information to answer the next question.*

Terry brought a variety of drinks for a party.  He has 2 cans of pop that are 355 mL each, a bottle of orange juice that is 1.25 L, and a 2 L bottle of apple juice.

193. How many milliliters of drinks does Terry have in total?

*Use the following information to answer the next question.*

Maria is putting new carpet in her house.  She bought one roll that is 6 m long.  She used 450 cm of it.

194. How much of the carpet is left?

    A. 1 m                             B. 1.5 m

    C. 2 m                             D. 2.5 m

*Use the following information to answer the next question.*

Rhonda and Julie took a road trip. Their first stop was 51 km away.

195. How far away was their first stop in meters?
   A. 510 m
   B. 5,100 m
   C. 51,000 m
   D. 510,000 m

*Use the following information to answer the next question.*

Kirsten is baking some cakes for her bakery. She needs 2,000 g of flour and 1,000 g of sugar.

196. What is the difference between the amount of flour and sugar needed in kilograms (kg)?
   A. 0.1 kg
   B. 1.0 kg
   C. 1.5 kg
   D. 2.0 kg

*Use the following information to answer the next question.*

Mark is packing boxes. One of the boxes has a mass of 8 kg, and the other box has a mass of 6 kg.

197. What is the total mass of the two boxes in grams?
   A. 14 g
   B. 1,400 g
   C. 14,000 g
   D. 140,000 g

198. How many inches are in 9 yd? _____ in

199. How many feet are in 12 yards?
   A. 1 ft
   B. 4 ft
   C. 36 ft
   D. 144 ft

200. How many ounces are there in 5 lb? _____ oz

*Use the following information to answer the next question.*

Carla wanted to measure the weight of her kitten. She put the kitten on a scale and found that it was 96 oz.

201. How much does Carla's kitten weigh in pounds?
   A. 4 lb
   B. 6 lb
   C. 10 lb
   D. 12 lb

*Use the following information to answer the next question.*

Mark had 3 pints of orange juice after he ran a marathon.

202. How many cups of orange juice did Mark drink?
 A. 4 c
 B. 5 c
 C. 6 c
 D. 7 c

203. If Daniel buys 5 gal of paint, what is the amount of paint in quarts that he will have?
 A. 3 qt
 B. 10 qt
 C. 13 qt
 D. 20 qt

204. How many grams are there in 2,000 mg?
 A. 1 g
 B. 2 g
 C. 10 g
 D. 20 g

205. How many grams are there in 8 kg?
 A. 80 g
 B. 800 g
 C. 8,000 g
 D. 80,000 g

206. How many meters are there in 8 km?
 A. 400 m
 B. 800 m
 C. 4,000 m
 D. 8,000 m

207. How many millimeters are there in 10 m?
 A. 100 mm
 B. 1,000 mm
 C. 10,000 mm
 D. 100,000 mm

**208.** Calculate the mean of the data set {125, 300, 150, 175, 50, 450, 150}.

*Use the following information to answer the next question.*

Sam surveyed eight of his friends to see how many pets they own. He recorded his results in the given table.

| Friend | Number of Pets |
|--------|----------------|
| Laurel | 2 |
| Mark | 0 |
| Scott | 3 |
| Virginia | 1 |
| Lee | 0 |
| Kayla | 1 |
| Mei | 1 |
| Kevin | 0 |

**209.** What is the mean number of pets owned by Sam's friends? _____

*Use the following information to answer the next question.*

James surveyed some of his classmates to find out how many people were in each of their families. He wrote their answers on a piece of paper.

2, 4, 5, 7, 5, 2, 2, 4, 4, 7, 3, 4, 5, 4, 5

210. Which of the following line plots shows the data James collected?

A.

B.

C.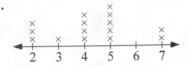

D.

*Use the following information to answer the next question.*

Mrs. Morris used the following steps to teach her students how to organize their data using a line plot:

1. Use a scale from the smallest number to the largest number, using equal spacing in between. Include the numbers in between even if they do not appear in the data set.
2. Record the data by placing an *X* above each number. If a number appears more than once, then an additional *X* can be placed above the original X.
3. Identify the largest number and smallest number of the data set.
4. Draw a number line with the smallest number on the left and the largest number on the right.

211. What is the correct order of Mrs. Morris's steps?

A. 3, 4, 1, 2

B. 1, 2, 3, 4

C. 2, 3, 1, 4

D. 4, 3, 2, 1

A data set is given.

{ 76, 45, 63, 91, 87, 73, 78, 81}

**212.** Calculate the range of the data set.

**213.** Find the range of the data set {135, 114, 249, 187, 196}.

**214.** Determine the mode of the data set {5, 6, 4, 2, 5, 3, 5, 1, 1, 2}.

*Use the following information to answer the next question.*

This table shows the frequency of values used in a set of data.

| Value | Frequency |
|-------|-----------|
| 2 | 4 |
| 8 | 3 |
| 5 | 1 |
| 3 | 1 |
| 6 | 1 |

**215.** The mode of the data in the given table is

A. 1  B. 2

C. 4  D. 8

**216.** Find the median of the numbers 76, 45, 63, 91, 87, 73, 78, and 81.

*Use the following information to answer the next question.*

The weights of 5 apples are recorded in the table.

| | |
|---|---|
| | 230 g |
| | 170 g |
| | 190 g |
| | 220 g |
| | 190 g |

**217.** What is the median for the weights of the apples?

    **A.** 170 g                 **B.** 190 g

    **C.** 220 g                 **D.** 230 g

Rick measured the volume of a rectangular prism by filling the prism with 98 centimeter cubes.

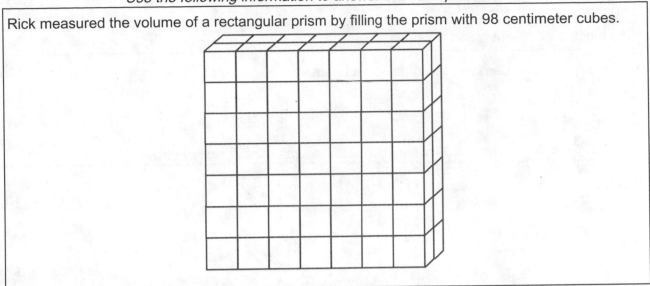

218. How many centimeter cubes did Rick put together to make each of the seven layers?

A. 7 cubes                          B. 9 cubes

C. 14 cubes                      D. 18 cubes

*Use the following information to answer the next question.*

An image of a cube is given.

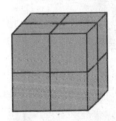

219. The volume of this cube can be represented as

A. $2 \text{ units}^3$                   B. $4 \text{ units}^3$

C. $6 \text{ units}^3$                   D. $8 \text{ units}^3$

*Use the following information to answer the next question.*

Richard needs to fill a rectangular fish tank that is 35 cm long, 25 cm wide, and 32 cm tall. The jug he is using to carry the water from the sink holds $4,000 \text{ cm}^3$.

220. How many trips to the sink will Richard have to make in order to fill the fish tank? _____

Laura has a rectangular sandbox that is 2 ft long, 3 ft wide, and 1 ft deep. She wants to make it 2 ft longer, 1.5 ft wider, and 1 ft deeper.

**221.** How much larger than her old sandbox will Laura's new sandbox be?

    **A.** 3 ft³                                **B.** 9 ft³

    **C.** 30 ft³                                **D.** 36 ft³

*Use the following information to answer the next question.*

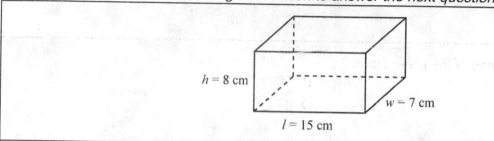

$h = 8$ cm      $w = 7$ cm      $l = 15$ cm

**222.** What is the volume of the given rectangular prism?

    **A.** 630 cm³                              **B.** 680 cm³

    **C.** 740 cm³                              **D.** 840 cm³

*Use the following information to answer the next question.*

A prism is given.

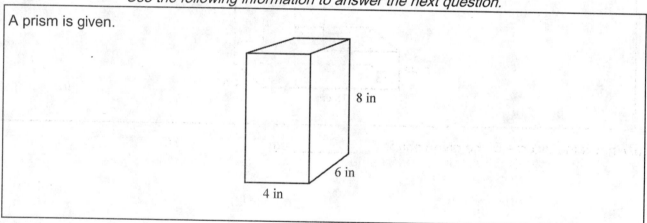

8 in

6 in

4 in

**223.** The volume of this prism is _____ in³.

*Use the following information to answer the next question.*

A rectangular prism is stacked on top of a cube.

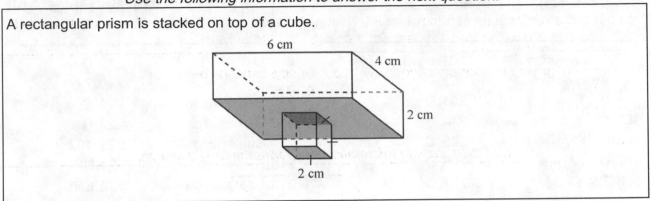

**224.** What is the total volume of the given figure?

    **A.** 48 cm$^3$                 **B.** 56 cm$^3$

    **C.** 51 in$^3$                  **D.** 62 in$^3$

*Use the following information to answer the next question.*

A shape is given.

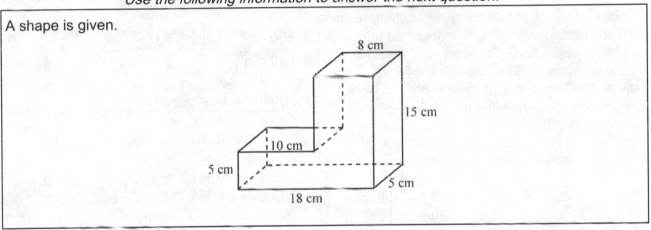

**225.** What is the volume of the given shape? _____ cm$^3$

# EXERCISE #1—MEASUREMENT AND DATA ANSWERS AND SOLUTIONS

| | | | |
|---|---|---|---|
| 192. See solution | 201. B | 210. D | 219. D |
| 193. See solution | 202. C | 211. A | 220. 7 |
| 194. B | 203. D | 212. See solution | 221. C |
| 195. C | 204. B | 213. See solution | 222. D |
| 196. B | 205. C | 214. See solution | 223. 192 |
| 197. C | 206. D | 215. B | 224. B |
| 198. 324 | 207. C | 216. See solution | 225. 850 |
| 199. C | 208. See solution | 217. B | |
| 200. 80 | 209. 1 | 218. C | |

## 192.

HINT: Smaller unit→ larger unit
Think division.

### Step 1
It is easier to compare measures when they are all in the same unit. Since three of the five measures are in liters, change the two measures expressed in millimeters into liters. When you convert millimeters to liters, you are converting a smaller unit to a larger unit. This means that the answer will be a smaller number. To get a smaller number, think division.
Since 1,000 mL = 1 L, convert 2,300 mL into liters by dividing 2,300 by 1,000.
$2,300 ÷ 1,000 = 2.3$
　　$2,300$ mL $= 2.3$ L
Convert 1,059 mL into liters by dividing 1,059 by 1,000.
$1,059 ÷ 1,000 = 1.059$
　　$1,059$ mL $= 1.059$ L

### Step 2
Now that all the measures are in the same unit (liters), order them from the least volume to greatest volume.

1. 0.9 L
2. 1,059 mL (1.059 L)
3. 1.25 L
4. 2,300 mL (2.3 L)
5. 2.5 L

## 193.

### Step 1
Ensure all values are in the same units.
Convert liters to milliliters.
To convert all liters to milliliters, multiply the number of liters by 1,000 mL.
$1$ L $= 1,000$ mL
$1.25$ L $= 1.25 × 1,000$ mL
　　　$= 1,250$ mL
$2$ L $= 2 × 1,000$ mL
　　$= 2,000$ mL

### Step 2
Add the volumes together.
$1,250 + 2,000 + 355 + 355 = 3,960$ mL
Terry brought 3,960 mL of drinks to the party.

## 194. B

### Step 1
Convert the centimeter measurements to meter measurements.
$1$ m $= 100$ cm
The length of the carpet that was used is 450 cm, so divide 450 cm by 100 cm.
$450 ÷ 100 = 4.5$
Maria used 4.5 m of carpet.

### Step 2
Use subtraction to determine how many meters of carpet are left.
$6$ m $– 4.5$ m $= 1.5$ m

**195. C**

Convert kilometers to meters to solve the problem.
1 km = 1,000 m
51 km = 1,000 m × 51
51 km = 51,000 m

Rhonda and Julie's first stop was 51,000 m away.

**196. B**

**Step 1**
Find the difference in weight between the flour and sugar.
2,000 g − 1,000 g = 1,000 g
The difference between the flour and sugar is 1,000 g.

**Step 2**
Convert grams into kilograms.
1,000 g = 1 kg
The difference between the flour and sugar in kilograms is 1.0 kg.

**197. C**

**Step 1**
Find the total mass of the two boxes in kilograms.
8 kg + 6 kg = 14 kg
The total mass of the two boxes is 14 kg.

**Step 2**
Convert kilograms into grams.
　　　1 kg = 1,000 g
14 kg × 1,000 g = 140 g
The total mass of the two boxes is 14,000 g.

**198. 324**

**Step 1**
Choose the correct conversion ratio.
1 yd = 36 in

**Step 2**
Use the ratio to convert the distance into inches.
To convert from a larger unit to a smaller unit, use multiplication.
9 × 36 = 324
There are 324 in in 9 yd.

**199. C**

**Step 1**
Choose the correct conversion ratio.
1 yd:3 ft

**Step 2**
Use the ratio to convert the distance into feet.
When converting from a larger to a smaller unit, use multiplication.
3 × 12 = 36
There are 36 ft in 12 yd.

**200. 80**

Since 1 lb is 16 oz, then 5 lb will equal 5 times as many ounces.
5 × 16 = 80 oz

There are 80 oz in 5 lb.

**201. B**

When converting from a smaller unit to a larger unit, use division.

Since 16 oz is 1 lb, you need to divide 96 by 16 to find the solution.
96 ÷ 16 = 6

96 oz is equal to 6 lb.

Carla's kitten weighs 6 lb.

**202. C**

**Step 1**
Choose the correct conversion ratio.
1 pt = 2 c

**Step 2**
Convert pints to cups.
You are going from a larger unit to a smaller unit, so you need to multiply.
3 × 2 = 6
Therefore, Mark drank 6 cups of orange juice.

**203. D**

**Step 1**
Choose the correct converting ratio.
1 gal = 4 qt

**Step 2**

Convert gallons to quarts.

Since you are converting from larger units to smaller units, you need to multiply.
5 × 4 = 20

Daniel will have 20 qt of paint.

### 204. B

Convert 2,000 mg to grams in order to solve this problem. To convert a smaller unit to a larger unit (milligrams to grams), use division.

Since 1,000 mg = 1 g, divide 2,000 mg by 1,000 to solve the problem.
2,000 mg ÷ 1,000 = 2 g

There are 2 g in 2,000 mg.

### 205. C

Convert 8 kg to grams.

When converting a larger unit to a smaller unit (kilograms to grams), use multiplication. Since 1 kg = 1,000 g, 8 kg will be equal to eight times as many grams.
8 kg × 1,000 = 8,000 g

There are 8,000 g in 8 kg.

### 206. D

To solve this problem, you need to convert 8 km to meters.

To convert a larger unit into a smaller unit (kilometers to meters), use multiplication.

Since 1 km = 1,000 m, 8 km will be equal to eight times as many meters.
8 km × 1,000 = 8,000 km

There are 8,000 m in 8 km.

### 207. C

Convert 10 m into millimeters.

To convert a larger unit into a smaller unit (meters to millimeters), use multiplication.
Since 1 m = 1,000 mm, 10 m will be equal to 10 times as many millimeters.
10 m × 1,000 = 10,000 mm

There are 10,000 mm in 10 m.

### 208.

**Step 1**

The mean of a set of data is defined as the ratio of the sum of the values to the number of values in the data set (in other words, taking the average of the data set).
Determine the sum of the given values.
$$\left(\begin{array}{c} 125 + 300 + 150 + 175 \\ +50 + 450 + 150 \end{array}\right) = 1,400$$

**Step 2**

Divide the total sum by the number of values. Since there are 7 values, divide by 7.
1,400 ÷ 7 = 200

Therefore, the mean of the data set is 200.

### 209. 1

**Step 1**

Add up the number of pets.
2 + 0 + 3 + 1 + 0 + 1 + 1 + 0 = 8

**Step 2**

Divide the sum by the number of friends. There are 8 friends, so divide the sum by 8.
8 ÷ 8 = 1

The mean number of pets is 1.

### 210. D

**Step 1**

Put the information in a frequency table.

| Number of Family Members | Number of Students |
|---|---|
| 2 | 3 |
| 3 | 1 |
| 4 | 5 |
| 5 | 4 |
| 6 | 0 |
| 7 | 2 |

**Step 2**

Draw a number line to show the number of family members.

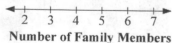

**Number of Family Members**

**Step 3**

Put an X above each number to show how many students have that many people in their family.

- Three students have 2 family members. Draw 3 Xs above the 2.
- One student has 3 family members. Draw 1 X above the 3.
- Five students have 4 family members. Draw 5 Xs above the 4.
- Four students have 5 family members. Draw 4 Xs above the 5.
- Two students have 7 family members. Draw 2 Xs above the 7.

This line plot shows the data James collected.

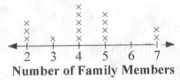

**Number of Family Members**

### 211. A

This is the order of steps for organizing data using a line plot:

- Identify the smallest number and largest number in the given data set.
- Draw a number line with the smallest number on the left and the largest number on the right.
- Use a scale from the smallest number to the largest number, using equal spacing in between. Include the numbers in between even if they do not appear in the data set.
- Record the data by placing an X above each number. If a number appears twice in a data set, then an additional X can be placed above the original X.

Therefore, the correct order of steps is 3, 4, 1, 2.

### 212.

**Step 1**

Place the numbers in order from least to greatest.
45, 63, 73, 76, 78, 81, 87, 91

**Step 2**

Subtract the lowest value from the highest value in the set.
The lowest value is 45, and the highest value is 91.
91 – 45 = 46
The range is 46.

### 213.

**Step 1**

Place the numbers in order from the lowest to the highest.
114, 135, 187, 196, 249

**Step 2**

Subtract the lowest value from the greatest value.
249 – 114 = 135
The range is 135.

### 214.

**Step 1**

Place the values in order from least to greatest.
1, 1, 2, 2, 3, 4, 5, 5, 5, 6

**Step 2**

Determine which numbers occur most frequently.
The numbers 1 and 2 each occur twice, and the number 5 occurs three times. The rest of the numbers occur once each. Therefore, the mode is 5 because it occurs more than any other number.

### 215. B

The mode is the value that occurs most often.

The number in the frequency column of the table tells how many times the particular value appears in the set of data.

Since 4 is the number with the greatest value in the frequency column (4 > 3 > 1), that means the number value of 2 is used four times, which is more than any other number in this set of data.

Therefore, the mode of the data in the given table is 2.

**216.**

**Step 1**

Place the values in order from least to greatest.
45, 63, 73, 76, 78, 81, 87, 91

**Step 2**

Determine the middle numbers.

There is an even number of values, so calculate the average of the two middle numbers.

The middle numbers are 76 and 78.

76 + 78 = 154

154 ÷ 2 = 77

Therefore, the median is 77.

**217. B**

**Step 1**

Place the values in order from least to greatest.
170, 190, 190, 220, 230

**Step 2**

Determine the middle number.

There is an odd number of values, so only one number is in the middle.

170, 190, 190, 220, 230

The median weight of the apples is 190 g.

**218. C**

Choice C is correct. Rick put 14 cubes together to make each of the seven layers.

Rick made 2 rows of 7 cubes in each row. 7 × 2 = 14

Another way to find the number of cubes in each layer is to divide the total number of cubes used (98) by the number of layers (7).

98 ÷ 7 = 14

**219. D**

**Step 1**

Determine the area of the base.

$a = l \times w$

2 × 2 = 4

The area of the base is 4 units².

**Step 2**

Determine the height.

The height of the cube is 2 units.

**Step 3**

Determine the volume.

$V$ = area of base × height

= 4 × 2

= 8

The volume of the cube is 8 units³.

**220. 7**

**Step 1**

Determine what is being asked.

The question is asking how many times 4,000 cm³ of water will need to go into the fish tank in order to fill it.

**Step 2**

Make a plan.

First, find the volume of the fish tank.

Next, find out how many jugs of water are needed by dividing the volume of the fish tank by the volume of the jug.

**Step 3**

Solve the problem.

Calculate the volume of the fish tank.

$V = l \times w \times h$

= 35 × 25 × 32

= 28,000

The fish tank holds 28,000 cm³ of water.

Calculate the number of jugs of water needed to fill the tank by dividing the volume of the fish tank by the volume of the jug.

$$\text{jugs needed} = \frac{V_{\text{fish tank}}}{V_{\text{jug}}}$$

$$= \frac{28,000}{4,000}$$

$$= 7$$

## Step 4

Decide if your answer is reasonable.

Use estimation to check the answer.

Estimate the volume of the fish tank that is 35 cm long, 25 cm wide, and 32 cm tall.

Since both the numbers 35 and 25 have digits that are in the middle for rounding, one number will be rounded up and the other number will be rounded down to make the estimation more balanced.

Thus, 35 will be rounded up to 40, and 25 will be rounded down to 20. Round 32 down to 30.

The estimated volume of the fish tank will be $40 \times 20 \times 30 = 24,000$.

The division of the estimated fish tank volume by the jug of water volume is $\frac{24,000}{4,000} = 6$.

This is very close to the original calculation, so the answer is reasonable.

Since 7 jugs of water are needed to fill the tank, Richard will need to make 7 trips to the sink.

## 221. C

### Step 1

Determine what is being asked.

The sandbox is 2 ft by 3 ft by 1 ft. It will be increased by 2 ft, 1.5 ft, and 1 ft.

This information needs to be used to find the difference in volume between the new measurements and the old measurements.

Your answer will be given in units cubed because it will be a volume. Also, because it is the difference between the two volumes, it has to be less than the volume of the new sandbox.

### Step 2

Make a plan.

First, find the volume of the original sandbox using the formula $V = lwh$.

Then, find the dimensions of the new sandbox by adding the increases to the original measurements.

Next, use the new measurements to find the volume of the expanded sandbox.

Finally, find the difference in volume by subtracting the old sandbox volume from the new sandbox volume.

### Step 3

Solve the problem.

Find the volume of the original sandbox.

$V_{old} = lwh$
$\quad = 2 \times 3 \times 1$
$\quad = 6 \text{ ft}^3$

Calculate the measurements of the new sandbox.

$l = 2 + 2 = 4 \text{ ft}$
$w = 3 + 1.5 = 4.5 \text{ ft}$
$h = 1 + 1 = 2 \text{ ft}$

Find the volume of the expanded sandbox.

$V_{new} = lwh$
$\quad = 4 \times 4.5 \times 2$
$\quad = 36 \text{ ft}^3$

Find the difference.

$36 - 6 = 30 \text{ ft}^3$

### Step 4

Decide if your answer is reasonable.

Your answer is in cubic feet and is smaller than the volume of the expanded sandbox, which is what you predicted in step 1. Therefore, your answer is reasonable.

Laura's new sandbox is 30 ft$^3$ larger than her original sandbox.

## 222. D

To determine the volume of the prism, use the volume formula. Substitute the numbers for the length (15 cm), width (7 cm), and height (8 cm).

$V = l \times w \times h$
$V = 15 \times 7 \times 8$
$V = 840 \text{ cm}^3$

The volume of the given rectangular prism is 840 cm$^3$.

## 223. 192

### Step 1

Write the formula for calculating volume.

$V = l \times w \times h$

**Step 2**
Substitute the given dimensions into the formula.
$V = 4 \times 6 \times 8$
$\quad = 192 \text{ in}^3$
Remember to include the unit when you write your answer.
The volume of the rectangular prism is 192 in³.

**224. B**

**Step 1**
Calculate the volume of each prism.
$V = l \times w \times h$
Volume of the cube:
$2 \times 2 \times 2 = 8 \text{ cm}^3$
Volume of the rectangular prism:
$6 \times 4 \times 2 = 48 \text{ cm}^3$

**Step 2**
Add the two volumes.
$48 + 8 = 56$
The total volume of the given figure is 56 cm³.

**225. 850**

$V_{\text{composite figure}} = V_{\text{small rectangular prism}}$
$+ V_{\text{large rectangular prism}}$

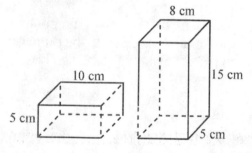

**Step 1**
Calculate the volume of the larger prism.
$V = l \times w \times h$
$V = (8) \times (5) \times (15)$
$V = 600 \text{ cm}^3$

**Step 2**
Calculate the volume of the smaller prism.
$V = l \times w \times h$
$V = (10) \times (5) \times (5)$
$V = 250 \text{ cm}^3$

**Step 3**
Add the volumes.
$600 + 250 = 850$
The total volume of the given figure is 850 cm³.

# EXERCISE #2—MEASUREMENT AND DATA

226. Jonas brought a water bottle containing 1.4 L of water to his track meet. How many milliliters of water were in the bottle?

227. The bicycle path at Victoria Park is 7.8 km long. How long is the path in meters?
  A. 78 m
  B. 780 m
  C. 7,800 m
  D. 78,000 m

*Use the following information to answer the next question.*

> Emma is taking two suitcases on a trip. The first suitcase weighs 14 kg, and the second suitcase weighs 10 kg.

228. What is the difference between the two suitcases in grams?
  A. 4 g
  B. 40 g
  C. 400 g
  D. 4,000 g

229. How many feet are in 60 In? _____ ft

230. How many ounces are in 80 lb? _____ oz

*Use the following information to answer the next question.*

> The capacity of a single bottle is 3 pt.

231. How many quarts is the total capacity of 12 of these bottles?
  A. 12 qt
  B. 18 qt
  C. 36 qt
  D. 72 qt

232. How many milligrams are there in 4 g?
  A. 200 mg
  B. 400 mg
  C. 2,000 mg
  D. 4,000 mg

**233.** How many kilometers are in 4,000 m?

    A. 3 km

    C. 5 km

                  B. 4 km

                  D. 6 km

**234.** Calculate the mean of the data set {6, 13, 40, 23, 35, 27, 31}.

*Use the following information to answer the next question.*

Mrs. Morris taught her students how to make a line plot and then gave the following data set for soccer scores:  3, 6, 8, 1, 2, 8, 13, 10, 1, 4, 8, 5, 6, 2

Becky wrote the following steps to show how to make a line plot using the data:

1. Identify the smallest and the largest numbers in the data set. Smallest: 1 Largest: 13
2. Draw a number line and write 1 on the far left and 13 on the far right.
3. Write the numbers 1, 2, 3, 4, 5, 6, 8, 10, 13 on the number line, using equal spacing between each number.
4. Record the data by placing an $X$ above each number.  If a number appears twice in the data set, record another $X$ above the first $X$.

**235.** Which of Becky's steps is **incorrect**?

    A. Step 1

    C. Step 3

                  B. Step 2

                  D. Step 4

A data set is given.

$$\{56, 43, 46, 64, 52, 59\}$$

**236.** Calculate the range of the data set.

**237.** Determine the mode of the data set {345, 323, 256, 252, 237, 342}.

**238.** Find the median of the numbers 56, 43, 46, 64, 52, and 59.

*Use the following information to answer the next question.*

Trina built a rectangular prism out of connecting cubes.

**239.** What is the volume of the rectangular prism Trina built?

A. 22 cubic units

B. 42 cubic units

C. 56 cubic units

D. 60 cubic units

*Use the following information to answer the next question.*

Ms. Sundeen is digging a vegetable garden in her backyard. She wants it to be 6 m long and 3 m wide, and she needs the soil to be 1 m deep.

**240.** If soil costs $11.00/m$^3$, how much will it cost Ms. Sundeen to buy soil for her garden?

A. $101.00

B. $132.00

C. $156.00

D. $198.00

A cube is shown.

5 cm

5 cm

**241.** What is the volume of this cube?

A. 100 cm$^3$

B. 125 cm$^3$

C. 225 cm$^3$

D. 625 cm$^3$

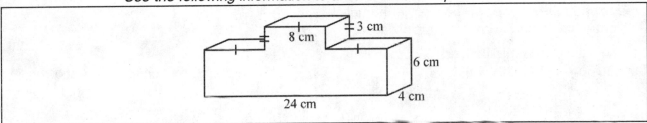

3 cm

8 cm

6 cm

24 cm

4 cm

**242.** What is the volume of the given composite figure?

A. 96 cm$^3$

B. 480 cm$^3$

C. 576 cm$^3$

D. 672 cm$^3$

# EXERCISE #2—MEASUREMENT AND DATA  ANSWERS AND SOLUTIONS

| | | | |
|---|---|---|---|
| 226. See solution | 231. B | 236. See solution | 241. B |
| 227. C | 232. D | 237. See solution | 242. D |
| 228. D | 233. B | 238. See solution | |
| 229. 5 | 234. See solution | 239. C | |
| 230. 1280 | 235. C | 240. D | |

## 226.

HINT: Larger unit → smaller unit
Think multiplication.

When you convert liters into milliliters, you convert a larger unit into a smaller unit.  This means that the answer will be a larger number. To get a larger number, think multiplication.

Since 1 L = 1,000 mL, convert 1.4 L to milliliters by multiplying 1.4 L by 1,000.

1.4 × 1,000 = 1,400
$\qquad$ 1.4 L = 1,400 mL

A quick way to multiply by 1,000 is to move the decimal point three places to
the right.  1.4 → 1,400

Remember:  When you move the decimal point to the right, you may need to add zeros if you do not have enough digits.

The bottle held 1,400 mL of water.

## 227.  C

1 km = 1,000 m
To convert 7.8 km to meters (larger unit to smaller unit), multiply 7.8 by 1,000.

7.8 × 1,000 = 7,800 m
A quick way to multiply by 1,000 is to move the decimal point three places to the right.
You need to add two zeros since there are not enough digits.

The path is 7,800 m long.

## 228.  D

### Step 1
Find the difference in weight between the two suitcases.
14 kg – 10 kg = 4 kg
The difference between the suitcases is 4 kg.

### Step 2
Convert kilograms into grams.
$\qquad$ 1 kg = 1,000 g
4 kg × 1,000 g = 4,000 g
The difference between the suitcases in grams is 4,000 g.

## 229.  5

### Step 1
Choose the correct conversion ratio.
1 ft:12 in

### Step 2
Use the ratio to convert the distance into feet.
Use division when converting from a smaller to a larger unit.
60 ÷ 12 = 5
There are 5 ft in 60 in.

## 230.  1280

Multiply to convert from a larger unit to a smaller one.

There are 16 oz in 1 lb.
80 lb × 16 oz = 1,280 oz

There are 1,280 oz in 80 lb.

## 231.  B

### Step 1
Calculate the capacity of 12 bottles.
3 × 12 = 36 pt

### Step 2
Determine the relationship between the units.
There are 2 pt in 1 qt.

### Step 3
Convert the units.
You are converting from smaller units to larger units.  This means you need to divide.
36 ÷ 2 = 18 qt

## 232. D

To solve this problem, convert 4 g to milligrams.

To convert a larger unit to a smaller unit (grams to milligrams), use multiplication. Since 1 g = 1,000 mg, 4 g will be equal to four times as many milligrams.
4 g × 1,000 mg = 4,000 mg

There are 4,000 mg in 4 g.

## 233. B

To convert a smaller unit to a larger unit (meters to kilometers), use division.

Since 1,000 m = 1 km, divide 4,000 m by 1,000 to solve the problem.
4,000 m ÷ 1,000 = 4 km

There are 4 km in 4,000 m.

## 234.

### Step 1
The mean of a set of data is defined as the ratio of the sum of the values to the number of values in the data set.
Determine the sum of the given values.
6 + 13 + 40 + 23 + 35 + 27 + 31 = 175

### Step 2
Divide the total sum by the number of values.
Since there are 7 values, divide by 7.
175 ÷ 7 = 25

Therefore, the mean of the data set is 25.

## 235. C

Step 1 is correct. Becky needs to be able to identify the smallest and largest numbers in the data set to determine how long the number line needs to be.

Step 2 is correct. Becky needs to draw a number line with the smallest number (1) on the far left and the largest number (13) on the far right.

Step 3 is incorrect. Becky needs to write all the numbers that are between 1 and 13 using equal spacing, even if they do not appear in the data set.

Step 4 is correct. Becky records her data using an X.

## 236.

### Step 1
Place the numbers in order from least to greatest.
43, 46, 52, 56, 59, 64

### Step 2
Subtract the lowest value from the highest value in the set.
The lowest value is 43, and the highest value is 64.
64 − 43 = 21
The range is 21.

## 237.

### Step 1
Place the values in order from least to greatest.
237, 252, 256, 323, 342, 345

### Step 2
Determine which numbers, if any, occur most frequently.
Each number occurs once in the data set. Therefore, there is no mode because no number occurs more than any of the others.

## 238.

### Step 1
Place the values in order from least to greatest.
43, 46, 52, 56, 59, 64

### Step 2
Determine the middle numbers.
There is an even number of values. The two middle numbers are 52 and 56.
Calculate the average of the two middle numbers.
52 + 56 = 108
108 ÷ 2 = 54

Therefore, the median is 54.

### 239. C

Choice C is correct. The volume of Trina's rectangular prism is 56 cubic units.

There are 7 connecting cubes in each of the 4 rows in the base layer.

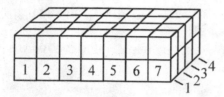

$$4 \times 7 = 28$$

There are 2 layers.

$$2 \times 28 = 56$$

### 240. D

**Step 1**

Determine what is being asked.

Ms. Sundeen's garden is 6 m by 3 m by 1 m, and the cost of soil is $11.00/m^3$. Use this information to find the total cost of the soil.

Your answer will be an amount of money, and it will have to be greater than $11.00 because that is the cost of soil for 1 $m^3$.

**Step 2**

Make a plan.

First, calculate the volume of the garden. Use the formula for the volume of a rectangular prism, $V = lwh$.

Next, find out the total cost of the soil by multiplying the volume of the garden by the cost for 1 $m^3$ of soil.

**Step 3**

Solve the problem.

Calculate the volume of the garden.

$V = lwh$
$\quad = 6 \times 3 \times 1$
$\quad = 18 \text{ m}^3$

Find the total cost of the soil. Multiply 18 by 11.

$$\begin{array}{r} 18 \\ \times\ 11 \\ \hline 18 \\ 180 \\ \hline 198 \end{array}$$

The total cost of soil for Ms. Sundeen's garden is $198.00.

**Step 4**

Decide if your answer is reasonable.

Your answer is a money amount greater than $11.00, which is what you predicted in step 1. You can also use estimation to check your answer. Round the volume of the garden to 20 $m^3$ and the cost of the soil to $10.00.

$$20 \times 10 = \$200.00$$

This is very close to your calculation, so your answer is reasonable.

### 241. B

**Step 1**

Write the formula for calculating volume.

$V = l \times w \times h$

**Step 2**

Substitute the given dimensions into the formula, and solve.

$V = 5 \times 5 \times 5$
$V = 125 \text{ cm}^3$

Remember to include the unit when you write the answer.

The volume of the cube is 125 $cm^3$.

### 242. D

To calculate the volume of the given composite figure, use the following formula:

$V$ = volume of top rectangular prism+ volume of bottom rectangular prism

Top prism:

$V$ = area of the base × height of object
$V = (l \times w) \times \text{height}$
$V = (8 \times 4) \times 3$
$V = 32 \times 3$
$V = 96 \text{ cm}^3$

Bottom prism:

$V$ = area of the base × height of object
$V = (l \times w) \times \text{height}$
$V = (24 \times 4) \times 6$
$V = 96 \times 6$
$V = 576 \text{ cm}^3$

$V$ = volume of top rectangular prism+ volume of bottom rectangular prism
$V = 96 \text{ cm}^3 + 576 \text{ cm}^3$
$V = 672 \text{ cm}^3$

# Geometry

# GEOMETRY

| Table of Correlations | | | | |
|---|---|---|---|---|
| Standard | | Concepts | Exercise #1 | Exercise #2 |
| 5.G | Geometry | | | |
| 5.G.1 | Use a pair of perpendicular number lines, called axes, to define a coordinate system, with the intersection of the lines (the origin) arranged to coincide with the 0 on each line and a given point in the plane located by using an ordered pair... | Plotting Points | 243, 244 | 255, 256 |
| | | Identify Points on a Cartesian Plane | 245, 246 | 257, 258 |
| | | Understanding the Cartesian Plane | | |
| 5.G.2 | Represent real world and mathematical problems by graphing points in the first quadrant of the coordinate plane, and interpret coordinate values of points in the context of the situation. | Plotting Points | 243, 244 | 255, 256 |
| | | Identify Points on a Cartesian Plane | 245, 246 | 257, 258 |
| | | Identifying Coordinates of the Vertices of a 2-D Shape | 247, 248 | 258, 259 |
| 5.G.3 | Understand that attributes belonging to a category of twodimensional figures also belong to all subcategories of that category. | Relating Different Types of Quadrilaterals | 249, 250 | 260 |
| | | Understanding Geometric Properties of Quadrilaterals | 251, 252 | 261 |
| | | Identifying Quadrilaterals | 253, 254 | 262 |
| 5.G.4 | Classify two–dimensional figures in a hierarchy based on properties. | Relating Different Types of Quadrilaterals | 249, 250 | 260 |
| | | Understanding Geometric Properties of Quadrilaterals | 251, 252 | 261 |
| | | Identifying Quadrilaterals | 253, 254 | 262 |

**5.G.1** *Use a pair of perpendicular number lines, called axes, to define a coordinate system, with the intersection of the lines (the origin) arranged to coincide with the 0 on each line and a given point in the plane located by using an ordered pair...*

## PLOTTING POINTS

A Cartesian plane is a grid that has two important lines called axes.

The horizontal line is called the **x-axis**. The vertical line is called the **y-axis**. The point where both lines meet is called the **origin**.

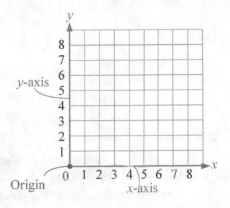

An ordered pair is two numbers inside brackets separated by a comma. An example of an ordered pair is (3, 5). The first number shows how many spaces over you need to count. The second number shows how many spaces up you need to count. If you are plotting the point (3, 5), start by counting over 3 spaces. Then, count up 5 spaces, and plot the point.

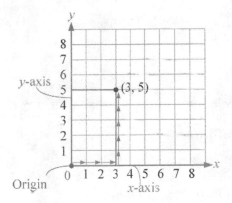

To plot points on a Cartesian plane, follow these steps:

1. Count over (along the *x*-axis) the same number of spaces as the first number In the ordered pair.
2. Count up (along the *y*-axis) the same number of spaces as the second number in the ordered pair.
3. Plot the point.

You can follow the same steps to plot more than one point at a time.

*Example*

Locate the coordinates (2, 2), (3, 4), and (4, 2) in the first quadrant of a Cartesian plane.

*Solution*

**Step 1**

Identify the location of (2, 2) on the Cartesian plane.

Trace your finger along the *x*-axis until you get to 2. Then, trace your finger up the *y*-axis until you get to 2. The point where the 2 on the *x*-axis and the 2 on the *y*-axis meet is where this coordinate point is located.

**Step 2**

Identify the location of (3, 4) on the Cartesian plane.

Move along the *x*-axis until you get to 3. Then, move up the *y*-axis until you get to 4. The point where the 3 on the *x*-axis and the 4 on the *y*-axis meet is where this coordinate point is located.

**Step 3**

Identify the location of (4, 2) on the Cartesian plane.

Move along the *x*-axis until you get to 4. Then, move up the *y*-axis until you get to 2. The point where the 4 on the *x*-axis and the 2 on the *y*-axis meet is where this coordinate point is located.

The points can be plotted in the first quadrant of the Cartesian plane as shown on the given diagram.

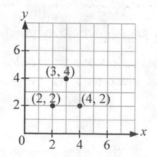

## IDENTIFY POINTS ON A CARTESIAN PLANE

To identify ordered pairs, follow these steps:

1. Count horizontally (to the right) from the *y*-axis.
2. Count vertically (up) from the *x*-axis.
3. Record the numbers within brackets separated by a comma. The horizontal count (*x*-coordinate) goes first, and the vertical count (*y*-coordinate) goes second.

## Example

Identify the ordered pairs for points *A*, *B*, *C*, and *D*.

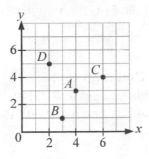

## Solution

Point *A*—Count 4 spaces right of the *y*-axis and 3 spaces up from the *x*-axis. The ordered pair for point *A* is (4, 3).

Point *B*—Count 3 spaces right and 1 space up. The ordered pair for point *B* is (3, 1).

Point *C*—Count 6 spaces right and 4 up. The ordered pair for point *C* is (6, 4).

Point *D*—Count 2 spaces right and 5 up. The ordered pair for point *D* is (2, 5).

## UNDERSTANDING THE CARTESIAN PLANE

A **Cartesian plane** is formed by the intersection of a horizontal and a vertical number line at a 90° angle. The horizontal and vertical number lines are called the *x*-axis and the *y*-axis, respectively. The lines intersect at a point called the origin.

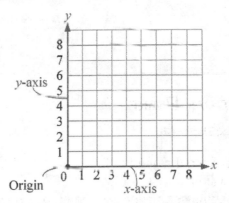

Points are plotted on a Cartesian plane and are identified as **ordered pairs**. An ordered pair consists of two numbers inside parentheses. They are always separated by a comma. An example of an ordered pair is (4, 2).

The first number in an ordered pair tells you how far you have to travel along the *x*-axis to reach the point. In other words, it tells you how many lines you have to move to the right to get to the point.

The second number in an ordered pair tells you how far you have to travel along the *y*-axis to reach the point. In other words, it tells you how many lines you have to move up to get to the point.

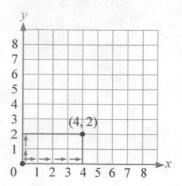

On the given Cartesian plane, you can see the point (4, 2). The first number (4) tells you that the point is four lines to the right of the origin. The second number (2) tells you that the point is two lines up from the origin.

*5.G.2*    *Represent real world and mathematical problems by graphing points in the first quadrant of the coordinate plane, and interpret coordinate values of points in the context of the situation.*

## IDENTIFYING COORDINATES OF THE VERTICES OF A 2-D SHAPE

The horizontal and vertical grid lines on a coordinate grid allow you to pinpoint coordinates when you are locating an object or drawing a design. The horizontal grid lines run from left to right, while the vertical grid lines run up and down.

*Example*

The triangle on the grid shows the ordered pairs where the points meet to make the shape.

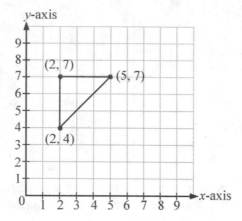

When you are writing the coordinates for an ordered pair, the order of the coordinates is important. Be sure to list the horizontal coordinate (*x*-axis) first and the vertical coordinate (*y*-axis) second (horizontal, vertical).

*Example*

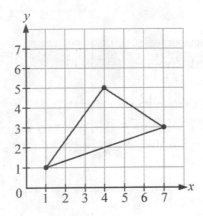

A triangle is formed by connecting points plotted on a grid.

Identify the coordinates of the vertices of the triangle.

*Solution*

When finding the coordinates for the vortices of a shape, always remember to read the *x*-coordinate first and then the *y*-coordinate.

The coordinates for the scalene triangle are (1, 1), (4, 5), (7, 3).

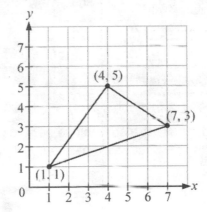

---

5.G.3    *Understand that attributes belonging to a category of twodimensional figures also belong to all subcategories of that category.*

## RELATING DIFFERENT TYPES OF QUADRILATERALS

Quadrilaterals are closed four-sided figures. Some examples of regular quadrilaterals are parallelograms, rectangles, rhombuses, squares, and trapezoids.

You can compare quadrilaterals by describing the kinds of sides and angles they have. For example, a rectangle and a square both have four right angles.

A **parallelogram** has two sets of parallel lines. The opposite sides of a parallelogram are parallel. A regular parallelogram like the one shown has two angles greater than right angles and two angles less than right angles.

Parallelogram

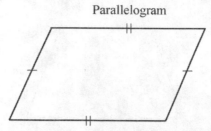

A **rectangle** is a kind of parallelogram because it also has two sets of parallel lines that are opposite each other. A rectangle is different from a parallelogram because it has four right angles.

Rectangle

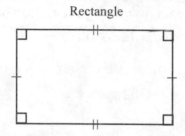

A **rhombus** is also a kind of parallelogram because it has two sets of parallel lines that are opposite each other. Also, it has two angles greater than right angles and two angles less than right angles. A rhombus has four sides of equal lengths. That makes it different from a regular parallelogram and a rectangle.

Rhombus

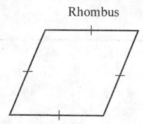

A **square** is a kind of parallelogram because it also has two sets of parallel sides that are opposite each other. A square is also a kind of rectangle because it has four right angles. It is also like a rhombus because it has four sides of equal lengths.

Square

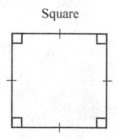

A **trapezoid** is different from any of the other shapes because it only has one set of parallel sides. It is like a parallelogram and a rhombus because it has two greater than right angles and two less than right angles.

Trapezoid

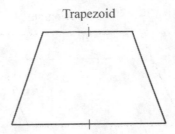

## UNDERSTANDING GEOMETRIC PROPERTIES OF QUADRILATERALS

A **quadrilateral** is a special kind of polygon. They are closed shapes with four sides. Examples of regular quadrilaterals include **rectangles**, **squares**, **parallelograms**, **rhombuses**, and **trapezoids**.

Quadrilaterals can be defined by the following attributes:

- Number of parallel sides
- Number of equal-length sides
- Number of right angles
- Number of equal angles

## NUMBER OF PARALLEL SIDES

Quadrilaterals may have parallel sides.
For example, a rectangle has two sets of parallel sides.

Rectangle

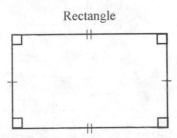

Other quadrilaterals may not have any parallel sides.
For example, the given quadrilateral does not have any parallel sides.

# NUMBER OF EQUAL-LENGTH SIDES

Quadrilaterals may have equal side lengths.

This rhombus has all four sides that are the same length.

Rhombus

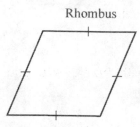

Quadrilaterals may not have equal side lengths

This quadrilateral does not have any sides that are equal.

# NUMBER OF RIGHT ANGLES

A right angle is an angle that forms a square, like the corner of a book. It looks like this:

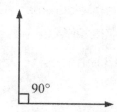

90°

Different quadrilaterals have different numbers of right angles. For example, a square has four right angles.

# NUMBER OF EQUAL ANGLES

Some quadrilaterals have angles that are equal. In the rhombus shown, you can see that the opposite angles are equal.

It is important to understand these properties because you can use them to describe quadrilaterals.

*Example*

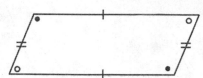

Describe the **geometric properties** of the quadrilateral.

*Solution*

**Step 1**
Describe the number of parallel sides.
This quadrilateral has two sets of parallel sides.

**Step 2**
Describe the equal side lengths.
This quadrilateral has opposite sides with the same lengths.

**Step 3**
Describe the number of right angles.
This quadrilateral does not have any right angles.

**Step 4**
Describe the number of equal angles.
This quadrilateral has opposite equal angles.

---

## IDENTIFYING QUADRILATERALS

Quadrilaterals are a special kind of polygon. They are closed shapes with four sides. Examples of quadrilaterals include rectangles, squares, parallelograms, rhombuses, and trapezoids.

All quadrilaterals can be described based on these features:

- Number of parallel sides
- Number of equal-length sides
- Number of right angles
- Number of equal angles

A trapezoid only has one pair of parallel sides. Some trapezoids may have two right angles, but at least two of the angles are not right angles. Some trapezoids may also have two pairs of equal angles. This trapezoid does not have any right angles.

Trapezoid

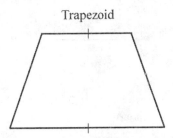

A parallelogram has two pairs of sides that are opposite each other. They are parallel and the same length. The angles in the opposite corners of a parallelogram are always equal.

Parallelogram

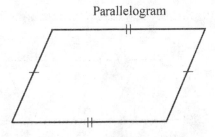

A rectangle is a special parallelogram. It has two pairs of sides that are opposite each other. They are parallel and the same length. A rectangle is special because the angles in all four corners are equal. Each corner has a right angle, so a rectangle has four right angles.

Rectangle

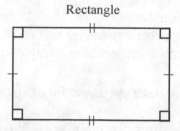

A square is a special rectangle. It has two pairs of sides that are opposite each other. These sides are parallel and the same length. A square also four right angles. A square is different from a rectangle because all four sides of a square are the same length.

Square

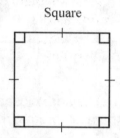

A rhombus is like a parallelogram, rectangle, and square. It has two pairs of sides that are opposite each other. They are parallel. Like a square, all four sides of a rhombus are equal in length. Like a parallelogram, angles in the opposite corners are always equal. The angles in a rhombus are not right angles.

Rhombus

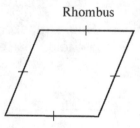

*Example*

Kyle draws four quadrilaterals.

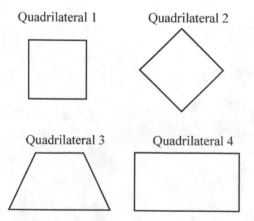

Which of Kyle's quadrilaterals is **not** a parallelogram?

*Solution*

### Step 1

Think about the features of parallelograms.

A parallelogram has two pairs of sides that are opposite each other. They are parallel and the same length. The opposite angles in a parallelogram are always equal.

### Step 2

Identify the features of each quadrilateral Kyle drew. Find the one that does not have the same features as the parallelogram.

Start with Quadrilateral 1. The opposite sides are equal. The opposite sides are also parallel and the same length. The opposite angles are equal. Quadrilateral 1 is a parallelogram.

Look at Quadrilateral 2. The opposite sides are equal, parallel, and the same length. The opposite angles are equal. Quadrilateral 2 is also a parallelogram.

Look at Quadrilateral 3. The two of the opposite sides are not equal. Two of the opposite sides are not parallel. Quadrilateral 3 cannot be a parallelogram.

Check Quadrilateral 4. The opposite sides are equal, parallel, and the same length. The opposite angles are equal. Quadrilateral 4 is parallelogram.

Quadrilateral 3 is not a parallelogram.

# EXERCISE #1—GEOMETRY

*Use the following information to answer the next question.*

Here is a set of coordinates.

(1, 5)(3, 3)(4, 2)(5, 0)

243. In which of the following graphs is the given set of coordinates plotted correctly?

A.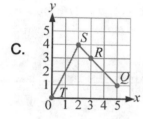

B.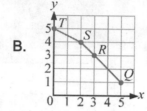

C.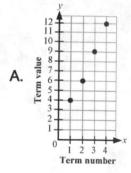

D.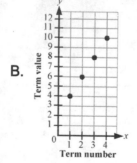

*Use the following information to answer the next question.*

Here is a set of coordinates.

(1, 4), (2, 5), (3, 7), (4, 11)

244. Which of the following graphs shows the given set of coordinates plotted correctly?

A.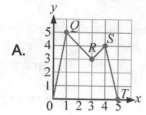

B.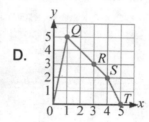

C.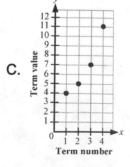

D.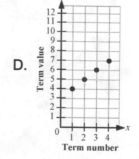

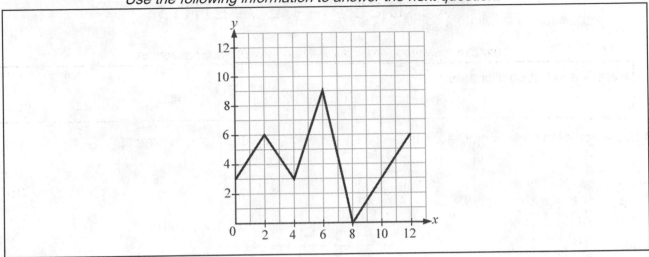

*Use the following information to answer the next question.*

245.Which of the following coordinates is **not** plotted on the given graph?

A. (8, 0)        B. (4, 3)

C. (9, 6)        D. (0, 3)

*Use the following information to answer the next question.*

Points *M*, *N*, *D*, and *P* are given on a Cartesian plane.

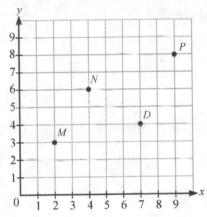

246.Which of the following ordered pairs does **not** identify one of these labeled points on the Cartesian plane?

A. (2, 3)        B. (4, 6)

C. (7, 7)        D. (9, 8)

*Use the following information to answer the next question.*

A shape is made by plotting points on the coordinate grid.

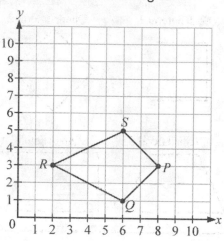

247. What are the coordinates for the points *P*, *Q*, *R*, and *S*?

A. *P*(8, 3), *Q*(6, 5), *R*(2, 3), *S*(6, 1)

B. *P*(2, 3), *Q*(6, 1), *R*(8, 3), *S*(6, 5)

C. *P*(8, 3), *Q*(6, 1), *R*(6, 5), *S*(2, 3)

D. *P*(8, 3), *Q*(6, 1), *R*(2, 3), *S*(6, 5)

*Use the following information to answer the next question.*

A shape is formed by points plotted on a coordinate grid.

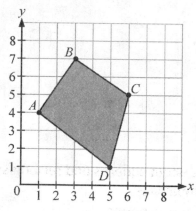

248. What are the coordinates of points *A*, *B*, *C*, and *D*?

A. *A*(1, 5), *B*(6, 5), *C*(3, 7), *D*(1, 4)

B. *A*(1, 4), *B*(6, 5), *C*(3, 7), *D*(5, 1)

C. *A*(4, 1), *B*(7, 3), *C*(5, 6), *D*(1, 5)

D. *A*(1, 4), *B*(3, 7), *C*(6, 5), *D*(5, 1)

*Use the following information to answer the next question.*

Kyle draws some quadrilaterals.

Quadrilateral 1    Quadrilateral 2

Quadrilateral 3    Quadrilateral 4

**249.** Which of Kyle's quadrilaterals is **not** a parallelogram?

Explain your answer using geometric words.

**250.** Which of the following statements about squares and rectangles is **true**?

A. Squares and rectangles are trapezoids.

B. Squares and rectangles are parallelograms.

C. Squares have fewer right angles than rectangles.

D. Squares have more parallel edges than rectangles.

251. Which of the following shapes has exactly one right angle?

A.

B.

C.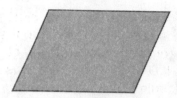

D.

252. Which of the following shapes has exactly one pair of sides that are equal in length?

A.

B.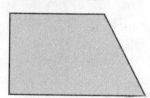

C.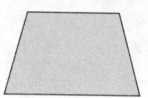

D.

253. Which of the following types of quadrilaterals both have opposite parallel sides and angles that measure 90°?

A. Square and rhombus

B. Square and rectangle

C. Rhombus and trapezoid

D. Parallelogram and trapezoid

254. Which of the following quadrilaterals has four sides of equal length and no right angles?

A. square

B. rhombus

C. rectangle

D. trapezoid

# EXERCISE #1—GEOMETRY ANSWERS AND SOLUTIONS

| | | | |
|---|---|---|---|
| 243. D | 246. C | 249. See solution | 252. C |
| 244. C | 247. D | 250. B | 253. B |
| 245. C | 248. D | 251. A | 254. B |

## 243. D

The term numbers are located to the left of the commas in the ordered pairs. and will be located on the *x*-axis of the graph.

The corresponding terms are located to the right of the comma in the ordered pairs, and will be located on the *y*-axis of the graph.

### Step 1

To locate the coordinates of (1, 5), start at 0, and move to the right (horizontally) to the 1. Then, move up (vertically) to the 5. The dot that represents the first set of coordinates will be located where the two lines cross. Call this dot *Q*.

### Step 2

To locate the coordinates of (3, 3), start at 0, and move to the right (horizontally) to the 3. Then, move up (vertically) to the 3. The dot that represents the second set of coordinates will be located where the two lines cross. Call this dot *R*.

### Step 3

To locate the coordinates of (4, 2), start at 0, and move to the right (horizontally) to the 4. Then, move up (vertically) to the 2. The dot that represents the third set of coordinates will be located where the two lines cross. Call this dot *S*.

### Step 4

To locate the coordinates of (5, 0), start at 0, and move to the right (horizontally) to the 5. The dot that represents the fourth set of coordinates will be located on the *x*-axis since the second coordinate is 0. Call this dot *T*. The given set of coordinates is plotted correctly in this graph.

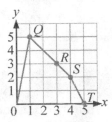

## 244. C

The *x*-coordinate is the term number, which is the first number in each ordered pair of coordinates. The *y*-coordinate is the corresponding term value, which is the second number in each ordered pair of coordinates.

Follow these directions as you check to see which graph has the coordinates plotted correctly:

1. For each coordinate, start at 0 and move to the right on the *x*-axis until you reach the term number you are looking for.
2. Move vertically until you reach the line that the corresponding term value from the *y*-axis is on.
3. The coordinate will be located where the two lines intersect.

This graph shows the given coordinates plotted correctly.

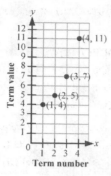

## 245. C

### Step 1

The first number in an ordered pair represents the term numbers that are represented on the x-axis (horizontal axis) of the graph.

To locate the first number of an ordered pair, start at the 0 position, and move to the right along the x-axis until you reach the particular number you are looking for.

### Step 2

The second number in an ordered pair represents the terms that are represented on the y-axis (vertical axis) of the graph.

To locate the second number of the ordered pair, start with the particular term number you just located, and move up the vertical line until you reach the line that the second number of the pair is located on. The ordered pair (coordinate) will be located where the two axes cross.

The coordinate (9, 6) is not plotted on the graph.

- Start at the 0 position, and move to the right along the x-axis until you reach the 9 position (the line between 8 and 10).
- Move up the 9 line until you reach the line that the 6 is on.
- There is nothing plotted where the two lines cross.

## 246. C

### Step 1

Identify the coordinates of the labeled points on the Cartesian plane.

Point M lies 2 units to the right of the origin and 3 units up from the origin. Therefore, the coordinates of M are (2, 3). Point N lies 4 units to the right of the origin and 6 units up from the origin. Therefore, the coordinates of N are (4, 6). Point D lies 7 units to the right of the origin and 4 units up from the origin. Therefore, the coordinates of D are (7, 4). Finally, point P lies 9 units to the right of the origin and 8 units up from the origin. Therefore, the coordinates of P are (9, 8).

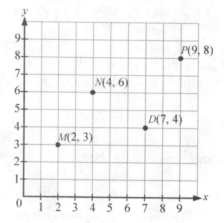

### Step 2

Identify the ordered pair that does not match one the labeled points.

Point (2, 3) is point M, point (4, 6) is point N, and point (9, 8) is point P. Point (7, 7) is not labeled.

## 247. D

When finding coordinates, remember to always read the x-coordinate first and then the y-coordinate.

- Point P is eight units to the right and three units up. The coordinates for point P are (8, 3).
- Point Q is six units to the right and one unit up. The coordinates for point Q are (6, 1).
- Point R is two units to the right and three units up. The coordinates for point R are (2, 3).
- Point S is six units to the right and five units up. The coordinates for point S are (6, 5).

The coordinates for the shape are P(8, 3), Q(6, 1), R(2, 3), S(6, 5).

**248. D**

When finding coordinates, remember to always read the *x*-coordinate first and then the *y*-coordinate.

- Point *A* is one unit to the right and four units up. The coordinates for point *A* are (1, 4).
- Point *B* is three units to the right and seven units up. The coordinates for point *B* are (3, 7).
- Point *C* is six units to the right and five units up. The coordinates for point *C* are (6, 5).
- Point *D* is five units to the right and one unit up. The coordinates for point *D* are (5, 1).

The coordinates for the shape are

*A*(1, 4), *B*(3, 7), *C*(6, 5), and *D*(5, 1).

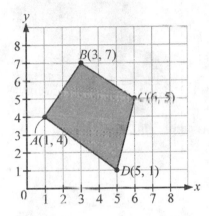

**249.**

| Points | Rationale |
|---|---|
| 4 | Applies knowledge of quadrilaterals, giving a complete and effective explanation. |
| | **Sample Answer:**<br>Parallelograms have two sets of opposite sides that are parallel. Quadrilateral 3 has one set of parallel sides (top and bottom), but the left and right sides are not parallel. That is why it is not a parallelogram. |

| Points | Rationale |
|---|---|
| 3 | Applies knowledge of quadrilaterals but may give an incomplete explanation. |
| | **Sample Answer:**<br>Number 3 is not a parallelogram because it has slanted lines that are not parallel. |
| 2 | Applies some knowledge of quadrilaterals, but may give a limited or partly incorrect explanation. |
| | **Sample Answer:**<br>Shape 3 is not because it does not have square corners like the others. |
| 1 | Applies some knowledge of quadrilaterals, but may not give an explanation. |
| | **Sample Answer:**<br>3 |

**250. B**

The relationships among the different types of quadrilaterals are shown in the given tree diagram.

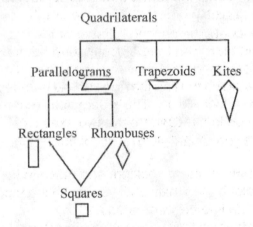

A rectangle is a parallelogram that has two pairs of parallel sides and four right angles.

Copyright Protected

A square is a parallelogram that also has two pairs of parallel sides and four right angles, but all four sides of a square are congruent.

### 251. A

Count the right angles on each of the shapes.

The kite has one right angle.

The rectangle has four right angles.

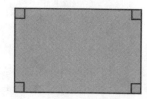

The parallelogram does not have any right angles.

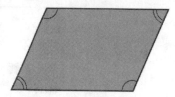

The trapezoid has two right angles.

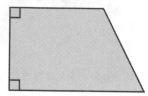

The only shape that has exactly one right angle is the kite.

### 252. C

Count the equal sides on each shape.

The rectangle, kite, and parallelogram all have two pairs of sides with equal lengths.

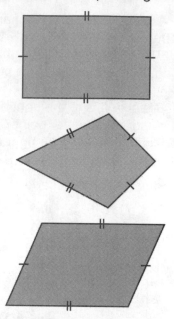

The trapezoid is the only shape that has one pair of sides with equal lengths.

### 253. B

A square is a type of quadrilateral in which all four sides are equal, opposite sides are parallel, and all angles measure 90°.

A rectangle is a type of quadrilateral in which the opposite sides are equal and parallel and all the angles measure 90°.

**254. B**

**Step 1**

Consider the characteristics of each given shape.

- A square has four sides of equal length and four right angles.
- A rhombus has four sides of equal length and no right angles.
- A rectangle has two sets of sides with equal side lengths and four right angles.
- A trapezoid may have one set of sides that are equal in length and may have one or two right angles, or no right angles.

**Step 2**

Identify the shape that matches the given characteristics.

A rhombus has four sides of equal length and has no right angles.

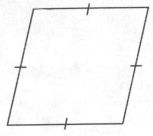

# EXERCISE #2—GEOMETRY

255. Which of the following figures correctly places the points *P*(3, 9), *Q*(8, 9), *T*(8, 4), and *S*(3,4) on the coordinate plane?

A.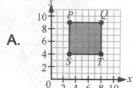

B.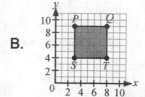

C.

D.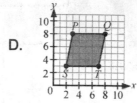

256. Which graph shows the point *P*(2, 7) plotted correctly?

A.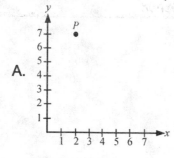

B.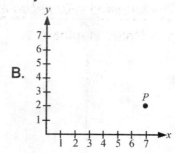

C.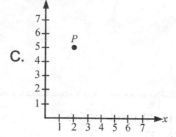

D.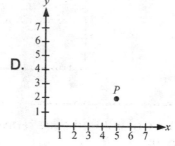

*Use the following information to answer the next question.*

A point is plotted on a graph, as shown.

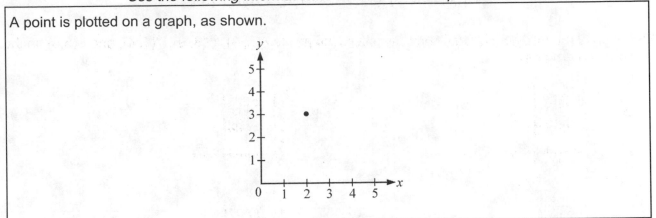

**257.** What is the position of this point?

**A.** (1, 1)

**B.** (2, 1)

**C.** (2, 3)

**D.** (5, 2)

*Use the following information to answer the next question.*

A student graphs the coordinates of a triangle.

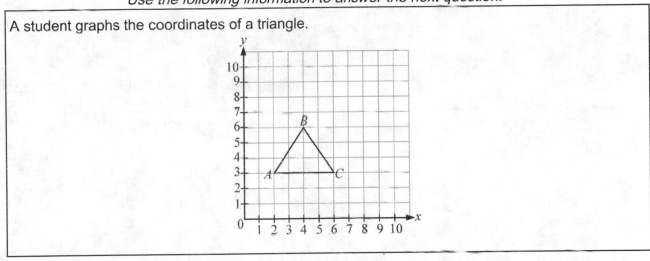

**258.** Which of the following sets of ordered pairs represents the three vertices of the triangle?

**A.** *A*(2, 3), *B*(6, 4), *C*(6, 2)

**B.** *A*(2, 3), *B*(4, 6), *C*(6, 3)

**C.** *A*(2, 2), *B*(2, 6), *C*(6, 8)

**D.** *A*(2, 2), *B*(1, 6), *C*(6, 2)

*Use the following information to answer the next question.*

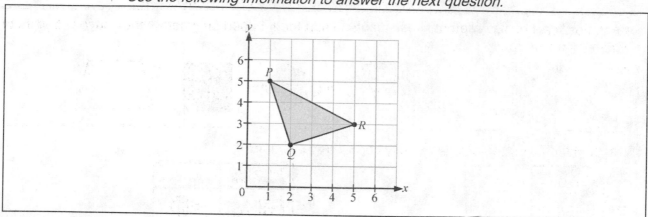

259. What are the coordinates of points P, Q, and R?

   A. P (5, 1), Q(2, 2), R(5, 3)          B. P(2, 2), Q(5, 3), R(1, 5)

   C. P(1, 5), Q(2, 2), R(3, 5)           D. P(1, 5), Q(2, 2), R(5, 3)

*Use the following information to answer the next question.*

Marnie says that a square is a special kind of rectangle.

260. Is she correct?

   Explain your answer using geometric words.

Jared has a set of quadrilaterals. He wants to sort them based on whether they have two pairs of parallel sides or not.

**261.** Which of the following tables correctly sorts Jared's shapes?

A.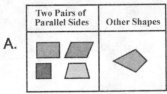

B.

C.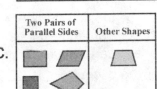

D.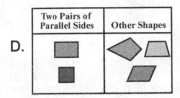

Ryan made a riddle about a quadrilateral. These are the clues he gave.

- I have 2 sets of parallel lines.
- Not all of my sides are equal in length.
- I am made up of 2 greater than right angles.
- I am also made up of 2 less than right angles.

**262.** Ryan's riddle is about which quadrilateral?

A.
Square

B.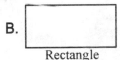
Rectangle

C.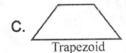
Trapezoid

D.
Parallelogram

# EXERCISE #2—GEOMETRY ANSWERS AND SOLUTIONS

| | | | |
|---|---|---|---|
| 255. A | 257. C | 259. D | 261. B |
| 256. A | 258. B | 260. See solution | 262. D |

## 255. A

The plotted points are identical to the coordinate plane given in A:

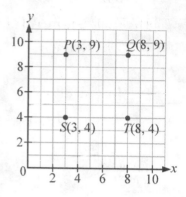

## 256. A

To plot point $P(2, 7)$ on a graph, move 2 units right from the origin on the $x$-axis and then 7 units up.

The correct graph, A, is shown below.

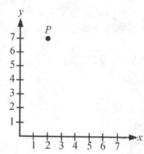

## 257. C

### Step 1

Determine the $x$-coordinate.

To locate the first number of the ordered pair, start at the 0 position on the bottom axis and move to the right until the number that is directly below the point is reached.

The first coordinate along the $x$-axis is 2.

### Step 2

Determine the $y$-coordinate.

To locate the second number of the ordered pair, start at the 0 position on the side axis and move up until the number that is directly across from the point is reached.

The second coordinate along the $y$-axis is 3.

### Step 3

Write the ordered pair.

The $x$-coordinate will be the first number of the ordered pair, and the $y$-coordinate will be the second number of the ordered pair.

The ordered pair for the given point is (2, 3).

## 258. B

To identify the coordinates of the vertices of the triangle, read the $x$-coordinate first and then the $y$-coordinate.

Point $A$ is 2 units to the right and 3 units up. The coordinates for point $A$ are (2, 3).
Point $B$ is 4 units to the right and 6 units up. The coordinates for point $B$ are (4, 6).
Point $C$ is 6 units to the right and 3 units up. The coordinates for point $C$ are (6, 3).

The coordinates of the vertices of the triangle are $A$ (2, 3), $B$ (4, 6), and $C$ (6, 3).

## 259. D

When finding coordinates, remember to always read the $x$-coordinate first and then the $y$-coordinate.

Point P is 1 unit to the right and 5 units up. The coordinates for point P are (1, 5).

Point Q is 2 units to the right and 2 units up. The coordinates for point Q are (2, 2).

Point R is 5 units to the right and 3 units up. The coordinates for point R are (5, 3).

Therefore, the coordinates for the design are P (1, 5), Q (2, 2), and R (5, 3), which correspond to **D**.

**260.**

| Points | Rationale |
|---|---|
| 4 | Expresses the relationship between squares and rectangles with a high degree of effectiveness. |
| | **Sample Answer:** Yes, Marnie is correct. They both have 4 straight sides and 4 right angles. The opposite sides are parallel. |
| 3 | Expresses the relationship between squares and rectangles with considerable effectiveness. |
| | **Sample Answer:** Yes, she is correct. They both have right angles and 4 sides. |
| 2 | Expresses the relationship between squares and rectangles with some effectiveness. |
| | **Sample Answer:** Yes, she is right. All the corners are square. A rectangle has 2 long lines, and a square has all the same, but they are all up and down or across. |
| 1 | Expresses the relationship between squares and rectangles with limited effectiveness. |
| | **Sample Answer:** They have square corners, but a rectangle is bigger. |

**261. B**

**Step 1**

Count the pairs of parallel sides on each shape. The square, the parallelogram, and the rectangle each have two pairs of parallel sides.

 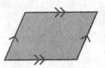 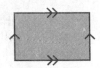

The trapezoid has only one pair of parallel sides.

The kite does not have any parallel sides.

**Step 2**

Sort the shapes.

Shapes that have two pairs of parallel sides go in the first column. Those shapes are the square, the rectangle, and the parallelogram. Shapes that do not have two pairs of parallel sides go in the second column. Those shapes are the kite and the trapezoid.

| Two Pairs of Parallel Sides | Other Shapes |
|---|---|
| | |

## 262. D

### Step 1
Consider the characteristics of each given quadrilateral.

- AA square has 4 sides that are of equal length and 4 right angles.
- BA rectangle has 2 sets of parallel lines, 2 sets of equal side lengths, and 4 right angles.
- CA trapezoid has 1 set of parallel lines. It could have no equal side lengths or it could have one set of equal side lengths. It could have any type of angles (right, greater than right, less than right).
- DA parallelogram has 2 sets of parallel lines, 2 sets of equal side lengths, 2 angles greater than right angles, and 2 angles less than right angles.

### Step 2
Identify the quadrilateral that meets all the clues that Ryan gave.

The parallelogram meets all the clues that Ryan gave.

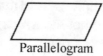

Parallelogram

# NOTES

NOTES

NOTES

# NOTES

# SOLARO Study Guides
## Ordering Information

Every SOLARO Study Guide unpacks the curriculum standards and provides an overview of all curriculum concepts, practice questions with full solutions, and assignment questions for students to fully test their knowledge.

**SOLARO**
Study Guides

Visit www.solaro.com/orders to buy books and learn how SOLARO can offer you an even more complete studying solution.

**SOLARO Study Guide—$29.95 each plus applicable sales tax**

| SOLARO Common Core State Standard Titles | |
|---|---|
| Mathematics 3 | Algebra I |
| Mathematics 4 | Algebra II |
| Mathematics 5 | Geometry |
| Mathematics 6 | English Language Arts 3 |
| Mathematics 7 | English Language Arts 4 |
| Accelerated Mathematics 7 (Int.) | English Language Arts 5 |
| Accelerated Mathematics 7 (Trad.) | English Language Arts 6 |
| Mathematics 8 | English Language Arts 7 |
| Accelerated Mathematics I | English Language Arts 8 |
| Mathematics I | English Language Arts 9 |
| Mathematics II | English Language Arts 10 |
| Mathematics III | English Language Arts 11 |
| Accelerated Algebra I | English Language Arts 12 |

**To order books, please visit**
www.solaro.com/orders

Volume pricing is available. Contact us at
orderbooks@solaro.com